Location-Based Services

The Morgan Kaufmann Series in Data Management Systems
Series Editor: Jim Gray, Microsoft Research

Location-Based Services
Jochen Schiller and Agnès Voisard

Database Modeling with Microsoft® Visio for Enterprise Architects
Terry Halpin, Ken Evans, Patrick Hallock, Bill Maclean

Designing Data-Intensive Web Applications
Stephano Ceri, Piero Fraternali, Aldo Bongio, Marco Brambilla, Sara Comai, and
Maristella Matera

Mining the Web: Discovering Knowledge from Hypertext Data
Soumen Chakrabarti

Advanced SQL: 1999—Understanding Object-Relational and Other Advanced Features
Jim Melton

Database Tuning: Principles, Experiments, and Troubleshooting Techniques
Dennis Shasha and Philippe Bonnet

SQL: 1999—Understanding Relational Language Components
Jim Melton and Alan R. Simon

Information Visualization in Data Mining and Knowledge Discovery
Edited by Usama Fayyad, Georges G. Grinstein, and Andreas Wierse

Transactional Information Systems: Theory, Algorithms, and Practice of Concurrency Control and Recovery
Gerhard Weikum and Gottfried Vossen

Spatial Databases: With Application to GIS
Philippe Rigaux, Michel Scholl, and Agnes Voisard

Information Modeling and Relational Databases: From Conceptual Analysis to Logical Design
Terry Halpin

Component Database Systems
Edited by Klaus R. Dittrich and Andreas Geppert

Managing Reference Data in Enterprise Databases: Binding Corporate Data to the Wider World
Malcolm Chisholm

Data Mining: Concepts and Techniques
Jiawei Han and Micheline Kamber

Understanding SQL and Java Together: A Guide to SQLJ, JDBC, and Related Technologies
Jim Melton and Andrew Eisenberg

Database: Principles, Programming, and Performance, Second Edition
Patrick and Elizabeth O'Neil

The Object Data Standard: ODMG 3.0
Edited by R. G. G. Cattell and Douglas K. Barry

Location-Based Services

Jochen Schiller

Agnès Voisard

ELSEVIER

AMSTERDAM · BOSTON · HEIDELBERG · LONDON
NEW YORK · OXFORD · PARIS · SAN DIEGO
SAN FRANCISCO · SINGAPORE · SYDNEY · TOKYO

Morgan Kaufmann is an imprint of Elsevier

MORGAN KAUFMANN PUBLISHERS

Acquisitions Editor	Lothlórien Homet
Acquisitions Editor	Rick Adams
Editorial Assistant	Corina Derman
Project Manager	Justin Palmeiro
Marketing Manager	Brent Dela Cruz
Cover Design	Yvo Riezobos Design
Cover Illustration	Getty Images
Full Service Provider	Graphic World Publishing Services
Composition	Cepha Imaging Pvt. Ltd.
Copyeditor	Graphic World Publishing Services
Proofreader	Graphic World Publishing Services
Indexer	Graphic World Publishing Services

Morgan Kaufmann Publishers is an imprint of Elsevier.
500 Sansome Street, Suite 400, San Francisco, CA 94111

This book is printed on acid-free paper.

Library of Congress Control Number: Application submitted.

ISBN: 1-55860-929-6

For information on all Morgan Kaufmann publications, visit our website at *www.mkp.com*

Printed and bound by CPI Group (UK) Ltd, Croydon, CR0 4YY
Transferred to Digital Print 2012

Foreword

Jim Gray, Microsoft Research/San Francisco

There is an explosion of technologies to communicate with mobile and occasionally-connected devices and sensors. Wireless networking (WiFi), cellular telephone (GSM), packet radio, radio frequency identifiers (RFID), smart personal object technology (SPOT), global positioning systems (GPS), and sensor networks are already with us. Many completely new communication innovations are on the horizon.

These technologies enable new applications. They allow mobile users to query their environment and they allow applications to monitor and track remote objects. People can ask about nearby services – for example a restaurant, and how to get there from here. Police, hospital, and taxi dispatchers can send the closest vehicle to where it is needed. Conversely, monitoring systems can track the flow of goods and monitor environmental parameters. Railroads, airfreight, wholesalers, retailers, and other transportation industries can track goods from their source to their final destination on the retail shelf. Environmental systems can monitor air quality, noise, streamflow, and other environmental parameters.

All these applications have strong spatial components – object location, proximity, and connectivity are the central organizing principle of these applications. This book takes a pragmatic approach to representing, organizing, and searching spatial data and object location. It views the problem from top to bottom. It starts with descriptions of some real applications and their requirements. It then explains ways to represent spatial information and explores algorithms to efficiently find nearby objects and paths to them. It then segues to a very informative description of the basic location and communication technologies for wireless communication (like GSM) and location (like GPS).

Location-based services are a vibrant and rapidly evolving application area with many active research groups, many products, and many interesting applications. This book provides a good picture of the current state of the art. It is a great introduction to this exciting field of location-based services.

Contents

Introduction

Jochen Schiller, Freie Universität Berlin
Agnès Voisard, Fraunhofer Institute for Software and Systems Engineering (ISST)
and Freie Universität Berlin

The term *location-based services* (*LBS*) is a recent concept that denotes applications integrating geographic location (i.e., spatial coordinates) with the general notion of services. Examples of such applications include emergency services, car navigation systems, tourist tour planning, or "yellow maps" (combination of yellow pages and maps) information delivery.

With the development of mobile communication, these applications represent a novel challenge both conceptually and technically. Clearly, most such applications will be part of everyday life tomorrow, running on computers, personal digital assistants (PDAs), phones, and so on. Providing users with added value to mere location information is a complex task. Given the variety of possible applications, the basic requirements of LBS are numerous. Among them we can cite the existence of standards, efficient computing power, and friendly yet powerful human–computer interfaces.

This book aims at understanding and describing in an accessible fashion the various concepts that serve as a support to mobile LBS. It is written by experts in the relevant topics. Major issues to be considered when dealing with LBS, together with their current solutions, are described formally and illustrated through a case study given as a reference at the beginning of the book.

The field of LBS, which emerged a few years ago, presents many challenges in terms of research and industrial concerns. This book focuses on some of the arising issues. Other important issues are not covered by the book, among them security, privacy, data availability, and pricing. Location-based services are often used via Web browsers and are in this case considered as a particular type of Web services. With this perspective, the major challenges to consider are the personalization of services, the ubiquity of services to the mobile user, and the chaining of services with the transmission of context, such as time, location, and possibly other dimensions like the user profile. The user profile typically includes basic user-related data, such as name and address, but possibly also preferences that have been set by the user or inferred by the system. Such aspects are not addressed in great detail in this book. For a thorough study of Web services the reader is referred to [ACKM03] and [B03], for mobile location services to [J03], and for common approaches supported by the World-Wide Web Consortium (W3C)—for instance in the context of the Semantic Web—to [WWW04]. A description of promising approaches for information delivery and exchange among many users who may be geographically grouped can be found in [JV04].

Note that a representative application example is that of 'Personalized Web Services for the Olympic Games in Beijing in 2008', carried out by the Fraunhofer Institute for Software and Systems Engineering in Dortmund and Berlin, Germany, and the Institut of Computing Technology (ICT) of the Chinese Academy of Sciences, located in Beijing, China in the SigSit joint-laboratory [SIGSIT04].

This book has two potential audiences: practitioners and researchers. The former will find solutions to many questions that may arise when handling such applications, both from a high-level viewpoint (the user's side) and from a technical viewpoint (e.g., which protocols are adapted to which situation). Researchers will discover the breadth and depth of the numerous research challenges in the different areas concerned.

The concepts described in this book range from general application-related concepts to technical aspects. We use a top-down approach, reaching from a high level of abstraction—the application—down to the various technical levels. The same set of concepts is studied at each level: requirements, services, data, and scalability. Moreover, all of the concepts described in this book are illustrated using a reference application given at the beginning of the book.

The book is structured in three major parts: application, data management and services, and communication, each of which is composed of two or three chapters. Following is a succinct description of each of them.

Part 1, composed of three chapters, is devoted to the general notion of LBS applications. Chapter 1, by Sarah Spiekermann from Humboldt-Universität zu Berlin, aims at setting the basis (vocabulary, concepts) of LBS, namely the various categories of applications and the requirements for an operational system. The interaction with end users (e.g., possible devices, GUI aspects) and the notions of horizontal and vertical services are also discussed.

Chapter 2, by Mark Strassman from Autodesk Inc. and Clay Collier from Kivera Inc., describes an example application, which actually became quite popular as a reference to LBS: the Find Friends application. The example is meant to illustrate most concepts seen so far as well as the chaining of services that exists in such applications.

Chapter 3, by Shashi Shekhar, Ranga Raju Vatsavai, Xiaobin Ma, and Jin Soung Yoo from the University of Minnesota, deals with navigation systems. It details the functionalities of intelligent navigation systems as well as their main algorithms.

Part 2, also composed of three chapters, is concerned with data management and services, which are at the core of such systems. Data organization and management, as well as system interoperability, are the prime focuses of this system.

Chapter 4, by Hans-Arno Jacobsen from the University of Toronto, focuses on middleware issues. It describes the requirements for LBS middleware platforms and the actual solutions in this area.

Chapter 5, by Christian Jensen from Aalborg University, deals with database aspects of LBS, and more precisely with database-centered management of static and dynamic data, data formats, and storage strategies.

Chapter 6, by Lance McKee from the Open GIS Consortium, Inc. (OGC), describes interoperability through standards. This chapter reports on the objectives and achievements of the special-interest group Open Location Services of the OGC.

Part 3, composed of two chapters, is devoted to the communication aspect of LBS (i.e., to technical aspects of wireless data information exchange).

Chapter 7, by Jörg Roth from the University of Hagen, relates to data collection, such as locating people and devices, locating services, and Service Location Protocols (i.e., IEEE/IETF location awareness technologies).

Chapter 8, by Holger Karl from the Technical University of Berlin, focuses on data transmission. Major mechanisms for transferring data in the context of wireless technologies as well as most common standards are described in this chapter.

ACKNOWLEDGMENTS

We wish to thank the MKP team we had the pleasure to work with, namely Rick Adams, Corina Derman, Jim Gray, and Josh Stevens, and especially Lothlórien Homet for her encouragements and her patience during the whole process.

References

[ACKM03]   G. Alonso, F. Casati, H. Kuno, and V. Machiraju. *Web Services: Concepts, Architectures and Applications.* Springer Verlag Publishers, Berlin/Heidelberg, 2003.

[B03]   D. K. Barry. *Web Services and Service-Oriented Architectures. Your Road Map to Emerging IT.* Morgan Kaufmann Publishers, San Francisco, CA, 2003.

[J03]   A. Jagoe. *Mobile Location Services: The Definitive Guide.* Prentice Hall, Upper Saddle River, NJ, 2003.

[JV04]   J. Schiller and A. Voisard. Information Handling in Mobile Applications: A Look Beyond Classical Approaches. In *Geosensor Networks.* S. Nittel and A. Stefanidis (Eds.), Taylor&Francis, London, 2004.

[SIGSIT04]   Sino-German Joint Laboratory of Software Integration Technologies (SigSit). Home page of the project "Personalized Web Services for the Olympic Games 2008 in Beijing", http://www.sigsit.org.

[WWW04]   The World-Wide Web Consortium (W3C) home page. http://www.w3.org/.

Part 1

LBS Applications

General Aspects of Location-Based Services

Sarah Spiekermann, Humboldt-Universität zu Berlin

CONTENTS

1.1   INTRODUCTION

Location services can be defined as *services that integrate a mobile device's location or position with other information so as to provide added value to a user.*

Location services have a long tradition. Since the 1970s, the U.S. Department of Defense has been operating the global positioning system (GPS), a satellite infrastructure serving the positioning of people and objects. Initially, GPS was conceived for military purposes, but the U.S. government decided in the 1980s to make the system's positioning data freely available to other industries worldwide. Since then, many industries have taken up the opportunity to access position data through GPS and now use it to enhance their products and services. For example, the automotive industry has been integrating navigation systems into cars for some time.

In traditional positioning systems, location information has typically been derived by a device and with the help of a satellite system (i.e., a GPS receiver).[1] However, widespread interest in location-based services (LBS) and the underlying technology as discussed in this book has really started to boost only in the late 1990s, when a new type of localization technology and new market interest in data services was sparked by mobile network operators. In approximately 1997, mobile networks were widely deployed in Europe, Asia, and the United States, and income from telephony services had proven to be significant to mobile operators. Yet, even though mobile voice services continue to be a major revenue generator for telcos, growth of mobile telephony is limited and the price per minute is decreasing. Consequently, operators have started to look around for means to stabilize their bottom line and find new areas for future growth. One major way to reap additional financial benefits of mobile networks apart from voice is to offer data services, many of which will be location enhanced.

Approximately 15% of current operator income in Western Europe and 20% in Asia is already based on data services. Most of this income is coming from Short Message Services (SMS). To grow the data business further, operators need to invest in new technologies, especially in mobile

---

1. Besides the GPS system, the former USSR has also started to offer free use of parts of its comparable system, the Global Orbiting Navigation Satellite System (GLONASS).

messaging (e.g., MMS, IM, email) and mobile Internet (Wireless Application Protocol [WAP]), and look for ways to optimize the user experience of this new product domain. User location is an important dimension in this new data-service world: Not only does it allow companies to conceive completely new service concepts (i.e., tracking applications), but it also has the potential to make many messaging and mobile Internet services more relevant to customers as information is adjusted to context (i.e., weather information adjusted to the region one is in). In addition, location information can considerably improve service usability.

As a result of these multidimensional benefits of location information, operators are coming to consider it as their "third asset" besides voice and data transmission. Important investments are being made to extract, use, and market it.

1.2   USAGE AREAS OF LOCATION-BASED SERVICES

Location services are mainly used in three areas: military and government industries, emergency services, and the commercial sector. As was previously mentioned, the first location system in use was the satellite-based GPS, which allows for precise localization of people and objects of up to 3 meters or more of accuracy. GPS is funded and controlled by the U.S. Department of Defense and was built primarily to serve military purposes. In the 1980s, however, the U.S. government decided to make the system freely available worldwide in order to spark innovation around satellite technology. This means that any other governmental, emergency, or commercial service has the possibility to integrate GPS into equipment and services. The result of this free availability of satellite positioning parameters has led to wide adoption of the American system. Air traffic control, sea port control, in-car navigation, freight management, and many emergency services worldwide have all opted to use the system and partly made their industries depend on it. Responding to this freely accessible monopoly for positioning data, the European Union (EU) decided in 2002 to build a comparable satellite system called Galileo, which is scheduled to start operations in 2008. Galileo is a joint initiative of the European Commission and the European Space Agency (ESA). Both GPS and Galileo run on a similar frequency, which from a military perspective is most interesting because blocking the other party's signal would result in impacting one's own as well.

Besides the military use of location data, emergency services have turned out to be an important application field. Every day, 170,000 emergency calls are made in the United States. Of those, one-third originate from mobile phones, and, in most cases, people do not know where they are precisely in order to guide support to the correct location [Tom03]. As a result, the U.S. Federal Communications Commission (FCC) set an October 2001 deadline for commercial wireless carriers to provide the caller's location information in a 911 emergency call. This means that when placing an emergency call from a mobile phone, a caller's phone position is automatically transmitted to the closest emergency station. Consequently, people in such situations do not have to explain at length where they are but are located in seconds. Ultimately, few carriers were able to meet the original deadline so the FCC relaxed the date for wireless E911 services. It is expected that it takes several years before the system reaches full coverage with high precision.

In Europe, the EU has followed a similar path. Statistics reveal that 50% to 70% of the 80 million "real" EU-wide emergency calls each year originate from mobile phones [HT02]. Some industry sources even argue that approximately 5000 lives could be saved each year in the region with automatic positioning of emergency calls. As a result, the EU Commission has passed Article 26 of the "Directive of universal service and users' rights relating to electronic communications networks and services (2002/22/EC of 7th March 2002)." This article asks member states to develop national regulations for mobile operators enforcing the automatic positioning of emergency calls: "Member states shall ensure that undertakings which operator public telephone networks make a caller location information available to authorities handling emergencies, to the extent technically feasible, for all calls to the single European emergency call number 112."

"Technical feasibility" in this context means that unlike in the United States, European regulators do not enforce the highest accuracy levels such as GPS for locating emergency cases. Although GPS allows a cell phone to be located accurately, European operators have the right to start out with the accuracy levels their mobile networks can provide right now. Because more than 80% of European operators have implemented so-called Cell-ID technology [CI03] for mobile positioning, only very low accuracy levels can be offered for now in emergency situations: 100 meters potentially in urban areas, but only up to 3-kilometer accuracy in rural areas. A debate has started whether the latter is enough

Table 1.1 Overview of LBS applications and level of accuracy required.

Application	Accuracy	Application	Accuracy
News	Low	Gaming	Medium
Directions	High	M-Commerce	Medium to High
Traffic Information	Low	Emergency	High
Point of Interest	Medium to High	Sensitive Goods Transportation	High
Yellow Pages	Medium to Low	Child Tracking	Medium to High
Car Navigation	Medium to High	Pet Tracking	Medium to High
Personal Navigation	High	Electronic Toll Collection	Medium to High
Directory Assistance	Medium to High	Public Management System	Medium to High
Fleet Management	Low	Remote Workforce Management	Low
Car Tracking	Medium to High	Local Advertisement	Medium to High
Asset Tracking	High	Location-Sensitive Billing	Medium to Low

Source: Bellocci, V., Genovese, S., Inuaggiato, D., and Tucci, M. (2002, July 18). "Mobile Location-Aware Services: 2002 Market Perspective," Ericsson, Division Service Architecture and Interactive Solutions.

accuracy in the mid-term and ethically defendable by operators in case of life losses.

The accuracy debate leads to the third area of location use and probably the most ubiquitous one in the future: the commercial use of positioning information. For some time, marketers have been unsure whether lower levels of accuracy as they are obtained from Cell-ID would be sufficient to launch compelling consumer and business services. Yet, early service examples show that the accuracy level required depends very much on the service. Even with Cell-ID, location information can successfully be integrated by operators into many existing and new applications that enhance current value propositions and usability.

At a high level, the company Ericsson has developed a scheme of what accuracy levels it considers to be necessary for different types of applications. Table 1.1 gives an overview of this scheme.

1.3   LBS APPLICATION TAXONOMY

Analysts and researchers have taken several approaches to classifying LBS applications. A major distinction of services is whether they are person-oriented or device-oriented.

◆ *Person-oriented LBS* comprises all of those applications where a service is user-based. Thus, the focus of application use is to position a person or to use the position of a person to enhance a service. Usually, the person located *can control the service* (e.g., friend finder application).

◆ *Device-oriented LBS* applications are external to the user. Thus, they may also focus on the position of a person, but they do not need to. Instead of only a person, an object (e.g., a car) or a group of people (e.g., a fleet) could also be located. In device-oriented applications, the person or object located is usually *not controlling the service* (e.g., car tracking for theft recovery).

In addition to this first classification of services, two types of application design are being distinguished: push and pull services [OV02].

◆ *Push services* imply that the user receives information as a result of his or her whereabouts *without having to actively request it.* The information may be sent to the user with prior consent (e.g., a subscription-based terror attack alert system) or without prior consent (e.g., an advertising welcome message sent to the user upon entering a new town).

◆ *Pull services*, in contrast, mean that a user actively uses an application and, in this context, "pulls" information from the network. This information may be location-enhanced (e.g., where to find the nearest cinema).

Some services such as a friend finder or date finder integrate both push and pull functionality.

Table 1.2 gives an overview of the LBS service dimensions with some application examples:

Most of the early location services in Europe have been pull services, especially information services. Push services have not come to flourish yet. Unproven economics and privacy concerns are the main reasons for this situation.

Economically, it is unclear to what extent push services can be profitable. On the cost side, it has been argued that push services take up disproportionate amounts of network resources because they require a constant update of users' locations. For example, in order to push a restaurant coupon to all mobile users who enter a certain area, the network of that area needs to be "paged" at regular intervals to request the cell phone number of all those users passing by. In other words, the entire location area is queried about whether new phones have entered the respective cell area and whether any of these users are subscribed to the service. Yet, some services involving push may not require network

Table 1.2 Categories and examples of LBS applications.

	Push Services	**Pull Services**
Person-oriented		
Communication	Ex. 1: You get an alert from a friend zone application that a friend has just entered your area. Ex. 2: A message is pushed to you asking whether you allow a friend to locate you.	Ex. 1: You request from a friend finder application who is near you.
Information	Ex. 3: You get an alert that a terror alarm has been issued by the city you are in.	Ex. 2: You look for the nearest cinema in your area and navigation instructions to get there.
Entertainment	Ex. 4: You have opted to participate in a location-based "shoot 'em up" game and are being attacked.	Ex. 3: You play a location-based game and look for another opt-in in your area to attack.
M-Commerce and Advertising	Ex. 5: A discount voucher is being sent to you from a restaurant in the area you are in.	Ex. 4: You look for cool events happening in the area you are in.
Device-oriented		
Tracking	Ex. 6: An alert is sent to you from an asset-tracking application that one of your shipments has just deviated from its foreseen route. Ex. 7: You get an alert that your child has left the playground.	Ex. 5: You request information on where your truck fleet currently is located in the country.

paging. An example of this is a friend finder service. Here, a message is pushed to a subscriber A indicating to him that somebody else (person B) wants to locate him. In this type of *passive* service, no cost-intensive network paging is required.

A factor that inflates the cost of push services is user profile management. In order to push a message to anybody, the recipient has to have expressed prior consent to receive messages. This is required not only by law [EU02] but also dictated by market forces. Unsolicited spamming of mobiles is certainly not a way to gain customers or increase service usage. By subscribing to a service such as a friend finder, a user indirectly gives consent that he or she is also willing to be contacted, storing preferences with the application service provider. In addition to consent and rules for contacting users, push applications need to store the history of messages sent (e.g., advertising coupons sent) in order to avoid duplication.

Given the cost side of push services, considerable revenue is necessary to make these services profitable. Revenue can be obtained by charging end users directly for receiving push messages (charging the recipient) or by charging the sender (e.g., an advertisement agency). So far, it is unclear to what extent end users are willing to pay for location-based services, including push services. A good pricing strategy that seems to have worked for some operators (such as Telia in Sweden) is to relate service usage to SMS pricing. Thus location-based games or friend finder applications that have no initial subscription charge, but rather a per-usage price similar to SMS, have seen some success in terms of service adoption. Charging senders such as advertising agencies, however, has not seen a viable business case yet. The currently required investment in IT infrastructure and network usage may drive the *cost per contact* for advertising agencies to a point where it does not make sense for them to integrate location. The cost would outweigh the benefits.

The second reason why push services in general and location-based push in particular are rarely seen today is that they raise considerable privacy concerns. The inherent character of the mobile network frequently updating one's position in the network already raises the notion of real-time tracking. Yet, getting push messages related to one's position may increase the perception of being observed for many users.

1.4 LBS AND PRIVACY

Many studies have shown that consumers care about their privacy and are wary of any intrusions. As a result, operators and marketers, but also friends among each other, must be careful and sensitive about the way they handle the localization of others. In addition to the perception of being observed, spamming has become another threat to the industry. Because location would considerably enhance the relevancy of messages, location-based spam messages may occur and considerably intrude on people's "right to be let alone." As a result of the relatively free distribution of mobile phone numbers (e.g., via Web-based SMS, SMS voting services), it is feared that a similar spamming problem could emerge in the mobile world as can be observed today on the Internet. Unsolicited messages pushed to mobile phones may be perceived as even more harmful by the recipients than email spamming. After all, the mobile phone is a trusted device, is carried close to the body, and has such a small display that attention is forced onto each message.

As a result of this potential threat, the EU Commission has recognized the issue in its Directive on Privacy and Electronic Communications (Directive 2002/58/EC).[2] Besides regulating many aspects of electronic communication, push messages that are "unsolicited" are explicitly covered (Article 13). Main points covered in the directive are as follows:

◆ Automated calling is only allowed in respect to subscribers who have given their PRIOR CONSENT.

◆ Only the body that a user has a purchase contract with is allowed to use contact details for direct marketing purposes.

◆ If the operator wants to do direct marketing, then the user must be given the opportunity to object, free of charge and in an easy manner, to the use of his or her contact data. This opportunity must be given at each message.

◆ Electronic messages that conceal the identity of the sender OR are without a valid reply address are prohibited.

Also, the use of location data in general is regulated, demanding in that (Article 9):

◆ Location data may only be processed when it is made anonymous OR with the consent of the user for the duration necessary for the provision of a service.

◆ The location service must INFORM the user, PRIOR to obtaining their consent, of the type of location data that will be processed, of the PURPOSE and DURATION of the processing, and whether the data will be transmitted to a third party.

◆ Users shall be given the possibility to withdraw their consent for the processing of location data at any time.

◆ Users must have SIMPLE MEANS, FREE OF CHARGE for temporarily refusing the processing of location data FOR EACH CONNECTION TO THE NETWORK.

For mobile operators, unsolicited push can lead to tremendous customer care cost. Unlike Internet access or Internet service providers (ISPs), mobile operators have a much more intimate relationship with

---

2. The full details of this legislation are included in the "DIRECTIVE 2002/58/EC of the European Parliament and of the Council of 12 July 2002 concerning the processing of personal data and the protection of privacy in the electronic communications sector (Directive on privacy and electronic communications)" at: http://europa.eu.int.

their customers. When something does not work with a user's PC, he mostly has to sort it out for himself. When something does not work with a user's mobile phone, though, the operator is usually contacted. Consequently, operators would most likely be the target for complaints of people who receive unsolicited push messages.

Foresight of such potential developments have led operators to take technological as well as contractual measures in addition to relying on EU regulation.

Vodafone, for example, has defined strict requirements regarding the privacy management capabilities of its location middleware technology. (Location middleware is described in more detail in Chapter 4.) As a result of industry pressure for privacy functionality, Vodafone now allows users to anonymize location requests by mapping the cell phone number to an alias in both mobile-initiated and mobile-terminated requests. Furthermore, it allows users to set privacy preferences on a per-service level, including the frequency with which somebody may be contacted, the time, the accuracy level, and the notification mode. Finally, it usually provides for a client interface that allows end users to directly turn localization on or off altogether.

Second to this technological approach, Vodafone has taken another important step forward to address privacy by formulating a Privacy Management Code of Practice. This code of practice is obligatory for all third parties who want to provide location services to Vodafone customers. Breach of the code is said to lead to serious consequences, such as termination of service contracting, cost recovery, and withholding of payments.

In its code of practice, Vodafone distinguishes two types of location services:

- *Active services*, where the end user initiates the location request (e.g., information services such as Find My Nearest Cinema).
- *Passive services*, where a third party locates an individual (locatee) at the request of another (the locator). Typical passive location services are friend finder services, location-based gaming, or fleet management.

For active services, it is assumed that a user is aware of being localized and agrees to this practice. Consequently, privacy protection measures do not need to be as restrictive as they are for passive services. Still, the code foresees that the user gets at least one "awareness message" that his or her position is being used. Also, Vodafone demands that information about the use of location shall not be "buried in terms and conditions," which embraces an open communication with the customer about the subject.

Passive services imply a higher risk of misuse by end users and application service providers. Consequently, Vodafone imposes stricter requirements in relation to this type of service, including the following:

- ◆ Explicit and written capture of consent of the locatee
- ◆ Clear information of the locatee of the nature of the locator *prior to consent*
  - • Name and mobile number of the locator
  - • Web site or customer support where further service information, terms, and conditions of the locator can be accessed
  - • Service name and service provider
  - • An exact description of the service
  - • Information on the duration and frequency of the location requests as well as circumstance
- ◆ Explicit and repeated notification of location requests happening
- ◆ Direct access of the locatee to a site that specifies who has the right to position oneself
- ◆ A direct and easy way to cancel a passive service

With these guidelines, Vodafone is establishing and driving privacy standards into the mobile industry that correspond to Fair Information Practices as they have been proposed (i.e., by the U.S. Federal Trade Commission—namely notice, choice, and access). This company's actions are a very good example of how market forces can drive the protection of privacy.[3]

1.5   LBS MARKETS AND CUSTOMER SEGMENTS

Besides overcoming technological and ethical barriers, marketing location services has been a challenge to operators. Many managers of the early days of LBS have been discouraged by a lack of success and usage take-up of the first services launched. One major challenge has been that the new

---

3. The Privacy Management Code of Practice referred to here was issued in its first version (1.0) in August 2003 by Vodafone UK. In the current chapter, only a selection of major practices are being covered.

applications were relying on technology that was very slow in penetrating the market: WAP-enabled and high-end data phones suited to make all of those promises of the mobile Internet come true. In addition to this lack of phones, the location market makers had to—and still have to—collect some initial market experience. Most services launched initially were "find-the-nearest" types of applications. Yet, only a small selection of those services have proven to actually meet demand. Finally, most lLBS were launched with a wait-and-see mentality, and little effort was put into their advertising, design, and elaboration. As a result, revenues were poor and many operators turned away from LBS disappointed and with a feeling that they would not have a business model.

However, as data phones with high-resolution color screens, more processing power, and faster data connections penetrate the market and early experiences are being exchanged about what works and what does not, LBS are coming back. Big operator groups have started to embrace the location asset as a means to differentiate their services. One major insight has been that localizing people is not a service in itself, but that location is merely an enabler to enhance existing services, improve usability, or develop new service concepts. As a result, the industry now often talks about location as a means to *enable* services as opposed to location-based services.

The location market is developed around both business and consumer services and can be broadly grouped into a vertical and horizontal service sphere.

The *vertical market* is characterized by users drawn from industry environments where the management of mobile location information is and has always been an integral part of the business [Gre00]. For example, the location of a taxi is fundamental to the operations of a taxi company in order to efficiently assign drivers to customers. Likewise, airports need to have air traffic control systems in place in order to ensure the security of planes. Police officers have traditionally used radio transmission to inform each other of their whereabouts to optimize response times in emergency cases.

The vertical market segment has been the historic base of the mobile location services industry, and many players in it developed proprietary systems for localization long before LBS achieved today's general commercial availability. Yet, despite location being of such vital importance, technologies such as automatic vehicle location (AVL) were only affordable by big-business customers. Thus, a large trucking organization was likely to have a system that enabled it to position its trucks on an electronic map, integrated with truck and driver management systems and logistics software. A small delivery company, however, or a medium-sized plumbing firm, typically relied on its drivers calling in to report their positions and be dispatched to the next job. For private customers, LBS were not accessible at all.

With the arrival of mobile phones serving as a replacement for many traditional built-in localization devices, the market is changing. Also, software packages such as fleet management software are being standardized and packaged for multiuse purposes. An example may illustrate this change and how it can affect the industry [Tak02]: In May 2001, NTT Communications (NTT Com) launched e-Transit, a service that provides, through the Internet, information about where a vehicle is located and how long it will take to reach its intended destination. Originally, the service had to be based on a GPS built into vehicles, leading to very high cost for potential customers: typically $800 to $1,200 just for the onboard communication unit. Because of this high cost, in June 2002, NTT Com added a service that can be used with commercially available GPS mobile phones. Use of these mobile phones enabled users to get a localization unit for less than 20% of the cost of existing preinstalled vehicle equipment: $25 is added as a setup fee to install e-Transit applications on handsets, and another $25 per month is being charged per mobile unit to use the service. The result of this new service design was that within the first 6 months of launch, NTT Com signed up hundreds of customers (mainly from the transportation industry), many of whom probably could not have afforded the original system.

In contrast to the vertical market, the *horizontal market* is characterized by users drawn from industry environments where the use of mobile location information is a new and added value to existing services (e.g., child tracking as a new form of security service or asset tracking for high-value goods to keep down theft insurance fees). Horizontal LBS can be offered to and paid for by business customers or by consumers.

Today, horizontal markets offer a big business potential for operators and third-party application developers. Because the location asset can be used to enhance traditional services, new marketing channels can be explored to reach a mass market. At the same time, traditional products can be repackaged and their value proposition can be enhanced with location. For example, traditional security companies can offer

Table 1.3 Location markets and segments.

	Business	**Consumer**
Vertical market	Airports	
	Taxi companies	
	Police	
	Home repair services	
	Emergency	
	High-value goods delivery	
Horizontal market	Asset tracking	Child tracking
	Automated toll	Tourist security

easy-to-use, real-time tracking of people and objects. Online dating companies can integrate location as a factor to match those members who are physically close to each other. The tourist industry can develop new service concepts around navigation and find-the-nearest information. Motor clubs can create packages around emergency and roadside assistance. The list of potential services is very long.

Table 1.3 gives an overview and examples of location markets and customer segments.

1.6   HOW TO MAKE IT HAPPEN: THE LBS COMMUNICATION MODEL AND RELATED INDUSTRY ISSUES

In order to make location applications work, the industry had to overcome several challenges of both a technological and economic nature over the past years. Technologically, the realization of LBS can be described by a three-tier communication model (Figure 1.1), including a positioning layer, a middleware layer, and an application layer.

The *positioning layer* is responsible for calculating the position of a mobile device or user. It does so with the help of position determination equipment (PDE)[4] and geospatial data held in a geographic information

---

4. Several position determination equipment (PDE) solutions have been implemented or are being proposed. These include handset-based technologies (e.g., GPS), network-based technologies (e.g., Cell-ID, Cell-IDTA), or a hybrid of the two (e.g., E-OTD, GPS).

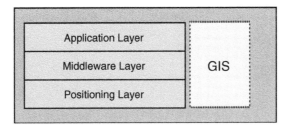

Figure 1.1 General LBS communication model.

system (GIS). While the PDE calculates where a device is in network terms, the GIS allows it to translate this raw network information into geographic information (longitudes and latitudes). The end result of this calculation is then passed on via a location gateway either directly to an application or to a middleware platform.

Originally, the positioning layer would manage and send location information directly to an application that requests it for service delivery. The *application layer* (which in the LBS industry is often and confusingly referred to as a "client") comprises all of those services that request location data to integrate it into their offering (e.g., a friend finder); however, as increasingly more LBS applications are being launched, many network operators have put a *middleware layer* between the positioning and application layer. Primarily, this is because PDE sits very deep in the network of a mobile operator, leading to complex and lengthy hookup of each individual new data service. Also, a middleware layer can significantly reduce the complexity of service integration because it is connected to the network and an operator's service environment once and then mitigates and controls all location services added in the future. As a result, it saves operators and third-party application providers time and cost for application integration. Figure 1.2 illustrates this concept.

Making application integration easy is vital for mobile operators in order to move to a so-called wholesale model for location data. The wholesale approach means that operators offer a kind of bulk access to the location of devices. An advertisement company, for example, can buy access to thousands of mobiles entering a certain location and then contact the devices with a push message. A roadside assistance company can offer its customers an automatic mobile positioning service for emergency purposes, but would have to buy the right to access this data

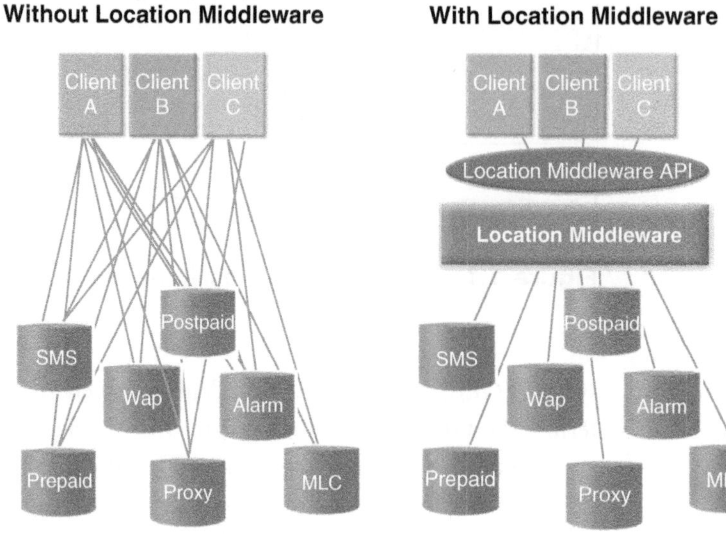

Figure 1.2 Application integration with or without middleware. Reprinted with permission from Openwave Systems, Inc. *http://www. openwave.com*

from an operator. Finally, many companies may want to take advantage of fleet management services. If a third-party company rather than an operator offers fleet management, then this company would have to purchase location data in bulk in order to realize the service. The examples show that the wholesaling of location data is an important business area for operators.

For quite a while, operators hesitated to embrace wholesaling, arguing that major privacy concerns would doom this model to failure. Here, location middleware can fulfill another role. On the downstream, it allows users to manage location access rights of third-party applications, while on the upstream it systematically anonymizes location information revealed. Thus, the location middleware takes over a similar role as an anonymizing proxy does on the Internet. In this way, many privacy concerns are addressed by an operator. Also, users get direct access to turn privacy on or off.

Finally, location middleware can be used to manage interoperability between networks for location data. Chapter 4 gives more details on the technological role of middleware in LBS. Chapter 6 in particular treats the issue of interoperability between networks as yet another major challenge of the LBS industry not covered here.

1.7   CONCLUSION

The use of location information in traditional and new markets will be ubiquitous. This chapter has introduced some of the ways in which the LBS market and its applications can be characterized, what and how the location information is used, and what challenges are being confronted. Mobile operators will be challenged to ensure themselves a place in this new service sphere, but being the providers (and often sponsors!) of location-enabled mobile phones, they have the greatest opportunity to do so. At the same time, third-party application developers help enable traditional industries to enhance the value proposition of their products by profiting from the availability of satellite and mobile positioning data. A new electronic communications service era is opening up.

References

[CI03]   *European Location-Based Services: Operator Status and Market Drivers* Concise Insight, Ltd., London, 2003.

[EU02]   EU Directive 2002/58/EC.

[Gre00]   J. Green, D. Betti, and J. Davison. *Mobile Location Services: Market Strategies*, OVUM, London, 2000.

[HT02]   *Caller Location in Telecommunication Networks in View of Enhancing E112 Emergency Services: Recommendation Towards a European Policy and Implementation Plan*, Helios Technology Ltd., prepared on behalf of the Directorate General Information Society, Brussels, Luxembourg, April 2002.

[OV02]   *Location: Not Quite Here Yet*, OVUM, London, 2002.

[Tak02]   M. Takeda, "Will GPS Mobile Phones Become the Driving Force in the GPS Applications Market?", *nG Mobile in Japan and Asia*, 1(7), July 22, 2002.

[Tom03]   Update on U.S. E911 Mandate, Mobile Location Services Conference, MLS, Amsterdam, 2003.

2

Case Study: Development of the *Find Friend* Application

Mark Strassman, Autodesk Inc.
Clay Collier, Iro Systems

CONTENTS

This chapter focuses on the development and deployment of a mobile friend finder application, showing a mass consumer use of LBS and the first live LBS application by any carrier in North America.

This chapter first introduces some background on mobile LBS applications and then delves further into the requirements and constraints of defining and building the application.

2.1   BACKGROUND

Location-based applications are one of the most anticipated new segments of the mobile industry. These new applications are enabled by GPS-equipped phones and range from Emergency 911 (E-911) applications to buddy finders (e.g., "let me know when my friend is within 1000 feet") to games (e.g., treasure hunt) to location-based advertising (e.g., "enter the Starbucks to your left and get $1.00 off a Frappuccino"). These services are designed to give consumers instant access to personalized, local content. In this case, local content is local to the consumer's immediate location. Some of these applications will couple LBS with notification services, automatically alerting users when they are close to a preselected destination. LBS proponents believe that these services will create new markets and new revenue opportunities for device manufacturers, wireless providers, and application developers.

The next generation of GPS devices *are* cell phones, and GPS features will probably be an invisible part of your next phone upgrade. In the United States, these GPS phone features were motivated by an FCC mandate, which required that wireless carriers provide E-911 service comparable to wireline 911. Traditional 911 services automatically deliver a caller's location to the appropriate public safety entity, based on the phone's fixed address. E-911 uses GPS and other technologies to detect the caller's location.

E-911 features require that wireless carriers make additional equipment investments. Although, at first glance, E-911 sounds like an expense with no obvious return, in reality it is an exceptional opportunity for carriers to offer new revenue-generating LBS.

In spring 2001, AT&T Wireless communicated to Kivera its goal of offering a mobile friend finder service, taking advantage of its new, location-aware GPRS service called mMode.

The goal was to provide enhanced LBS solutions for people to stay in touch with their friends and family, to be able to find one another, and to get directions to local shops and restaurants. AT&T Wireless created the first-ever Find Friend application, built on top of Kivera's Location Engine. The application was to be delivered over mMode (essentially a WAP variant) to provide the following capabilities:

◆ Deliver relevant user information about the location of a friend or family member's mobile cell phone position.
◆ Calculate driving directions from a mobile cell phone position to an address or point-of-interest (POI).
◆ Provide for selection of a business POI meeting place between two mobile cell phone positions.
◆ Provide for selection of a business POI in proximity to a mobile phone position.

2.2 LBS PLATFORM CONSIDERATIONS

Before delving into the actual AT&T application, it is critical to assess the two overall areas that contribute to the quality of results from any LBS application: the mapping data and the LBS Engine software.

2.2.1 Data Capture and Collection

LBS applications typically use information from several content databases:

◆ The road network (digital maps)
◆ Business and landmark information, often referred to as Yellow Pages, or POI information
◆ Dynamic data such as traffic and weather reports

DIGITAL ROAD DATABASES
Building LBS applications starts with the collection of road data. The United States alone contains millions of individual road segments. Map database vendors collect and convert raw geographic content into digital formats. The map data are captured in many ways, ranging from satellite imagery to scanned maps to manually digitizing paper maps. Some vendors physically drive each road segment in GPS-equipped cars,

recording every change of direction and photographing road signs to keep track of specific road conditions such as turn and height/weight restrictions.

Each vendor's data are different, which accounts for some of the discrepancy in the maps and routes generated. Some data are extremely accurate but have only partial coverage. Some vendors provide complete coverage but have data with positioning errors and geometry problems.

Map data are stored in a vector format composed of line segments (links) representing the roads and connecting points representing intersections or other road features. Each link has start and end points and may also incorporate shape points to model the curvature of the road. In addition to geometry, the data contain feature attributes such as one-way streets, exit signage, prohibited turns and maneuvers, vehicle-height restrictions, bridges, tunnels, and street addresses.

The complexities of modeling the idiosyncrasies of the road system are significant. Consider an example such as the Golden Gate Bridge in San Francisco. The bridge has moveable dividers that split the road into one-way sections in each direction and a shared lane that changes direction before morning and evening rush hours. To model this system accurately, a vendor needs to double-digitize the shared lane and flag the lanes with time-of-day restrictions for closures. Or consider the challenge of the European roundabout or traffic circle. Each road meeting at the circle is typically two-way, but the circle permits travel in only one direction. Information on data models and algorithms associated with road (network) data can be found in Chapter 3, Navigation Systems, and Chapter 5, Database Aspects of Location-Based Services.

POINT-OF-INTEREST INFORMATION

One of the most popular LBS applications is Yellow Pages, or concierge services. Mobile concierge-type services help users locate businesses near a specified location. These services help answer questions such as, "Where is the airport?" "Where can I find a Chinese restaurant?" or "Where is the nearest gas station?" Some services will even make hotel or dinner reservations, order flowers, and coordinate other fetch-and-get tasks. Concierge applications use business and landmark information that has been compiled into POI databases. Integrating the map database with the POI database creates a detailed, digital representation of the road network and business services available along it.

These POI databases contain the kind of detailed information typically found in a phone directory and add value to the map database's geographic content. As is the case with a map database, POI databases collected from multiple vendors can be merged to form a single, comprehensive data set. Each record in an individual POI database is geocoded, or assigned a latitude/longitude coordinate, before being combined with other POI databases. After multiple POI databases are integrated, the resulting "super" POI database is indexed and each record is assigned a unique identifier so that it can be associated to a link in the map database.

In addition to permitting the merge of multiple POI data sets, some LBS technology providers let vendors add their own unique POI information to the data set. For example, retail corporations can have store locations digitized, allowing prospective customers to search for the stores closest to them. This allows LBS application developers to contribute unique value to the data and/or to address specific vertical markets.

Integrating the map database with the POI database yields a detailed, digital representation of the road network with the accuracy and coverage necessary for high-quality LBS. Some providers, in the rush to get to market, have not taken stringent steps to guarantee the quality of their map databases. Although some vendors handle conflation using rigorous techniques such as Selective Area Merging, many rely on haphazard, manual data-integration methods that result in inaccurate and incomplete product offerings. Only providers who use high-quality data and data-merging methodologies can offer technology for creating superior LBS applications.

DYNAMIC DATA

Those who drive to work daily are keenly aware that the optimal route from Point A to Point B can change profoundly during commute hours. Traffic jams, accidents, road construction, and inclement weather can all affect a road's "arterial capacity," or its supported traffic speed. This situation can significantly change the true "fastest" route.

Daily traffic conditions, obviously, cannot be coded into a map database a priori. To accommodate changing road features, well-designed Location Engines are designed to work with dynamic data and to use it to supplement and/or override existing map information. Time-critical applications such as E-911 and fleet management depend on LBS engines with dynamic data capabilities because they allow dispatchers to react almost instantaneously to changing conditions.

2.2.2   The Location Engine

The heart of any LBS system is the Location Engine, which contains the software components that add intelligence to digital map data. The quality of these modules is just as important as data quality for generating accurate results. Software functions such as geocoding, reverse geocoding, and routing are key technologies built into the Location Engine (see Figure 2.1).

GEOCODING AND REVERSE GEOCODING

Geocoding is a feature of all geospatial applications. Geocoding converts a street address to a latitude/longitude (x, y pair of coordinates) position so it can be accurately placed on a map. In the case of either geocoding or reverse geocoding, accuracy is critical to the quality of the results.

Geocoding becomes a much more difficult process when complete addresses are not available. One of the biggest problems of many Internet-based mapping applications is figuring out misspelled addresses. Although only a few of these applications will choke on abbreviations (e.g., "ln" instead of "lane"), most cannot handle phonetic spellings. Unfortunately, in the real world, we are not always given complete and accurate street names.

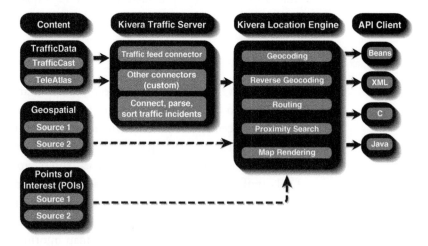

Figure 2.1 Kivera's Location Engine architecture.

To address this problem, some Location Engines utilize *metaphone* or *soundex* algorithms that use "sounds like" rules to perform address matches when the spelling or pronunciation of a location is not clear. This "fuzzy matching" facility dramatically enhances the engine's ability to find and geocode addresses.

The opposite function of geocoding is *reverse geocoding*, the process of deriving the location of the nearest road segment to a point with a specified longitude/latitude. The derived information, which includes world coordinates, address location, and directional distances from reference points, can then be used for routing or searching for points of interest.

ROUTING

Routing is the technique of calculating the optimal course, based on specific criteria, between an origin and destination. Although most people simply want the "best" route, most LBS software can calculate a variety of "best" routes, including the shortest route, fastest route, fewest-turns route, or nonfreeway route.

A routing engine evaluates the numerous ways a driver might travel over the streets, while accounting for various attributes of the street networks. Routing engines typically examine five attributes while calculating a route, including speed, length of link, travel time, turn restrictions, and one-way indicators. There are usually an enormous number of possible routes between any two points, and the speed and quality of route generation is one of the hallmarks of great LBS engines.

Starting at the route origin, the software uses a technique called the A* (A-star) algorithm to calculate the optimal route. During an A* calculation, all of the possible routes from a given point are considered. The cumulative time and distance to each node is tracked, as well as an estimate of the remaining distance. Routes are arranged from fastest to slowest, and slow routes are discarded when they intersect with faster routes having points in common. The A* algorithm is described in Chapter 3, Navigation Systems.

PROXIMITY SEARCHES

Proximity searches use POI database information to find businesses or landmarks near a specified location. Users can search for locations of ATMs, gas stations, restaurants, hotels, or other establishments.

2.2.3   *The LBS Platform*

The map database, POI database, geocoding, and routing software form the basic components that application developers use to build custom LBS applications (see Figure 2.2). Some LBS vendors have chosen to build their businesses around marketing LBS directly to consumers and/or to provide off-the-shelf packages, such as store finders, to businesses. These applications are attractive to companies that do not need highly customized solutions.

Other vendors target customers such as telcos, voice portals, auto clubs, and E-911 providers, which require custom-built solutions that may include unique features or which need to interface with company-specific databases. These enterprises cannot use a packaged application but need a scalable LBS platform with a set of core services for building applications. Such a standards-based tool set needs application programming interfaces (APIs) that adhere to industry standards such as Java, C, and XML. Other application logic can be layered on top of these location services to build almost any LBS application imaginable.

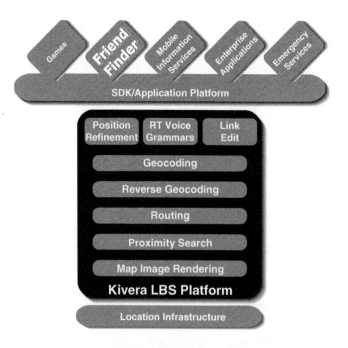

Figure 2.2 Kivera's LBS platform.

With the advent of GPS-equipped cell phones and the continued rise of in-car GPS and navigation devices, the LBS market is poised for enormous growth. Location-based technology is being used to create a wide variety of new location-aware applications, such as AT&T's revolutionary Find Friend offering.

2.3 AT&T'S *FIND FRIEND* APPLICATION

Working with Kivera, AT&T crafted a specific set of requirements for the Find Friend application, ensuring an application that would offer powerful LBS functionality, with a user-friendly front end, making the application accessible to the general mobile-phone-using public.

2.3.1 *User Interface*

The sole user interface for the Find Friend application is the mMode service on AT&T mobile phones. This program offers a simple, WAP-browser-like interface for accessing all of the Find Friend functionality.

The user metaphor for a friend finder application is much like an instant messenger program, yet it is location-aware. The sequence works as follows:

1. First, the user (let us call him Bob) adds selected friends and family members to his friend finder list. This is done simply by typing the friend's (let us call her Ruby) AT&T wireless phone number in the appropriate screen.

2. The friend (Ruby) then receives a text message on her phone, asking if Bob can add her to his friend finder list, enabling him to track her location.

3. If she replies in the affirmative, Ruby is added to Bob's friend list.

4. Bob can now choose Ruby from his friend list and choose "find friend." After querying the location of Ruby's phone, her location (street address or closest intersection) is transmitted to Bob's phone. Ruby is also sent a message, telling her that Bob has located her with the application. (If Ruby ever wants to "hide" from Bob, she can choose to "remain invisible" when powering on her phone.)

5. Once Bob has located Ruby, he can get directions to her location and find restaurants (or other points of interest) near her, or between her and Bob, so that the two can meet.

Figure 2.3 represents the interface flow of a generic friend finder application:

Figure 2.3   Interface flow of a generic friend finder application.

2.3.2   *Find Friend Core LBS Functionality*

GEOCODING/REVERSE GEOCODING

The application must receive latitude/longitude coordinates pinpointing the location of a user's mobile phone and resolve these positions to an address or cross street, city, and state (in the United States). In AT&T's case, these positions come from a Nortel Gateway Mobile Location Centre (GMLC), which looks up the position of a cell tower location. (Further friend finder applications could achieve even more precise accuracy by obtaining the latitude and longitude from GPS chips embedded in emerging mobile phone hardware.)

PHONE LOCATION DISPLAY

Once a phone's location has been reverse geocoded, it will display a description of the mobile phone position, including city and state. It will also display neighborhood information if found within a certain number of miles from the phone location. Distance criteria is to be a system set parameter.

DRIVING DIRECTIONS

A Find Friend user should be able to retrieve driving directions from the origin address or the mobile phone position to the destination address, and potentially provide a route map for email to an end user. A WAP interface for Driving Directions is provided, as well as interfaces for setting route origin and destination. Screens for route results, including trip summary and step-by-step narrative, are developed.

POINT-OF-INTEREST (POI) SEARCH BY PROXIMITY

A user must be able to search for stores, restaurants, and other points-of-interest near his current location, near his friend's location, or at a point between him and his friend. These POIs should be arranged in categories. Features include sort results by proximity and return a maximum of 18 results. POI information should include name, street address, phone number, and category. To access this functionality, WAP interfaces for selecting a POI category and setting the radius for search are provided. Screens for POI results and individual POI records are developed. The POI results list includes name and distance in miles. An individual record screen includes name, distance, address, and phone number.

NEIGHBORHOOD SEARCH BY PROXIMITY

This functionality would allow the phone user to search for neighborhood point data by proximity, allowing the user to know the neighborhood in which his friend is located, and provide driving directions from the phone's location to a given neighborhood.

DETERMINE CITY/NEIGHBORHOOD BETWEEN TWO POSITIONS

This functionality allows two mobile phone users to get directions to a point between them. The application provides for a single function call that identifies a middle point between two coordinate positions and searches for the closest neighborhood or NavTech city point in proximity to that point if NavTech data is used. Features include a maximum of five results, an algorithm for setting the radius for a proximity search based on the distance, a return code for positions with an exact match, and a return code for straight-line distances greater than a system set parameter.

SEARCH FOR ALL FRIENDS

This function allows a user to locate the whereabouts of everyone in his friend list, allowing the user to, for instance, determine what night club to go to or where to find a party of friends. This application function call calculates the straight-line distance between mobile phone position and an array of mobile phone positions. Features include distance returned in miles, a description of mobile phone location for each position, and a return code for positions with an exact match.

2.4   CONCLUSION

People and objects are becoming increasingly "locatable." As GPS-based technology proliferates, there will be new opportunities to deliver personalized, accurate content and applications based on location. Location services will move even further from today's paper map model. We have already started to see location-based advertising, location-aware games, and location-responsive instant-messaging systems. The technology used in GPS devices will likely be extended to develop futuristic location-sensitive watches, cameras, and appliances. As the market evolves, the development of unique LBS applications will be limited only by the talent of programmers and the imagination of marketers.

The building blocks of these new applications are robust LBS platforms, which must have highly accurate and comprehensive map databases, excellent Location Engines, and well-developed APIs. Exceptional applications will use the best and most accurate data, the fastest and most reliable routing and mapping algorithms, packaged with the most imaginative consumer appeal.

AT&T's Find Friend application is a forward-thinking and visionary step in making the first wireless LBS application available to the general public. Following this lead, future mobile devices will be used more frequently to access such dynamic and personal, geo-relevant content. LBS technology and applications will be a key driver of the mobile services market. The full value of geographic data will be derived from the deployment of location-based applications that apply this content in ways that help people better navigate their world.

3

Navigation Systems: A Spatial Database Perspective

Shashi Shekhar, Ranga Raju Vatsavai, Xiaobin Ma, and Jin Soung Yoo
University of Minnesota

CONTENTS

3.1   INTRODUCTION

Navigation systems that guide objects moving from one place to another have progressed recently with the rapid advances in positioning, communication, and spatial data storage and processing technologies. The easy availability of satellite-based global positioning systems has revolutionized all forms of automated navigation. Other positioning technologies such as handsets that use user input and networks that use one of the many location-determining methods are also showing continued advances. The proliferation of such location-aware devices provides us with opportunities to develop a diverse range of location-based applications, many of which will use user location-specific information.

Location-based services (LBS) provide the ability to find the geographical location of a mobile device and then provide services based on that location [OpenLS]. The Open GIS Consortium (OGC) recently initiated the OpenLS standard, which addresses the technical specifications for LBS, to enhance a range of personal, governmental, industrial, and emergency mobile applications. Location-based systems and geographic information systems (GIS) share many common features. At the heart of the OpenGIS Location Services (OpenLS) standard lies the GeoMobility server, which comprises abstract data types (ADTs) and the core services through which a service provider can provide location application services and content to any service point on any device. The core services are location utilities services, directory services, presentation service, gateway service, and route determination service.

These location-based application services require a spatial database (SDB) server, which provides effective and efficient retrieval and management of geospatial data. Spatial database systems serve various spatial data (e.g., digital road maps) and nonspatial information (e.g., route guidance instruction) on request to the client. SDB servers provide efficient geospatial query-processing capabilities such as find the nearest neighbor (e.g., gas station) to a given location and find the shortest path to the destination. The SDB system acts as a back-end server to the GeoMobility server. Thus SDB servers play a crucial role in implementing efficient and sophisticated navigation system applications. This chapter introduces navigation systems from a spatial database perspective.

Section 3.2 briefly reviews the history of navigation systems and provides a generic architecture of a typical navigation system based on

OpenLS specifications. In the subsequent sections, each component of this architecture is presented in detail. Section 3.3 presents various components of SDBs using a digital road map as an example. Section 3.4 introduces gateway service, and Section 3.5 addresses location utility service. Section 3.6 presents the components of directory service. Section 3.7 addresses route determination service and Section 3.8, presentation service. The chapter concludes with a discussion on future research needs.

3.2 NAVIGATION SYSTEMS

A modern navigation system is an integrated collection of position and orientation sensors and computing and communication hardware and software used to facilitate the movement of people, vehicles, and other moving objects from one place to another. It includes methods for determining position, course, and distance traveled. The platform could be anything from land-based vehicles to space-based satellites. So while navigation is the process that guides the movement of an object between two points in space, navigation systems are the hardware and software components that facilitate automated and intelligent navigation. As such, navigation systems cover a broad spectrum of integrated technologies that allow accurate determination of the geographic coordinates of the (moving) objects, their velocity, and height.

The history of navigation is as old as human history, although early navigation was limited to following landmarks and memorizing routes. Historical records show that the earliest vehicle navigation dates back to the invention of the south-pointing carriage in China around 2600 B.C. A brief discussion of other historic vehicle navigation systems can be found in [Zha97]. Well-known navigation devices that were extensively used in early navigation are the magnetic compass and the odometer. The 17th-century discovery of chronometer by John Harrison provided accurate local time at sea, which helped in solving the long-known problem of estimating longitudes [SA03]. The use of navigation devices in automobiles began in the early 20th century. Many modern-day automobiles are equipped with devices that are capable of determining the current location and then dynamically displaying and updating the current position on digital road maps.

Over the centuries, various kinds of technologies have been tried for navigation. The discovery of global positioning systems (GPS) has changed the face of modern navigation forever. In modern vehicle navigation, the second-generation guidance system developed by the U.S. Department of Defense in the mid-1980s, known as the Navigation Satellite Timing and Ranging (NAVSTAR) global positioning system, is becoming widely used. The positional accuracy of civilian GPS receivers has been improved to $+/-$ 10 meters. Submeter accuracy can also be obtained through differential GPS. Navigation inside confined spaces, such as buildings, can be achieved through indoor location-sensing devices. The commonly used sensors for indoor navigation are infrared and short-range radios. Some example indoor navigation systems are Active Badges [WHFG92], Active Bat [HHS + 99], ParcTAB [AGS + 93], Cricket system [PCB02], and the radio frequency identification (RFID) systems [HSK04].

This ability to accurately determine the position of moving objects gave rise to new services known as location-based services. LBS uses accurate and real-time positioning systems and GIS to determine the location of a moving object. The information generated by these systems is sensitive to the current position of the user and can be used to advise users about current conditions such as weather and traffic. Thus navigation systems are the backbone of the location-based services.

The OGC recently initiated the OpenLS standard to address the technical specifications for LBS. The core of LBS applications is the back-end SDB server, which provides efficient storage, management, and processing capabilities for geospatial data. The limitations of earlier navigation systems, which were confined to simple positioning devices and paper-based maps (e.g., road maps, navigation charts), have been diminished with the availability of accurate digital road maps and digital communication systems. The SDB server provides dynamic information on demand to aid automated navigation. Thus navigation systems along with SDBs provide us with opportunities to develop innovative applications ranging from a simple trip plan to complex mobile object monitoring and management systems.

The general architecture of a modern navigation system is shown in Figure 3.1. The components can be broadly classified into four subsystems: the SDB server, the GeoMobility server, communication systems, and the location-aware clients. Client-side components include position-aware devices that range from personal digital assistants (PDAs) and cellular phones to cars, ships, airborne vehicles, and laptops. The client can be totally independent; in that case, the devices can also include small (static) SDBs (e.g., CD/DVD-ROMs); however, in many

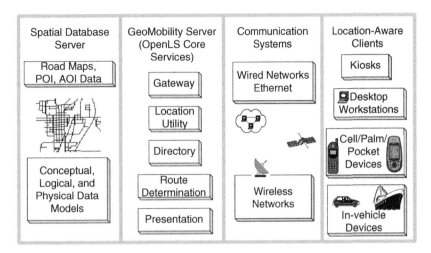

Figure 3.1   Architecture of a modern navigation system.

location-based service applications, the client depends on a server for various services and communicates with the server through wireless and Internet network technologies.

The server-side components include a Web server, a large SDB server, and the application server. The client and server interact through wireless communications. Client-side devices use various visual interfaces (e.g., graphical user interface [Bon93; Mac96; ST91], voice recognition [YLM95; Rab95]) to interact (query and presentation) with the server. Building applications that integrate heterogeneous technological pieces in a viable way is impossible without the help of standards, and OpenLS [OpenLS] is such a standard. Several other standards are similar or address specific issues; for example, Location Interoperability Forum's (LIF) standard addresses location determination methods, and ISO TC/ 204 deals with navigation data formats. The discussion in this chapter is based on the OpenLS standard and describes how the various subsystems work together to form various navigation system applications.

3.2.1   *Spatial Database Server*

An SDB [Guting94; SCR + 99; SC02; RSV01] management system aims at the effective and efficient management of data related to a space in the physical world (e.g., geographic or astronomical space). An SDB server is an essential component for building efficient navigation system applications. It provides conceptual, logical, and physical data modeling facilities to build and manage spatial databases. It serves various spatial (e.g., digital road maps) and aspatial information (e.g., route guidance instructions) on request to the client. It also provides various geospatial query-processing capabilities, such as find the nearest neighbor (e.g., restaurant) to a given location and find the shortest route between two points. It acts as a back-end SDB server to the GeoMobility server. Commercial examples of SDB management systems include Oracle Spatial [SDC], DB2 Spatial Extender [DB2Spatial], and ESRI's Spatial Database Engine [ESRI].

3.2.2   *Open Location Services and GeoMobility Server*

The OGC is an international consortium for developing publicly available geoprocessing specifications. Most of these specifications have been adopted by the industry, and as a result an extremely successful interoperable geospatial infrastructure now exists. The OGC recently initiated an Open Location Services Initiative [OpenLS], which aims at the development of interface specifications that facilitate the use of location and other forms of spatial information in the wireless Internet environment. The purpose of the Initiative is to produce open specifications for interoperable location application services that will integrate spatial data and processing resources into the telecommunications and Internet services infrastructure [OpenLS]. The OpenLS specification allows the deployment of interoperable location-based products and services that will have a far-reaching impact on industry and society.

The *GeoMobility server* is an OpenLS platform through which content/service providers can deliver and service location-based applications. The core services are Location Utilities Service, Directory Service, Presentation Service, Gateway Service, and Route Determination Service.

◆ *Location Utilities Service.* The OpenLS utilities specification provides two services, geocoding and reverse geocoding, and an abstract data type named as Address. The geocoder service is a network-accessible service that transforms a description of a location into a normalized description of the location with point geometry. The reverse geocoder service maps a given position into a normalized description of a feature location.

◆ *Directory Service.* The directory service provides a search capability for one or more points of interest (e.g., a place, product, or service with a fixed position) or area of interest (e.g., a polygon or a bounding box). An example query is "Where is the nearest Thai restaurant to the EE/CS department?"

◆ *Presentation Service.* This service deals with visualization of the spatial information as a map, route, and/or textual information (e.g., route description).

◆ *Gateway Service.* This service enables obtaining the position of a mobile terminal from the network.

◆ *Route Determination Service.* This service provides the ability to find a best route between two points that satisfies user constraints. This service and other network analysis capabilities are described in Section 3.7.

3.2.3 Communication Systems

Telecommunications have undergone significant changes in the last 30 years. In the 1970s, analog communications gave way to digital communications and circuit-switching technology gave way to packet-switching technology. In the early 1980s, the original ARPANET began to evolve into the current Internet. In its early days, the Internet comprised a handful of small networks at universities and defense establishments. Explosive growth of the Internet began during the late 1980s, at the same time personal computers revolutionized the home computing environment.

The Internet can be viewed as the interconnection of thousands of Local Area Networks (LANs) and Wide Area Networks (WANs). Ethernet is the most widely installed LAN technology to connect multiple computers together to enable applications such as file sharing, electronic mail, and Internet access. WANs are simply the interconnection of two or more LANs using some form of telecommunication medium. Asynchronous Transfer Mode (ATM) has been widely adopted for WAN interconnections. Most modern WAN protocols, including TCP/IP and X2.5, are based on packet-switching technologies. ATM combines the best of both worlds (i.e., the guaranteed delivery of circuit-switched networks and the efficiency of packet-switched networks).

The most recent advance in telecommunications is wireless telephony, commonly known as cell phones. Cell phone usage grew exponentially in the United States during the 1990s. More history of communications can be found in [ComSoc]. Today, wireless communication plays an important role in navigation systems. It is what makes user mobility over large geographic areas possible. Both analog and digital wireless systems are used in current communication systems. However, some wireless communication applications such as paging may still need access to wired networks (e.g., Public Switched Telephone Network), and the Internet readily provides countless access points for wireless subnetworks. Some navigation systems such as short-range beacons (used for vehicle to roadside communications) also need wired networks to transfer information from the beacon heads to the navigation management center. Navigation devices communicate with the roadside beacon acceptor, which then transfers information to the navigation center. Location-based services are thus dependent on both wired and wireless networks.

3.2.4   *Location-Aware Clients*

Client-side devices in the architecture of a modern navigation system consist of three basic components: a position and orientation module, a computing module consisting of display and storage, and a communication module. Each client-side module may not necessarily be equipped with all three modules but still can be part of a location-based application. For example, a PDA without a positioning module can utilize the gateway service to obtain its current location. Client-side devices vary widely in nature and function; example devices include but are not limited to PDAs, cell phones, laptops, and land, sea, and airborne vehicles. Client devices may additionally be equipped with visual display units (e.g., touch screens) and voice recognition systems. Stand-alone (or thick) clients can store SDBs locally, either on CD-ROMs, DVDs, or hard disks; however, many location-based clients may need to access GeoMobility Servers.

3.3   SPATIAL DATABASES

3.3.1   *Digital Road Maps*

Location-based services depend heavily on digital road maps, postal addresses, and point-of-interest data sets. These maps are indispensable for any location-based utility that involves position- (e.g., street address) or route-based queries. Current road navigation systems use digital road maps available on CDs or DVDs, but many applications (e.g., emergency services) require dynamic updates from back-end SDB servers. Traditionally, digital road maps were available through governmental departments (e.g., state departments of transportation); however, due to commercial demand, several private-sector companies have begun to offer digital road maps with additional points of interest and areas of interest information. Table 3.1 summarizes various digital road map sources along with important characteristics. Given a wide variety of heterogeneous digital road map databases, it is imperative to understand data quality before building any LBS application.

Table 3.1 Digital road map sources.

Source	Provider	Coverage	Comments
TIGER [TIGER]	U.S. Department of Commerce, Census Bureau	USA	Aggregated from many sources, e.g., USGS, State DOTs, etc. Accuracy inadequate for OLSs in many areas
State base map [MNDOT]	State department of transportation, e.g., MN/DOT	Minnesota, USA	Digitized from 1:24,000 USGS paper map
Navtech [NAVTECH]	Navigation Technologies Corporation	USA, North America, Western Europe	Best accuracy for urban areas
Etak [ETAK]	Tele Atlas	USA, Canada, Western Europe, Hong Kong, Singapore	Best accuracy for urban areas
GDT [GDT]	Geographic data technology	USA, Canada	Better accuracy for nonurban areas
Digital Map 2500 [GSI93]	Geographical Survey Institute (GSI), Japan	Japan	The spatial data framework (SDF2500) includes roads and railways for city planning and as well for Japan as a whole
Philips-Digital Map Data [PDMD03]	Graticule	Great Britain, Europe	Street data specialized for navigation available at different scales

Data quality refers to the relative accuracy and precision of a particular GIS database. These facts are often recorded as a part of metadata. Digital road maps are an important category of geospatial data. The purpose of a geospatial data quality report is to provide detailed information for a user to evaluate the fitness of geospatial data for a particular use. To provide a data quality report based on geospatial data standards, a digital data producer is urged to include the most rigorous and quantitative information available on the components of data quality. In fact, data quality is a part of the geospatial metadata defined by the Federal Geographic Data Committee (FGDC) [FGDC01]. The metadata standard documents the content, quality, condition, and other characteristics of data so that geospatial digital data users can evaluate the data fitness for their purpose. This standard provides a common set of terminology and definitions for the documentation of spatial data, including information on identification, data quality, spatial data organization, spatial reference, entities and attributes, distribution information, and metadata references. There are several map accuracy standards, including the well-known National Map Accuracy Standard (NMAS) [NMAS] and the American Society for Photogrammetry and Remote Sensing (ASPRS) standard [ASPRS]. There are four components of data quality standards:

1. *Lineage.* Refers to the narrative of source materials (e.g., USGS quad sheets) used and procedures (e.g., map projection, map generalization) applied to produce the product.

2. *Positional Accuracy.* Defines expected error in position of features (e.g., landmark points). For example, an NMAS-compliant map guarantees 90% of features within 40 feet of their true position at 1:24,000 scale. New standards (e.g., ASPRS) revised this accuracy for well-defined points.

3. *Attribute Accuracy.* Defines expected error in attributes (e.g., road names). For example, a road map may claim 90% accuracy for a road name attribute.

4. *Completeness.* Defines the fraction of real-world features depicted on a map. For example, a road map includes 99% of available streets.

For current digital road maps, positional accuracies, which are of the most concern in navigation systems, vary greatly for different map sources. Following is a summary of accuracy claims from different sources:

◆ TIGER: mean error = 281 feet (90 m), Median error = 166 feet (50 m). 90th percentile from 110 m to 440 m across different sources
◆ Basemap: 40 feet at 1:24,000 scale, 166 feet at 1:100,000 scale using NMAS
◆ NavTech: 97% accuracy, percent error = linear combination of 13 component errors
◆ Etak: 40 feet at 1:24,000 scale (cover 70% of U.S. population), 166 feet at 1:100,000 scale (covers another 25% of U.S. population), using NMAS
◆ GDT: In enhanced regions, 5 m to 7 m

3.3.2 Data Model of Digital Road Maps

This section presents techniques related to the data modeling of a location-based application. The focus is a digital road map. Database applications are modeled using a three-step design process [EN01]. In the first step, all of the available information related to the application is organized using a high-level *conceptual data model*. The second step, also called the *logical modeling* phase, is related to the actual implementation of the conceptual data model in a commercial database management system (DBMS). The third and final step, modeling of the *physical design*, deals with the nuts and bolts of the actual computer implementation of the database applications.

CONCEPTUAL DATA MODEL

At the conceptual level, the focus is on the data types of the application, their relationships, and their constraints. The actual implementation details are left out at this step of the design process. Plain text combined with simple but consistent graphic notation is often used to express the conceptual data model. The Entity Relationship (ER) model is one of the most widely used conceptual design tools, but it has long been recognized that it is difficult to capture spatial semantics with ER diagrams. The first difficulty lies with geometric attributes, which are complex, and the second difficulty lies with spatial relationships. Several researchers have proposed extensions to the existing modeling languages to support spatial data modeling. The pictogram-enhanced ER (PEER) model

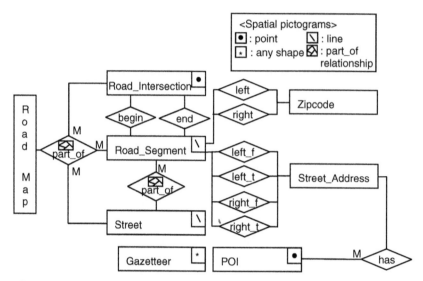

Figure 3.2 A PEER diagram for a digital road map.

proposed in [SVCB99] is used to show the conceptual model of a digital road map.

Figure 3.2 shows a PEER diagram for a digital road map. Spatial networks (e.g., road maps) are modeled as graphs, where vertices are points embedded in space. *Graph* consists of a finite set of *vertices* and a set of *edges*. In a digital road map, vertices represent road intersections and edges represent road segments, which are lines connecting two intersections. Sometimes labels (e.g., name) and weights (e.g., miles, travel time) are attached to each vertex and edge to encode additional information. A road segment is modeled with (a range of) street addresses, which is commonly used in geocoding (i.e., assigning a coordinate to a given address such as "511 Washington Ave") and reverse geocoding (i.e., finding the address given a coordinate), as suggested in [VW01]. The street addresses are divided into left-side addresses and right-side addresses. Each side keeps two end addresses: from and to. The zip code information of a street address is used for searching a map when the exact address is unknown. The left-side and right-side zip codes are also attached to the road_segment. Two edges are *adjacent* if they share a common node. A sequence of adjacent edges constitutes a *path*. At the conceptual level, a path is modeled as a street. This diagram also includes Point of Interest (POI) and Gazetteer entities for supporting directory service of the OpenLS standard.

LOGICAL DATA MODEL

The logical modeling phase is related to the actual implementation of the conceptual data model in a commercial DBMS. Data are organized using an implementation model without any regard to actual storage details. Examples of implementation models are hierarchical, network, relational, and object-oriented models. A hybrid object-relational data model is also gaining popularity and being implemented in current commercial SDBs. [SVCB99] provided the grammar-based translation scheme for mapping a pictogram-extended ER model onto an object-relational model. This mapping uses OGC simple feature specification for SQL [OGC98]. The SQL functions (methods) specified by the OGIS specification fall into three categories: (1) basic functions on the Geometry data types, (2) operators for testing topological relationships, and (3) functions that support spatial analysis. The OGIS standard specifies the data types and the operations on these data types that are essential for spatial applications such as GIS.

Although relational database management systems (RDBMS) provide a fixed set of data types, object-relational database management systems (ORDBMS) support recently standardized SQL3, which allows user-defined data types. This mechanism allows user-defined complex spatial data types such as point, line, and polygon. The actual mapping between a PEER model and OGIS/SQL3 logical model is guided through the definition of grammar and the translation rules. In general, entity pictograms translate into appropriate data types in SQL3, and the relationship pictograms translate into spatial integrity constraints.

Table 3.2 shows a relational schema for the digital road map example. There are six tables: Road_Map, Road_Intersection, Road_Segment, Street, POI, and Gazetteer. The Road_Map table is represented as an adjacency_list graph in order to support routing algorithms (see Section 3.7). The relationships of left-side and right-side zip codes, and the four street address relationships for geocoding, are placed as attributes in the road_segment relation. In addition, commercial database companies have introduced the notion of providing application-specific packages, which provide a seamless interface to the database user. For example, Oracle provides a *Spatial Data Cartridge* package [SDC] for GIS-related applications.

PHYSICAL DATA MODEL

In the physical data modeling phase, issues related to storage, indexing, and memory management are addressed. Physical database design is

Table 3.2 Relational schema for a digital road map.

Table Name	Primary Key	Attributes	Secondary Indices
Road_Map (A nested table)	Map_Id	Cover_area, nodes with adjacency lists	CCAM on road map
Road_Intersection	Intersection_Id	Coordinate	
Road_Segment	Segment_Id	Begin_intersect_Id, End_intersect_Id, Shape, Street_Id, Distance, Left_ zipcode, Right_ zipcode, Left_from_street_addr, Left_to_street_addr, Right_from *street* addr, Right_to_street_addr	R-Tree B+tree B+tree
Street	Street_Id	Street_name, Street_type, Direction, Speed, Oneway	
POI	POI_Id	Type, Name, Address, Coordinate	B+tree R-Tree
Gazeter	Type	Name, Address	

critical to ensure reasonable performance for various queries written in an elegant but high-level logical language such as SQL, which provides no hints about implementation algorithms or data structures. Historically, physical database design techniques such as B+ tree index are credited for the large-scale adoption of relational database technology by providing reasonable response time for SQL queries of many kinds. Well-known file organizations are hashed files and ordered files; however, ordered file organization cannot be used directly for spatial objects (e.g., location of a city) because no natural total order is defined on points in a multidimensional space. This situation has given rise to several mapping techniques such as Z-order and Hilbert curves, also known as space-filling curves. Even though there is no ideal mapping technique, the mapping of points in multidimensional space into one-dimensional values will enable the use of the well-known B+ tree indexing structure.

A fundamental idea in spatial indexing is the use of approximations. This allows index structures to manage an object in terms of one or more spatial keys, which are much simpler geometric objects than the object itself. The prime example is the *bounding box* (the smallest axis-parallel rectangle enclosing the object). For grid approximations, space is divided into cells by a regular grid, and the object is represented by the set of cells that it intersects. Well-known spatial indexing structures are R-tree and several variants of it. An R-tree is a height-balanced tree that is the natural extension of a B-tree for *k*-dimensions. Objects are represented in the R-tree by their minimum bounding rectangle (MBR). Figure 3.3 shows a set of spatial objects (MBRs) in a two-dimensional space and an R-tree for the set of MBRs. These well-known indexing methods provide efficient query processing involving point and range queries.

For the digital road map example, B+ tree can be used on street address attributes of road_segment for geocoding (see Table 3.2). For example, to transfer from a given address, "511 Washington Ave, Minneapolis, MN" to a coordinate, first find the road segment using secondary indices on street addresses and then search for a coordinate of the given address through connected road segments. For reverse geocoding (i.e., finding the street address given a coordinate), we can use an approximation method using a spatial index (e.g., R-tree in which the road segment is indexed in terms of one spatial key). The nearest road segment object to a query point gives the street address. Similarly, in the POI table, B+ tree can be used for text-based searches (e.g., name) and R-tree, which is defined on point coordinates, might be used for supporting proximity queries (point query, range query, and nearest neighbor query).

Several location-based services, especially those that deal with network databases (e.g., road networks), have to deal with efficient network computations. Figure 3.4 shows three different representations of a graph.

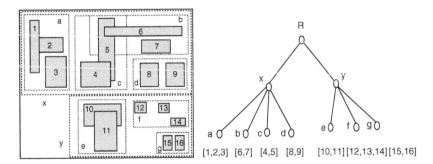

Figure 3.3   A collection of spatial objects and its R-tree hierarchy. Shekhar, Shashi; Chawla, Sanjay, Spatial Databases: A Tour, 1st Edition, © 2003. Reprinted by permission of Pearson Education, Inc., Upper Saddle River, NJ.

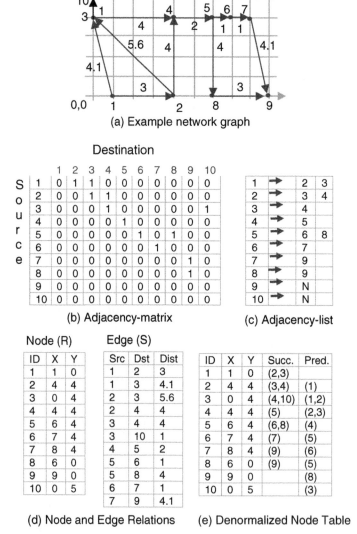

Figure 3.4   Three different representations of a graph.

The *Adjacency-matrix* and the *Adjacency-list* are two well-known main-memory data structures for implementing graphs. In the *Adjacency-matrix,* the rows and the columns of a graph represent the vertices of the graph. A matrix entry can be either 1 or 0, depending on whether there is an edge between the two vertices, as shown in Figure 3.4(b). The *Adjacency-list* structure is efficient for queries that involve enumerating the vertices of a graph: Find all neighbors of *v*. The *Adjacency-list* data structure is an array of pointers. Each element of the array corresponds to a vertex of the graph, and the pointer points to a list of immediate neighbors of the vertex, as shown in Figure 3.4(c); however, main-memory data structures are not suitable for database applications because the database is usually too big to fit in main memory at one time.

Directed graphs can be implemented in a relational model using a pair of relations for the nodes and edges of the graph. The *Node* (R) and the *Edge* (S) relations are shown in Figure 3.4 (d). A denormalized representation is shown in Figure 3.4 (e). The directed graph representation is often used to speed up shortest path computation. This representation of a node table contains coordinates, a list of successors, and a list of predecessors. This representation is used to model the digital road map example (Road_Map table in Table 3.3).

[SL97] have proposed a new spatial access method called the Connectivity-Clustered Access Method (CCAM) for general network databases. CCAM clusters the nodes of the network via graph partition. In contrast with the previous topological ordering-based approach, CCAM assigns segments to the data page by a graph partitioning approach, which tries to maximize the connectivity residue ratio. Each data page is kept at least half full whenever possible. In addition, an auxiliary secondary index is used to support the Find(), get-a-Successor(), and get-Successors() operations. B+ tree with Z-order can also be used to

Table 3.3 Query types for directory service.

Type	Subtype	Query Attribute	Query Example
Attribute Query	Unique Attribute Query	A unique identifier (e.g., the name (of restaurant), address	Where is the Red Dragon Chinese restaurant?
	Property Attribute Query	Some property or attribute (e.g., the type of restaurant, named reference category, keyword list)	Where are the Chinese restaurants?
Proximity Query	Point Query	Pointed location (e.g., highlighted location)	Where am I?
	Range Query	Spatial region within some distance of some other location (e.g., within boundary)	Which Chinese restaurants are within 500 meters of my hotel?
	Nearest Neighbor Query	Some point location (e.g., nearest (to my hotel))	Where is the nearest Chinese restaurant to my hotel?

index road maps. Other access methods, such as the R-tree or Grid File, can alternatively be created as secondary indexes in CCAM to suit an application.

3.4   GATEWAY SERVICE

Gateway service is the interface between the Open Location Services Platform and Mobile Positioning Servers through which the platform obtains near real-time position data for mobile terminals.

Positioning and orientation devices are vital to any navigation system. This chapter is concerned only with land-based navigation systems, so here positioning means the determination of the coordinates of a vehicle, person, or any moving object on the surface of the earth. There are three types of positioning systems commonly in use: stand-alone, satellite-based, and terrestrial radio-based [Zha97].

3.4.1   Stand-Alone Positioning Systems

Deduced (or "dead") reckoning (DR) is the typical stand-alone technique to determine "current position" with reference to a "starting position," and was commonly used by sailors before the development of celestial navigation. In order to determine the current position, DR incrementally integrates the distance traveled and the direction of travel relative to the known start location. In earlier times, direction used to be determined by magnetic compass, and the distance traveled was computed by the time of travel and the speed of the vehicle. In modern land-based navigation, however, various sensor devices can be used to compute accurate direction and distance traveled by the vehicle. Example sensors are differential odometers, gyroscopes, magnetic compasses, and transmission pickup sensors.

3.4.2   Satellite-Based Positioning Systems

The Navigation Satellite Timing and Ranging (NAVSTAR) global positioning system is the well-known satellite-based positioning technology that is widely used in modern vehicle navigation. GPS consists of three parts: (1) the space segment (which is a constellation of 24 operational satellites), (2) the user segment (GPS receivers), and (3) the control segment (consisting of monitoring stations, ground antennas, and the coordinating master control station). The 3D coordinates (latitude, longitude, and altitude) of a GPS receiver can be calculated from the simultaneous observation of three or more satellites with a positional accuracy of 10 meters. Using differential GPS, which combines signals from satellites and ground-based sources with known fixed locations, a positional accuracy of submeter can be achieved. Following is a sample format of GPS data (GPGGA) from the Trimble GPS receiver, where $GPGGA is the message id ($GP) followed by time, position, and fix related data (GGA), and UTC represents coordinated universal time. This structure is confined to the National Marine Electronics Association's NMEA-0183 Version 2.30 format [NMEA].

$GPGGA	UTC	Latitude	Lat. Dir. (S/N)	Longitude	Long. Dir. (E/W)	Data Quality	...

3.4.3 (Terrestrial) Radio-Based Positioning Systems

Radio-based positioning systems are designed for specific applications (e.g., offshore navigation) and are generally managed by government and military/naval agencies. Terrestrial positioning systems commonly employ direction or angle of arrival (AOA), absolute timing or time of arrival (TOA), and differential time of arrival (TDOA) techniques to determine the position of a vehicle. The radio navigation systems commonly operate in three frequencies: low ($< 300\,kHz$), medium ($300\,kHz$–$0.3\,MHz$), and high (0.3–$10\,GHz$) frequency. Well-known radio navigation systems are DECCA (operated by some European governments), Omega (developed by the U.S. Navy Submarine Service), and LORAN-C (operated by the U.S. Coast Guard).

Indoor navigation systems generally use infrared and short-range radios. A recent article shows the popularity of inexpensive radio frequency identification (RFID) tags for tracking moving objects inside retail stores. The mobile networking community uses a technique known as Cell Identification (Cell-ID).

3.5 LOCATION UTILITY SERVICE

The OpenLS utilities specification provides two services: geocoder and reverse geocoder, and an abstract data type named Address. The geocoder service is a network-accessible service that transforms the description of a location into a normalized description of the location with point geometry. Conversely, the reverse geocoder service maps a given positioning into a normalized description of a feature location.

3.5.1 Geocoding

Geocoding is the process of assigning an x, y coordinate (e.g., latitude, longitude) to a given address. Once such point geometry is computed, the given address can be displayed on a map. "Address interpolation" is a well-known geocoding technique. Given a street segment with start and end coordinates, and an associated address range (e.g., a tuple from the Road_segment table defined in the Logical Data Modeling section), we can interpolate the (approximate) location of any given address that falls within the given range by simply dividing the length of the road segment by the number of houses. In case of ambiguities, the approximate location can be computed as the centroid of the zip code.

3.5.2 Reverse Geocoding

As the name suggests, reverse geocoding is exactly the opposite of geocoding (i.e., find the address given an x, y coordinate). Reverse geocoding occurs virtually all the time; find an address (e.g., a landmark, a restaurant) given my current location. But because the coordinates predicted by the GPS receiver contain errors, we need to identify the most likely segment of the road network given the predicted location. This task is commonly known as *map matching*. Map-matching techniques can be broadly classified as geometric, probabilistic, and fuzzy.

GEOMETRIC

The geometric techniques utilize only the predicted location(s) and the road segments. The well-known geometric techniques are point-to-point matching, point-to-curve matching, and curve-to-curve matching. In point-to-point matching, the objective is to find the closet node n_i to the measured position p (e.g., the location predicted by GPS). Generally, the Euclidean distance is used to find the distance between p and n_i. The number of nodes n_i is quite large in a road network; however, this number can be reduced using a range query with a suitable window size and the appropriate spatial access method (e.g., R-tree, CCAM). In point-to-curve matching, the objective is to find the closest curve from the measured point. Here we find the minimum distance between a

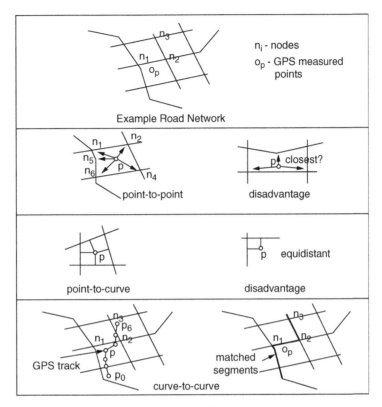

Figure 3.5 Geometric map-matching techniques.

p and the line segments l_i. Both of these methods have limitations. A more accurate geometric method, curve-to-curve matching, uses the piecewise linear curve (generated by connecting the points predicted by a GPS) to find the closest line segment. These methods are summarized in Figure 3.5, and more details on these methods can be found in [BK96].

PROBABILISTIC

Using sensor-specific error models, the probabilistic algorithms first compute a confidence region along the measured track (e.g., GPS track). A map overlay (or spatial join) of this estimated region with the road network layer gives the road segment on which the vehicle is traveling. If more than one road segment is found within the estimated region, however, then the most probable road segment is estimated using various checks (e.g., road network topology, history). More rigorous probabilistic models for map matching can be found in [PSS01;KJL00].

FUZZY LOGIC

Expert rules, such as amount of distance traveled and directional changes in the heading of the vehicle, are assigned fuzzy membership functions. A map-matching module then evaluates the sensor (GPS) measurements and road networks to find the matching segment and position of the vehicle. More details on probabilistic and fuzzy map matching can be found in [Zha97].

3.6 DIRECTORY SERVICE

The directory service of location-based services provides a search capacity for one or more Points of Interest (POI). A POI is a place, product, or service with a fixed position, typically identified by name rather than by address and characterized by type. A POI may be used as a reference or a target point in many query types (see Table 3.3). The query types can be divided into two types: (1) attribute queries, based on nonspatial attributes, and (2) proximity queries, based on spatial attributes. An attribute query is subdivided into a unique attribute query or a property attribute query. The unique attribute query amounts to a pinpoint White Pages query, which constrains the request by the identifier. The property attribute query is a normal Yellow Pages query constrained by nonunique attributes. Attribute queries are well supported by the query-processing methods of traditional relational databases.

Proximity queries are based on spatial objects and are divided into three types: point queries, range queries, and nearest neighbor queries.

3.6.1 Point Query (PQ)

Given a query point P, find all spatial objects O that contain it:

$$PQ(p) = \{O \mid p \in O.G \neq \phi\}$$

where $O.G$ is the geometry of object O. The spatial query-processing method of a point query can be used by a spatial index. First, in the filter step, the spatial objects are represented by simpler approximations such as the MBR. Determining whether a query point is in an MBR is less expressive than checking if a point is in an irregular polygon. The spatial operator, contain, can be approximated using the overlap relationship among corresponding MBRs. In the refinement step, the exact geometry of each element from the candidate set is examined.

3.6.2   Range Query (RQ)

Given a query polygon P, find all spatial objects O which intersect P. When the query polygon is a rectangle, this query is called a *window query*.

$$RQ(p) = \{O | O.G \cap P.G \neq \phi\}$$

If records are ordered using a space-filling curve (say Z-order), then the range of Z-order values satisfying the range query is determined. A binary search is used to get the lowest Z-order within the query answer. The data file is scanned forward until the highest Z-order satisfying the query is found. Range query can also be processed in a top-down recursive manner using spatial index structures (e.g., R-tree). These methods work in the same manner as in the point query. The query region is tested first against each entry (MBR, child-pointer) in the root. If the query region overlaps with MBR, then the search algorithm is applied recursively on entries in the R-tree node pointed to by the child-pointer. This process stops after reaching the leaves of the R-tree. The selected entries in the leaves are used to retrieve the records associated with the selected spatial keys.

3.6.3   Nearest Neighbor Query (NNQ)

Given a query point P, find the spatial object O with the smallest distance to P:

$$NNQ(p) = \{O | dist(O.G, P.G) \leq dist(O'.G, P.G)\}$$

Here O' are all other spatial objects except O. The most common type of nearest neighbor search is the point k-Nearest Neighbor (KNN) query, which finds the k point objects that are closest to a query point. Conceptually, one strategy for the nearest neighbor query applies to a two-pass algorithm. The first pass retrieves the data page D containing query object P to determine *dist*, the minimum distance between any objects in D to P. The second pass is a range query to retrieve objects within distance *dist* of P for determination of the nearest object. This approach reuses the spatial index algorithm for spatial selection (e.g., point query and range query). Most of the current research on KNN query is based on utilizing different spatial index structures such as R-trees or Quad-trees. The representative algorithm in a branch-and-bound manner was proposed originally by [RKV95]. The algorithm traverses a spatial index tree in a depth-first manner to visit entries with a

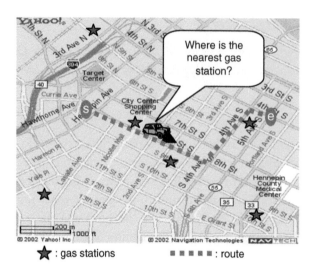

: gas stations   : route

Figure 3.6   An example of a nearest neighbor query. Background map courtesy of Yahoo! and NAVTEQ.

minimum distance from a query point. A similar technique for moving query point is described in [SR01].

Figure 3.6 shows a typical example of NNQ on a road network. Consider a situation in which a mobile user is on his way to a destination and wants to find the nearest gas station close to the route. Some recent studies have proposed NNQ techniques to solve this problem. Figure 3.7 shows four different ways to find the nearest neighbor on a road network. In the figure, the circle represents a current location on the route and the large diamond represents the nearest neighbor found by each method. Each method generates a different nearest neighbor. In Figure 3.7(a), the route is regarded as several consecutive line segments. [TPS02] proposes a continuous nearest neighbor search method for a query point (current location of the user) that is moving on a trajectory. This approach generates a result consisting of a set of <point, interval> tuples in which a point is the nearest neighbor in the corresponding interval. Figure 3.7(b) shows a neighborhood query generation model that takes account of the current position and the past/future trajectories of the moving points [IKK02]. Most NNQ methods use Euclidean distance as the distance measure. In LBS, however, especially those that deal with spatial network databases (e.g., road networks), the Euclidean distance may not properly approximate the real road-distance. Figure 3.7(c) presents [FW02]'s method for searching the nearest neighbor from a

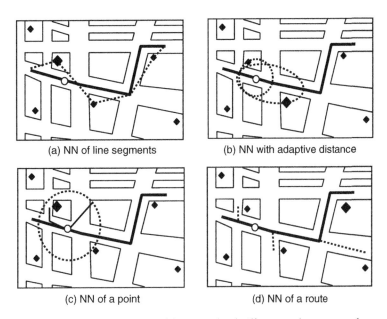

(a) NN of line segments   (b) NN with adaptive distance

(c) NN of a point   (d) NN of a route

Figure 3.7 Nearest neighbor methods illustrated on a road network.

query point on the road network. The algorithm consists of two interactive steps: a filtering step using Euclidean distance and a refinement step using road-distance.

Figure 3.7(d) shows another variation of NNQ [SY03], which tries to find the nearest neighbor having a minimum detour length from the predetermined route. The nearest neighbor in Figure 3.7(d) is very different from the other nearest neighbors in Figure 3.7. One approach for this problem uses an approximation method of finding the closest pair [CMTV00] between two spatial data sets (spatial object points and intersect points of the route), where each set is indexed by an R-tree, and rechecked it with the road-distance. Another approach uses an "Allocate" operation, which divides the road network into service areas of a given set of spatial objects. For all points P in the service area of a spatial object O_i, road_distance(P,O_i) $<=$ road_distance(P,O_j), $\forall_{j \neq I}$, only those service areas that intersect with a given route are considered for determining the nearest neighbor.

Most queries are composed from a fixed set of basic operations. These basic relational operations form the building blocks for the composition of all complex queries. Query processing maps high-level queries into a composition of basic relational operators and then optimizes them.

3.7 ROUTE DETERMINATION SERVICE

Route determination services address finding route and navigation information between locations. Route determination should support the following two services. The first deals with the determination of a new route; given a start location, end location, optional waypoints, and a set of route criteria, find the best path. Possible criteria are fastest, shortest, easiest, pedestrian, public transportation, avoid locations/areas, avoid highways, avoid tollways, avoid U-turns, and avoid ferries. The second service deals with the determination of alternate routes. The new (alternate) route should have minimal overlap with the existing route. After determining the route, returned combined information are route summary information, route maneuver and advisory information, route geometry, maps of the route and maneuvers, and turn-by-turn instructions, in presentation format.

3.7.1 Path-Query Processing

Path-query processing is an important ingredient in spatial network applications. Support for navigation, route planning, and traffic management essentially reduces to providing *path options* based on some application-dependent criterion. For example, a well-known graph operation is determining the "shortest" path between two points A and B on a road network where the "shortest" criterion could be based on distance, travel time, or some other user-specified constraint. Underlying the computation of all path queries are *graph traversal* algorithms, which search for paths by traversing from one node to another along the edges of a graph. As we have seen before, searching for paths is a recursive operation, and therefore the adjacency lists of nodes have to be repeatedly transferred from secondary storage to the main memory buffer. Graph traversal algorithms form the backbone of all path computation algorithms. Examples of well-known graph traversal algorithms are breadth-first, depth-first, and Dijkstra's and best-first A*. The description of breadth-first and depth-first search algorithms can be found in any basic data structures textbook. Memory-bounded and hierarchical search algorithms are described in the next subsection. Examples showing how all of these algorithms work are provided at the end of this section.

DIJKSTRA'S ALGORITHM

Dijkstra's algorithm can be used to solve the single-source (partial transitive closure) problem. Given a source node v, Dijkstra's algorithm will compute the shortest path from the source node v to all other reachable nodes using a best-first search where frontier nodes are ranked by their path lengths to the source. Dijkstra's algorithm is a classic shortest-path search algorithm that can be found in many books, including [SC02].

BEST-FIRST A* ALGORITHM

Best-first search has been a framework for heuristics that speed up algorithms by using semantic information about a domain. A* (A-star) is a special case of the best-first search algorithm. The cost function from node s to d is of the form $cost(s, d) = g(s, v) + h(v, d)$, among which $cost(s, d)$ is total cost, $g(s, v)$ is the cost from s to v, and $h(v, d)$ is the estimated cost from v to d. It uses an estimator function $h(v, d)$ (also known as f-cost) to estimate the cost of the shortest path between nodes v and d. The A* search without estimator functions is not very different from Dijkstra's algorithm. The pseudo-code is shown in Figure 3.8. The procedure terminates when it finds destination node d as the best node.

```
procedure A*(G(V,E),v,d,f);
{
    var: integer;
    foreach  u in V do {if (v,u) is edge then g(v,u) = edge(v,u) else g(v,u) = inf;
    g(v,v) = 0; path(v,u):= null}
    frontierSet := [v]; exploredSet := emptySet;
    while not_empty(frontierSet) do
    {
            select w from frontierSet with minimum(g(v,w)+ h(w,d));
            frontierSet := frontierSet - [w]; exploredSet := exploredSet + [w];
            if(u = d) then terminate
            else {
                    fetch( w.adjacencyList);
                    foreach < u, g(w,u)> in w.adjacencyList
                    if g(v,u) > g(v,w) + edge(w,u) then
                    {
                            g(v,u) := g(v,w) + edge(w,u);
                            path(v,u) := path(v,w) + (w,u);
                            if frontierSet ∪ exploredSet ∈ u then
                                    frontierSet := frontierSet + [u];
                    }
            }
    }
}
```

Figure 3.8 Best-first A*.

This procedure can terminate quickly if the shortest path from s to d has fewer edges. It does not have to examine all nodes to discover the shortest path, as in the case of many other algorithms (e.g., Dijkstra). Furthermore, the estimator can provide extra information to focus the search on the shortest path to the destination, reducing the number of nodes to be examined. The best-first A* search algorithm is complete and optimal.

MEMORY-BOUNDED SEARCH ALGORITHMS

Previously introduced algorithms assume that the system has unlimited memory that can hold all information used in these search algorithms. In reality, however, many systems have memory limitations, so we need algorithms that work with given memory bounds.

Let us consider a search tree of maximum depth m and branching factor b. Let us also assume that a solution (destination node) can be found at depth d. The time and space (memory) requirements for simple breadth-first and depth-first search algorithms are $O(b^d)$, $O(b^d)$ and $O(b^m)$, $O(bm)$, respectively. It is easy to see that the memory requirements are much higher as the problem size increases for breadth-first as compared to depth-first search algorithms. Although the depth-first search has modest memory requirements, it may get stuck going down the wrong path. This pitfall can be avoided by limiting the depth of the search path. Finding a good depth limit is not an easy task, however, and this limitation has led to the development of the iterative deepening search algorithm. The iterative deepening search algorithm combines the benefits of depth-first and breadth-first algorithms; it is optimal, complete, and has modest memory requirements $O(bd)$. We now present two algorithms, IDA* and SMA*, that are designed to work with modest memory requirements.

IDA*

The IDA* algorithm is a logical extension of the iterative-deepening search algorithm. The algorithm is similar to best-first A* presented previously; however, instead of a best-first search strategy, we use an iterative-deepening search. The algorithm [RN95] shown in Figure 3.9 proceeds in the same manner as depth-first; however, it uses a cost function (f-cost) to limit the search depth, rather than a fixed depth-limit. The f-cost of a node is given by $f(n) = g(n) + h(n)$, where $g(n)$ is the cost of the path from the start node to node n and $h(n)$ is the estimated cost of

```
function IDA* (problem) returns a solution sequence
  inputs: problem, a problem
  local variables: f-limit, the current f-cost limit
      root, a node
      root ←MAKE-NODE(INITIAL-STATE[problem])
      f-limit ← f-COST (root)
  loop do
      solution,f-limit ← DFS-CONTOUR(root,f-limit)
      if solution is non-null then return solution
      if f-limit = ∞  then return failure; end

function DFS -CONTOUR (node, f-limit) returns a solution sequence and a
  new f- COST limit
  inputs: node, a node
      f-limit, the current f-COST limit
  local variables: next-f , the f-COST limit for the next contour, initially ∞
  if f-COST [node] > f-limit then return null, f-COST [node]
  if GOAL-TEST [problem] (STATE[node]) then return node, f-limit
  for each node s in SUCCESSOR (node) do
      solution, new-f ←DFS-CONTOUR (s, f-limit)
      if solution is non-null then return solution, f-limit
      next-f ← MIN (next-f,new-f);end
  return null, next-f
```

Figure 3.9   IDA* algorithm.

the path from the node n to the destination node. First, each iteration expands all of the nodes inside the contour for the current f-cost. If a solution is not found, then the search extends over to the next contour line (f-cost). Once the search inside a given contour is complete, a new iteration is started, using a new f-cost for the next contour.

IDA* is complete and optimal under the same conditions as A*; however, it requires memory proportional to the longest path it explores. Although bd, branching factor time depth, is a good estimate of the storage requirement in most cases, IDA* suffers from duplicate computations because it remembers only the current cost between iterations.

SMA*

The simplified memory-bounded A* algorithm tries to avoid the duplicate computations of IDA* by remembering as much history as the memory permits and not just the f-cost, as in the case of IDA*. If there is no memory left and the algorithm still needs to generate a successor, the most unpromising node (i.e., the shallowest and highest f-cost node) is dropped from the queue. The SMA* algorithm is optimal and complete if enough memory is available; otherwise, it returns the best

Algorithm SMA* (start):
OPEN = {start};
USED ← 1;

loop

        if empty(OPEN) **return** FALSE;
        best ← deepest least-f-cost leaf in OPEN;
        if (d = best) return TRUE;
        u ← next-successor(best);
        f(u) ← max(f(best), g(u) + h(u));
        if (completed(best)), BACKUP(best);
        if (S(best) all in memory, remove best from OPEN.
        USED ← USED + 1;

        if (USED > MAX) **then**
                delete shallowest, highest-f-cost node in OPEN;
                remove it from its parent's successor list;
                insert its parent on OPEN if necessary;
                USED ← USED - 1;
        endif
        insert u in OPEN.
end of loop

Procedure BACKUP(n)
if n is completed and has a parent **then**
        f(n) ← least f-cost of all successors;
        if f(n) changed, **BACKUP**(parent(n)).

Figure 3.10 The SMA* search algorithm.

solution that can be found using the given memory. A simplified SMA* algorithm [Rus92] is shown in Figure 3.10. SMA* uses a binary tree of binary trees data structure to store the current node (OPEN) sorted by f and depth, respectively. MAX is a global variable used to represent the maximum number of nodes that can be fit into memory, and the USED variable is used to keep track of how many nodes are currently in memory. Each node contains its g, h, and f-costs, as well as the minimum f-cost of its examined successors. S(n) denotes n's successor list. A node with no unexamined successors is called complete.

HIERARCHICAL STRATEGIES

Hierarchical algorithms decompose a large spatial graph into a boundary graph and a collection of fragment graphs, each of which is much smaller than the original graph. Hierarchical graphs are particularly useful in reducing input/output (I/O) costs and main-memory buffer requirements for processing queries on graphs that are too large to fit inside the main-memory buffers.

The basic idea of a hierarchical algorithm for computing a shortest path is to decompose the original graph into a set of smaller-fragment graphs and a summary graph called a *boundary* graph. Proper construction of the *boundary* graph allows an optimality, preserving decomposition of the shortest path query on the original graph into a set of shortest path queries on the smaller graphs.

The hierarchical graph has a two-level representation of the original graph. The lower level is made up of a set of fragments of the original graph. The higher-level graph consists of the boundary nodes and is called the boundary graph. Boundary nodes are defined as the set of nodes that have a neighbor in more than one fragment, i.e.,

$$N_i \in BN \Leftrightarrow \exists E_{i,j}, E_{i,k} | FRAG(k) \neq FRAG(j)$$

Edges in the boundary graph are called boundary edges, and the boundary nodes of a fragment form a clique (i.e., they are completely connected). The cost associated with the boundary edge is the shortest-path cost through the fragment between the boundary nodes. A boundary edge is associated with a fragment identifier. A *boundary path* is the shortest path through the boundary graph.

The hierarchical algorithm is composed of three steps: (1) finding the relevant boundary-node pair in the boundary graph, (2) computing the boundary path, and (3) expanding the boundary path. The first step in determining the shortest path is to compute the boundary node through which the shortest path leaves the source's fragment and enters the destination's fragment. If both the source and destination are boundary nodes, then the algorithm is trivial. If the source is an internal node and the destination is a boundary node, then the boundary node through which the shortest path leaves the source's fragment is found by querying the fragment graph for the cost of the path from the source to all boundary nodes of that fragment, and by querying the boundary graph for the cost of the shortest path from all boundary nodes of the source's fragment to the destination. The source-boundary-destination path with the lowest aggregate cost determines the appropriate boundary node.

The case where the source is a boundary node and the destination is an internal node is similar, but the roles of the source and destination are reversed. When both the source and destination are internal nodes, the appropriate boundary node pair is found by querying the fragment graphs to determine the cost of the shortest path from the internal nodes to all boundary nodes of the fragment. Next, the boundary graph is queried to compute the shortest-path cost between all pairs of boundary nodes. The path with the lowest aggregate cost determines the boundary-node pair. Once the appropriate boundary-node pair has been determined, the boundary graph is queried to determine the shortest path between those boundary nodes. The final step is to expand the boundary path by querying the fragments for the shortest path through them. Adjacent nodes in the boundary path form source/destination pairs on which the shortest-path query can be run on in a fragment. For more details and related techniques, see [JHR95; JHR98; JP02; JSQ00].

We now briefly analyze how each algorithm described in the previous section performs on the example graph shown in Figure 3.4(a). Let us assume that the source node is 1 and the goal node is 9. The estimated cost h from a given node n to the goal node 9 is shown in Table 3.4.

In the first iteration, Dijkstra's algorithm explores edges (1,2) and (1,3) and then selects node 2 (as $cost(1,2) < cost(1,3)$) and set cost $g(1,2) = 3$. In the next iteration, it picks node 3 (as the $[cost(1,2) + cost(2,4)] > [cost(1,3) + cost(3,10)]$ and $[cost(1,2) + cost(2,3)] > [cost(1,3) + cost(3,10)]$). Applying the same logic, it examines other nodes from adjacency lists and puts them into the frontier set. This process continues ÿmpro the algorithm finds the shortest path from node 1 to node 9.

On the other hand, best-first A* uses an improved heuristic cost function, which also considers the cost between the current node and the

Table 3.4 Estimated cost to goal node (9).

Node (n)	$h(n)$
1	8
2	5
3	9.8
4	6.4
5	5
6	4.5
7	4.1
8	3
10	10.3

Table 3.5   Summary of path-finding results.

Algorithm		Solution
Dijkstra		1,2,4,5,6,7,9
A*		1,2,4,5,6,7,9
IDA*	f-limit = 16	1,2,4,5,6,7,9
SMA*	Mem = 5	No solution
	Mem = 6	1,2,4,5,8,9
	Mem = 7	1,2,4,5,6,7,9
Hierarchical (with A*)		1,2,4,5,6,7,9

destination node. At first iteration, it picks up node 2 (because the $[g(1,2) + h(2,9)] < [g(1,3) + h(3,9)]$). It then examines nodes 3 and 4, which are neighbors of node 2. The cost through node $4 (g(1,4) + h(4,9) < g(1,3) + h(3,9))$ is minimum to reach node 9. So as compared to Dijkstra's, A* will not expand node 3 at this iteration. Applying the same logic, best-first A* examines all necessary nodes in the following iterations. Finally, it will find the shortest path from node 1 to node 9. In the case of the IDA* algorithm, we first set the contour line to be the f-limit of $h(1,9)$, which is 8. In the first iteration, we find a new f-limit by finding the minimum f-cost that is greater than the current f-limit. This means the search expands from node 1 to node 2 because $g(1,2) + h(2,9)$, which gives the new contour line, is less than $g(1,3) + h(3,8)$. Applying similar logic, in the next iteration we find the minimum cost of the path through 1-2-4 as the new f-limit. Finally, we get path 1-2-4-5-6-7-9 as the optimal path.

To illustrate how SMA* works, we have chosen three memory bounds of 5, 6, and 7 nodes, respectively. If we can store information for only one node (i.e., node 1) and node 1 is not the destination node, we stop. When we have enough memory to store information for two nodes, then we can expand the search from node 1 to nodes 2, 3, and none of these are destination nodes. Because we cannot find a path to the destination node, we stop. As summarized in Table 3.5, we cannot find a solution up to a memory bound of 5; however, for memory bound 6, we do find a solution, although not an optimal one. For a memory bound of 7, we find an optimal path.

In the case of the hierarchical strategy, we first cut the graph between nodes 4 and 5 to get two fragments, $\{1, 2, 3, 4, 10\}$ and $\{5, 6, 7, 8\}$. The boundary graph consists of nodes 4 and 5, and the edge (4,5). Now finding the optimal path reduces to finding the optimal paths in these two subgraphs and that pass though the boundary nodes; that is, path(1,4) + path(4,5) + path(5,9). Using A* in the first fragment results in the optimal path of 1-2-4, and in the second fragment results in 5-6-7-9. The global optimal path is obtained by combining these subpaths. Table 3.5 summarizes the results of applying all of these algorithms on the network graph shown in Figure 3.4(a).

3.8   PRESENTATION SERVICE

Presentation services display road maps and overlay routes, points of interest, object locations, and/or text information such as route descriptions on a road map. Currently, most presentation services are provided based on a visual interface framework; however, in the future a voice-based user interface will likely be adopted, especially in in-vehicle navigation systems, to help drivers who are already overloaded with driving tasks. Apart from easy-to-use visual and audio interfaces, presentation service requires efficient route-guidance algorithms to dynamically process and present the guidance instructions.

Route guidance is the process that guides travelers along a route either by prepared printouts of the desired route in pretrip guidance or by output of an en route guidance module in real time. In either case, a route-planning module and a positioning system are required. When using prepared printouts or maps for pretrip guidance, an explicit route-planning module is not required, but some route-planning function should be executed before the traveling route has been acquired. Nowadays, en route guidance is a desirable feature for in-vehicle navigation systems. These display simple (visual or auditory) icons to advise drivers of forthcoming actions (e.g., right/left-turn ahead) in real-time. The idea is to convey route information to drivers that is relevant to the next few minutes of driving based on current position and without distracting drivers from driving tasks. Various guidelines for designing in-vehicle information systems with applications to route guidance can be found in [GLPS93].

There are two kinds of en route guidance models: a centralized model and a distributed model. In a centralized model, the traveler communicates with a management center, which traces the traveler's location, speed, and other information. It is the management center's responsibility to compute the route and broadcast this information to the traveler. In a distributed model, the route computation is performed by the guidance unit at the hand of the traveler; such guidance units require high computation ability.

In en route guidance, static route guidance assumes that the travel cost, which includes travel distance, travel time, and minimum turn, is static. In real situations, however, the travel cost varies at different times. Dynamic route-guidance systems consider the changing situation, calculate the travel cost on-the-fly with dynamic information, and recommend new routes to the traveler.

3.9   CONCLUSION

Earlier navigation systems, which were limited to simple positioning devices and static paper maps (e.g., road maps, navigational charts), have evolved into much more sophisticated navigation systems comprising satellite-based precise positioning systems (GPS)-enabled portable digital assistants. These devices have local memories to support small digital maps and have wireless communication ports for getting dynamic spatial information from remote back-end SDB servers. Spatial databases play a central role in modern location-based applications. Location-based services will not achieve their full potential unless there is a cohesiveness between disparate components and conformance with open standards. Recent industry trends show that key players in this sector (ESRI's ArcIMS, Intergraph's IntelliWhere, MapInfo, Cquay, Webraska) are developing interfaces to standard open platforms, such as OpenLS.

The current portable PDAs have limited memories and display units. These limitations dictate the need for efficient main memory spatial processing algorithms and intelligent user interfaces. Emergency applications, which require real-time dynamic spatial data from remote SDB servers, are limited by the limited bandwidth provided by present wireless communication devices. In order to reduce the amount of information transferred over networks, we need efficient compression techniques. Additional research is needed to progressively transmit the data based on importance. These research needs are summarized in Table 3.6.

Table 3.6 Research need in modern navigation systems.

Navigation System Component		Research Needs
Server	Gateway	Indoor location sensing
		100% coverage of location sensing despite GPS shadows
	Location utility	Improving map accuracy
		Improving effectiveness of map matching using additional information such as long-term and short-term histories
	Directory	Nearest neighbor (e.g., facility) to a route (segment)
	Route determination presentation	Alternate paths
		Safe visual and audio interfaces
		Cartographic generalization
		Adaptive (client-specific) result generation
Client	PDAs	Improving memories, display sizes, processing power
		Computing under limited resources
		Smart caching, prefetching
Communications		Improving bandwidths
		Efficient map compression algorithms
		Progressive transmissions

ACKNOWLEDGMENTS

This work was partially supported by Army High Performance Computing Research Center contract number DAAD19-01-2-0014 and NSF Grant EIA-0224392. The content of this work does not necessarily reflect the position or policy of the government, and no official endorsement should be inferred. We also gratefully acknowledge the support received from the Minnesota Department of Transportation. We would like to thank spatial database research group members for their valuable comments and input. We would also like to express our thanks to Kim Koffolt, whose comments have improved the readability of this paper.

References

[AGS⁺93]   N. I. Adams, R. Gold, B. N. Schilit, M. M. Tso, and R. Want. "An Infrared Network for Mobile Computers." In *Proc. USENIX Symp. On Mobile and Location Independent Computing*. Cambridge, Massachusetts, 1993.

[ASPRS]   American Society for Photogrammetry and Remote Sensing, "ASPRS Interim Accuracy Standards for Large-Scale Maps," *http://www.asprs.org/asprs/resources/standards.html*

[Bon93]   G. Bonsiepe. "Interpretations of Human User Interface." *Visible Language*, 24(3):262–285, 1993.

[CMTV00]   A. Corral, Y. Manolopoulos, Y. Theodoridis, and M. Vassilakopoulos. "Closest Pair Queries in Spatial Databases." ACM SIGMOD, 2000.

[ComSoc]   IEEE Communications Society. "Communications History." *http://www.ieee.org/organizations/history_center/comsoc/techhist.html*

[DB2Spatial]   IBM. "DB2 Spatial Extender for Linux, UNIX and Windows." *http://www.306.ibm.com/software/data/spatial/*

[BK96]   D. Bernstein and A. Kornhauser. "An Introduction to Map Matching for Personal Navigation Assistants." The New Jersey TIDE Center's technical report, 1996, *http://www.njtide.org/reports/mapmatchintro.pdf*

[EN01]   R. Elmasri and S. B. Navathe. *Fundamentals of Database Systems*, with E-book, 3rd edition. Addison-Wesley, New York, 2001.

[ESRI]   Environmental Systems Research Institute, ArcSDE, *http://www.esri.com/software/arcgis/arcinfo/arcsde/index.html*

[ETAK]   Tele Atlas, Products and Services, *http://www.na.teleatlas.com*

[FGDC01]   Federal Geographic Data Committee, *http://www.fgdc.gov*, Geospatial Metadata, April 2001.

[FW02]   J. Feng and T. Watanabe. "Fast Search of Nearest Target Object in Urban District Road Networks." Pan-Yellow-Sea International Workshop on Information Technologies for Network Era (PYIWIT), 2002.

[GDT]   Geographic Data Technology, Product Catalog, *http://www.geographic.com*

[GLPS93]   P. Green, W. Levison, G. Paelke, and C. Serafin. *Preliminary Human Factors Design Guidelines for Driver Information Systems*. The University of Michigan, Ann Arbor, MI, Transaction Research Institute, Technical Report No. UMTRI-93-21.

[GSI93]   Geographical Survey Institute, "Digital Map Series: Digital Map 2500 (Spatial Data Framework)," 1993, Japan.

[Guting94]   R. H. Guting. "An Introduction to Spatial Database Systems." *VLDB Journal*, 3:357–399, 1994.

[HHS+99]   A. Harter, A. Hopper, P. Steggles, A. Ward, and P. Webster. "The Anatomy of a Context-Aware Application." In *Proc. 5th Annual ACM/IEEE Intl. Conf. On Mobile Computing and Networking* (Mobicom), 1999.

[HSK04]   M. Hazas, J. Scott, and J. Krumm. "Location-Aware Computing Comes of Ages." *IEEE Computer*, 37(2), Feb. 2004.

[IKK02]   Y. Ishikawa, H. Kitagawa, and T. Kawashima. "Continual Neighborhood Tracking for Moving Objects Using Adaptive Distances." *IDEAS*, 2002.

[JHR95]   N. Jing, Y. W. Huang, and E. Rundensteiner. "Hierarchical Path Views: A Model Based on Fragmentation and Transportation Road Type." In *Proc. 3rd ACM Workshop on Geographic Information Systems*, November 1995.

[JHR98]   N. Jing, Y. W. Huang, and E. Rundensteiner. "Hierarchical Encoded Path Views for Path Query Processing: An Optimal Model and Its Performance Evaluation." *IEEE Transactions on Knowledge and Data Engineering*, 10(3), May/June 1998.

[JP02]   S. Jung and S. Pramanik. "An Efficient Path Computation Model for Hierarchically Structured Topological Road Maps." *IEEE Transactions on Knowledge and Data Engineering*, 14(5), Sept/Oct 2002.

[JSQ00]   G. R. Jagadeesh, T. Srikanthan, and K. H. Quek. "Heuristic Techniques for Accelerating Hierarchical Routing on Road Networks." *IEEE Transactions on Intelligent Systems*, 3(4), December 2000.

[KJL00]   W. Kim, G. I. Jee, and J. G. Lee. "Efficient Use of Digital Road Map in Various Positioning for ITS." In *Proc. Position Location and Navigation Symposium, IEEE*, 2000.

[Mac96]   V. Machiraju. *A Survey on Research in Graphical User Interfaces*. Department of Computer Science, University of Utah, August 1996.

[MNDOT]   Minnesota Department of Transportation, Basemap, *http://rocky.dot.state.mn.us/basemap/*

[NAVTECH]   Navigation Technologies, *http://www.navtech.com*

[NMAS]   U.S. Geological Survey. "National Map Accuracy Standards." *http://rocky-web.cr.usgs.gov/nmpstds/nmas.html*

[NMEA]   National Marine Electronics Association, The 0183 Standard, *http://www.nmea.org*

[OGC98]   OGC, "Simple Features Specification (for OLE/COM, CORBA, SQL)", *http://www.opengis.org/techno/specs.htm*

[OpenLS]   OGC, "Open Location Services Initiative (OpenLS)", *http://www.openls.org/about.htm*

[PCB02]   N. B. Priyantha, A. Chakraborty, and H. Balakrishnan. "The Cricket Location-Support System." In *Proc. Sixth ACM Intl. Conf. On Mobile Computing and Networking*, 2002.

[PDMD03]   Graticule, "Philips – Digital Map Data," 2003, *http://www.graticule.com*

[PSS01]   J. Pyo, D. H. Shin, and T. K. Sung. "Development of a map matching method using the multiple hypothesis technique." In *Proc. 2001 IEEE Intelligent Transportation Systems Conference*, pages 23–27, 2001.

[Rab95]   L. R. Rabiner. "The Impact of Voice Processing in Modern Telecommunications." *Speech Communications*, 17(3–4):217–226, November 1995.

[RKV95]   N. Roussopoulos, S. Kelleym, and F. Vincent. "Nearest Neighbor Queries." In *Proc. 1995 ACM SIGMOD Intl. Conf. On Management of Data*, pages 71–79, ACM Press, 1995.

[RN95]   S. Russell and N. Norvig. *Artificial Intelligence: A Modern Approach*. Prentice Hall, Englewood Cliffs, NJ, 1995.

[RSV01]   P. Rigaux, M.O. Scholl, and A. Voisard. Spatial Databases: With Applications to GIS. Morgan Kaufmann Publishers, 2001.

[Rus92]   S. Russell. "Efficient Memory-Bounded Search Methods." In *Proc. 10th European Conf. On Artificial Intelligence*, pages 1–5, Wiley.

[SA03]   D. Sobel and W. J. Andrewes. *The Illustrated Longitude*. Walker & Company, New York, 2003.

[SC02]   S. Shekhar and S. Chawla. *Spatial Databases: A Tour*. Prentice Hall, Englewood Cliffs, NJ, 2002.

[SCR+99]   S. Shekhar, S. Chawla, S. Ravada, A. Fetterer, X. Liu, and C. T. Lu. "Spatial Databases—Accomplishments and Research Needs." *IEEE Transactions on Knowledge and Data Engineering*, 11(1):45–55, 1999.

[SDC]   Oracle, "Oracle Spatial," *http://otn.oracle.com/products/oracle9i/datasheets/spatial/spatial.html*

[SL97]   S. Shekhar and D. R. Liu. "CCAM: A Connectivity-Clustered Access Method for Networks and Network Computations." *IEEE Transactions on Knowledge and Data Engineering*, 9(1), January 1997.

[SR01]   Z. Song and N. Roussopoulos. "K-Nearest Neighbor Search for Moving Query Point," In *Proc. 7th International Symposium on Advances in Spatial and Temporal Databases (SSTD)*, 2001.

[ST91]   J. W. Sullivan and S. W. Tyler (Eds.). *Intelligent User Interfaces*. ACM Press, New York, 1991.

[SVCB99]   S. Shekhar, R. R. Vatsavai, S. Chawla, and T. E. Burk. "Spatial Pictogram Enhanced Conceptual Data Models and Their Translation to Logical Data Models." Integrated Spatial Databases, Digital Images, and GIS, *Lecture Notes in Computer Science*, Vol. 1737, 1999.

[SY03]   S. Shekhar and J. S. Yoo. "Processing In-Route Nearest Neighbor Queries: A Comparison of Alternative Approaches." In *Proc. 11th ACM Intl. Symp. On Advances in Geographic Information Systems*, ACM-GIS 2003.

[TIGER]   U.S. Census Bureau, **T**opologically **I**ntegrated **G**eographic **E**ncoding and **R**eferencing system, *http://www.census.gov/geo/www/tiger/index.html*

[TPS02]   Y. Tao, D. Papdias, and Q. Shen. "Continuous Nearest Neighbor Search." In *Proc. 28th Very Large Data Bases Conference*, 2002.

[VW01]   M. Vazirgiannis and O. Wolfson. "A Spatiotemporal Model and Language for Moving Objects on Road Networks." In *Proc. 7th Intl. Symp. On Spatial and Temporal Databases*, SSTD, 2001.

[WHFG92]   R. Want, A. Hopper, V. Falcao, and J. Gibbons. "The Active Badge Location System." Technical Report 92.1, 1992, ORL, 24a Trumpington Street, Cambridge, CB2, 1QA.

[YLM95]   N. Yankelovich, G. A. Levowt, and M. Marx. "Designing Speech Acts: Issues in Speech User Interfaces." CHI 95 Conference on Human Factors in Computing Systems, Denver, CO, May 7–11, 1995.

[Zha97]   Y. Zhao. *Vehicle Location and Navigation Systems*. Artech House, 685 Canton Street, Norwood, MA, USA, 1997.

Part 2

Data Management and
Services in LBS

Middleware for Location-Based Services

Hans-Arno Jacobsen, University of Toronto

CONTENTS

4.1   INTRODUCTION

Generally speaking, an information service is a network-accessible and computer-based system to collect, process, filter, transmit, and disseminate data that represents information useful for a specific purpose or individual. Along the same lines, a location-based service (LBS) refers to the additional integration of position location information as part of the data processed by the information service. Thus an LBS provides and delivers information to its users in a highly selective manner, by taking users' past, present, or future location and other context information into account. An LBS is often even more generally defined as any value-added service offered in a wireless environment that exploits mobile terminal location position information.

Examples comprise route-planning applications, where a repository of map information is queried to determine a possible path between two points (e.g., the Map-on-the-Move application [YJK98]); push-based targeted advertisement (e.g., an XML-based selective information dissemination service [FJL+01a]), where a user profile is maintained by the information system and notifications are delivered to users as pertinent data correlated with users' locations and interests becomes available. Further applications are the friend finder system (see Chapter 2) and location-based games, where correlations between a number of moving users must be established; and tracking applications, where a number of moving objects must be tracked simultaneously and queries about the state of individuals or groups of objects must be processed.

These application categories have fundamentally different characteristics and impose a wide spectrum of requirements on the underlying middleware platform. Database-centric lookup services, as used in the route-planning scenario, for instance, require the concurrent execution of queries on large amounts of stored data, whereas the selective information dissemination–based scenarios require the correlation of just-in-time information with large amounts of stored user profiles. As we will see later, these are two very different problems. To date, they are not adequately supported by the same platform technology.

Often, location services and location application services are distinguished. A location service provides specific geographic location information about mobile terminals, such as cell phones, personal digital assistants (PDAs), or with sensors tagged on moving objects. A location *application* service refers to the information service that exploits this location information about a mobile terminal to offer highly customized information content to the mobile user or to third parties (i.e., other mobile terminals or static users and applications). Many early location application services were based on the user providing the necessary position information voluntarily by submitting a street name or a zip code to the application.

This chapter focuses on location application services and the middleware technology required for supporting their operation. No distinction is made between the two categories, and we uniquely refer to this kind of application as location-based services or location-based applications, always assuming that the required location information exploited by the ulterior information service is made available somehow. To back up this assumption, state-of-the-art location position identification technology is reviewed as follows.

We define middleware (aka middleware platform or middleware system) as a set of services that facilitate the development and deployment of distributed applications in heterogeneous environments. Middleware consists of a set of services exposing interfaces, a programming model, and an interaction model to the application developer. For the context of LBS, this refers to the services, abstractions, and models that implement mobile user coordination, information correlation, and information dissemination. A major component of LBS is the integration of location or position information. Thus it is important to understand the capabilities and limitations of existing position localization technologies and how they enable and constrain application development and deployment.

The objective of this chapter is to identify LBS application categories, identify requirements they impose on underlying middleware platforms, understand capabilities and limitations of position localization technology and their implications for middleware and the applications that can be offered, and survey standard middleware models applicable in this space.

4.2 APPLICATIONS

Location-based services are often broken down into two main categories: business-to-consumer (B2C) and business-to-business (B2B) applications (e.g., see Durlacher Research [DRL01], A. Sanchez and L. Telleria

Table 4.1   Classification and characterization of location-based services applications.

Service category	Example application	Characteristics
Infotainment services	Finder applications (e.g., route, location, friend, store, restaurant, gas station, and parking) Information requests (e.g., tourist, travel, news) Games, see below	Mobile user-initiated, query-based, and request-driven Pull-based model Location information is either transmitted with request or assessed by service
Tracking services	Goods, vehicle, and fleet People (e.g., child care, elderly, sick, and offenders) Security of entities (e.g., cars) Maintenance and assistance Workforce dispatching Supply-chain and inventory	Tracking requests are often initiated by a remote monitoring entity and not by the mobile entity per se State-based nature of application (i.e., often a state is kept between requests about objects tracked) Pull-based and push-based
Selective information dissemination	Targeted content dissemination (e.g., advertisements, information)	Proactive, event-based, and condition triggered A priori stateless
Location-based games	Treasure hunts Territory defense and claiming Scavenger hunts	Proactive, event-based, and condition triggered Correlation of location of multiple mobile terminals Maintenance of state between subsequent location requests
Emergency support services	Emergency 911 Ambulance, fire, police dispatching Roadside assistance	Mobile-user-initiated and pull-based A priori stateless
Location-sensitive billing	Call billing Toll payment Purchase of goods and services	Proactive, event-based, and condition triggered A priori stateless

[ST03], and Zeimpekis et al. [ZGL03]). Table 4.1 presents a classification that introduces a further division into subcategories. To better understand the requirements imposed by different applications on the underlying middleware model a finer-grained classification of application is helpful. This classification is as follows:

1. *Infotainment services.* Services to meet user requests on how to reach a given destination; where to find a particular service (e.g., automated teller machine, restaurant, parking, or gas station); how to find another mobile user (see friend finder application presented in Chapter 2); and

how to localize the current position (on a map) of a lost user are commonly referred to as infotainment services. A service request can often be further refined by correlating it with dynamic information about the environment, such as road and weather condition, traffic information, or other events of interest to the requester. Infotainment services are a valuable asset for travelers and tourists alike.

Characteristic for most of these services is their pull-based nature; the mobile user submits a request to receive information (i.e., actively pulls information from the service). The location of the mobile user drives the request evaluation at the server side. Mobile terminal location information, user context, and any other profile information may be used to derive personalized content returned to the user; however, detailed personalization is not a prerequisite for these kinds of services.

2. *Tracking services.* These services track the geographic whereabouts of, with mobile terminals equipped, entities (e.g., users, trucks, and packages) and support requests to establish the location of these entities, their progress and state change along a route, or perspective future location. Applications include fleet tracking, taxi monitoring and dispatching, workforce management, mobile supply-chain management, child support and security, tracking of elderly and sick persons, and goods and package tracking. This latter example is often supported by tracking the object as it passes through a statically fixed control point (i.e., a bar code reader). Active badge systems fall in this category as well [WHGF92].

Characteristic for these kinds of applications is the potentially very large number of entities that must be tracked simultaneously, the need to maintain state between different tracking points, and the inverse nature of the tracking request initiator (i.e., a remote monitoring entity is tracking the objects). Applications are pull- and push-based in nature.

3. (*Selective*) *information dissemination services.* This category refers to services that disseminate content to mobile users correlated with the subscriber's location, context, and profile. A prime example is (selective) advertisement dissemination. Disseminated content may include e-coupons or simply advertisements. At one extreme, all users entering the range of a particular dissemination source could receive notifications. At the other extreme, highly selective correlations

between a user's interests and the advertisement content could selectively target individual users.

Characteristic for this category is the push-based character of the application. That is, the dissemination is initiated by the supporting middleware technology, with little or no user intervention. The support of selective content correlation requires a user profile and requires user identification information to be available for each user location quote.

4. *Location-based games.* Essentially part of the infotainment category, location-based games are mostly targeted at the young mobile user market and aim at getting users on the air. Gaming models include visiting different parts of a city (i.e., network cells) to retrieve information or further direction requests and finding peer-mobile users. This category of services is presently under intense development. No distinct characterization from the previous service classes is obvious.

5. *Emergency support services.* These services have driven the development and deployment of location positioning technology in North America and are referred to as the E-911 services. The E-911 mandate, imposed by the Federal Communications Commission (FCC), requires that network operators be able to provide position information of a mobile 911 caller with a specified accuracy. This information serves police, fire fighters, ambulances, and automotive support crews.

These services rely entirely on the available position location technology and do not, by themselves, impose any specific requirements on the middleware technology.

6. *Location-sensitive billing.* Location-sensitive billing refers to the potential to dynamically bill a mobile user based on its present location. Calls that originate within the close vicinity of a wired phone or the user's home line are charged as wired calls versus entirely mobile calls.

From a middleware perspective, no special support is required for this kind of service. A call is classified as being wired or mobile, and different accounting records are generated.

Table 4.1 classifies location-based services and lists example applications for each category.

4.3   LOCATION-BASED SERVICE CHARACTERISTICS

From the previous discussion of applications, the following conceptual characterization of LBS can be extracted. Unless stated otherwise, these characteristics are all orthogonal and can be combined in an arbitrary manner. To fully support present and future LBS, the underlying middleware technology must support these application characteristics.

◆ *Push- versus pull-based applications.* In a pull-based application service, requests are initiated by the mobile terminal (i.e., the user). In a push-based application, the infrastructure autonomously and proactively pushes information to mobile terminals based on the occurrence of an event or the trigger of a condition.

◆ *Direct versus indirect profile.* A personalized application correlates a service request with requester profile information. This profile information about the requester may be gathered directly from the user in a subscription phase or may be obtained indirectly, either by observing the requester's interaction pattern or by obtaining the information from third parties. A profile may also contain information about the requester's current context. Clearly, privacy concerns and privacy policies play a crucial role and must be adhered to, but they are not linked to the characteristic itself and are not further discussed here.

◆ *Availability of profile information.* Profile information can either be made available at request time or be already available to the LBS. In the former case, the most likely placement of the profile information would be the mobile terminal. Each information request would submit part or all of the profile. A selective push model cannot be supported with this approach, but it has the advantage of keeping user profile information protected and not exposed, for ulterior exploitation, at the service site. On the downside, this may lead to request payloads that are considerably larger than they would be otherwise.

◆ *Interaction scenarios.* The interacting entities, mobile terminals and LBS, more generally speaking, service requester and service provider, can be either mobile or stationary. This gives rise to four distinct interaction scenarios. In the first scenario, both requester and provider are stationary and there is no need for dynamic management of location information, as it is statically known. Conventional information services are good examples of this category. In the second and third cases, either requester or provider are mobile and stationary, respectively. Both cases are symmetrical; however, their interpretation and instantiation depends on how the application is modelled (i.e., which entity is seen as the information provider and which as the information requester). For example, for vehicle tracking applications, the vehicle emitting location information can be interpreted as the provider, whereas the LBS would take on the role of the information requester (i.e., the location information of the vehicle). In the fourth scenario, both requester and provider are mobile, while the LBS takes on the role of a (stationary) coordinator. Examples of this scenario are applications where mobile users are interested in each others' locations (e.g., friend finder applications and location-based games). Examples that do not explicitly rely on a central coordinator are location-based ad-hoc applications, where information requester and provider reside on mobile terminals that run the entire application in a coordinated fashion without relying on a given network infrastructure.

◆ *Source of location information.* Location information may either be provided voluntarily by the user or made available by the network infrastructure or by a third party. In the first case, the location information is part of the service request; in the other cases, it may either be queried by the location-based application or be transmitted by the mobile terminal.

◆ *Accuracy of location information.* Depending on the location positioning technology used in the network infrastructure, different degrees of accuracy for localization requests of mobile terminals result. These range from being able to place a mobile terminal within a radius of several kilometers to several meters. This factor greatly affects the kind of application that can be supported.

◆ *Statefulness of interaction.* An interaction is classified as *stateful* if the LBS maintains state across multiple service requests and as *stateless* if no such state is maintained and each request is processed independently of past requests. In tracking applications, it may, for instance, be important to keep track of past object locations to calibrate a prediction scheme for future predictive behavior.

◆ *Kind of information sources.* Location-based services are based on the effective correlation of information originating from several sources. We distinguish between static and dynamic information sources. Static information sources refer to databases about the geographic environment (e.g., different kind of maps, location of attractions, and major buildings). Dynamic information sources offer information about changing environmental conditions, such as road, traffic, and weather conditions and major event information. The location information of mobile terminals can be classified as dynamic with very frequent changes. User profiles constitute a further source of information. Depending on its availability, it is either statically available to the information service or dynamically provided with each information request. Lastly, information provided by (third-party) content providers constitutes a further source of information. Unless persistently stored and replayed by the information service, it is commonly very short lived, such as advertisement content.

Table 4.2 provides a taxonomy of location-based services against their characteristics based on the analysis in this section.

4.4   REQUIREMENTS IMPOSED ON MIDDLEWARE

As for the number of potential users who may take advantage of LBS, we can consider that, to date, there exist millions of mobile wireless telecommunication service subscribers. In many countries, this number is larger than the number of Internet/PC users [Sim02]. A U.S. mobile carrier, for example, is reported to have had 27 million subscribers in April 2000 [Sim02], and on August 6, 2000, 18 months after the introduction of i-mode in Japan, the number of subscribers to NTT DoCoMo's i-mode service topped 10 million [MMJ00]. The same rate of adoption is occurring with IEEE 802.11 devices, which result in quickly growing adoption of wireless LANs by several companies. All of these users could easily become clients to widely available location-based services. From this discussion and the previous classification of applications, the following functional and nonfunctional requirements emerge for location-based middleware [Jac01, CJ02].

Location-based middleware platforms must do the following:

◆ Manage the mobility inherent to all LBS applications by supporting disconnected operations and supporting mobility-awareness in the middleware.

◆ Manage changes in the underlying network topology that may occur in very dynamic settings, such as ad-hoc location-based services.

Table 4.2 Taxonomy of location-based services categories against application characteristics.

	Infotainment	Tracking	Dissemination	Games	Emergency	Billing
Push vs. pull	Pull	Push toward tracking entity Tracking entity pull	Push	Pull and push	Pull and push	Push toward billing infrastructure
Direct vs. indirect profile	Both types of profiles possible	Direct profiles	Both types of profiles possible	Both types of profiles possible	Direct profiles	Direct profiles
Availability of profile	Request-time/on device and stored/at service	Stored/at service	Request-time/on device and stored/at service	Stored/at service	Stored/at service	Stored/at service
Interaction	Mobile requester and stationary provider	All four cases	Mobile requester and stationary provider	All four cases	Mobile requester and stationary provider	Mobile requester and stationary provider
Source of location information	Mobile terminal and network	Mobile terminal and network	Network	Mobile terminal and network	Network	Network
Accuracy of location position	Less than 1 km accuracy is desirable Outdoor	Less than 200 m accuracy is desirable Outdoor	Less than 1 km accuracy is desirable Outdoor	Less than 100 m accuracy is desirable Outdoor	Less than 20 m accuracy is desirable Outdoor/Indoor	Less than 0.5 km accuracy is desirable Outdoor/Indoor
State/stateless	Stateless	State-based	Stateless	State-based	Stateless	Stateless
Static/dynamic source	Mostly static	n/a	Static and dynamic	Static and dynamic	n/a	n/a

- Manage millions of information consumers and consequently millions of subscriptions.
- Manage a potentially very large number of information providers (in some cases, comparable with the numbers of information consumers).
- Propagate notifications for thousands of information consumers simultaneously, which results in managing large amounts of content sent to the system for filtering, matching, and correlating.
- Manage high volatility of users' interests (e.g., profile updates, insertion, deletion).
- Process diverse content formats, ranging from topic-tagged blobs and collections of attribute-value pairs to HTML and XML marked-up data, as well as easily support evolving and future data formats.
- Support heterogeneous notification channels (e.g., email, Internet protocols, fax, phone, WAP, i-mode, ICQ, SMS) and notification delivery protocols (e.g., UDP TCP, IIOP, RMI, SMTP, SOAP, WAP).
- Support approximate subscriptions and approximate events to enhance system flexibility by increasing the expressiveness of the filtering language and the publication language.
- Support high availability despite node failures (e.g., guarantee notification delivery).
- Perform accounting functions (i.e., information producer accounting, information consumer and subscriber accounting) and support incentive-driven reimbursement schemes and pricing models (e.g., for advertisement and for e-coupon distribution).
- Perform security functions, such as subscriber and publisher authentication, secure content distribution (e.g., not all subscribers may be allowed to receive all publications that match their subscriptions).
- Support privacy consideration, allowing subscribers to opt for the propagation of their location information to selected applications only.
- Support high rates of information input (e.g., news, location information per user).
- Support different content formats (e.g., XML, HTML, WML, or ASCII).

As can be seen from this list, the requirements are quite varied and affect all middleware system layers.

4.5   END-TO-END SYSTEM ARCHITECTURE

A middleware system is loosely defined as the set of services that facilitates the development and deployment of distributed applications in heterogeneous environments. The objectives of a middleware system are to abstract the details of the underlying operating system, network substrate and protocols, mask possible failures, and even mask the distribution of interacting (sub-)systems. The middleware's application programming interfaces (APIs) are often standardized by international standard bodies or widely accepted as standard solutions, so-called de facto standards. Standard APIs give rise to application portability and system interoperability.

LBS middleware is more specialized, but with much the same objectives. It aims at facilitating the development and deployment of LBS applications in heterogeneous network environments. LBS middleware has to bridge protocols and network technology dominant in the telecommunications world with wireless technology and Internet technology. It is commonplace that LBS middleware has to integrate subsystems connected via Signaling System 7 (SS7) network technology, IP-based Internet networks, and the latest wireless technology. Standards that are emerging in this domain are the Wireless Access Protocol (WAP), interoperability standards propagated by the OpenGIS consortium [OGC], and the efforts of the Location Interoperability Forum (LIF) to standardize mobile positioning technology.

LBS middleware is either deployed within the network operator's network or hosted by an application service provider. In the deployment context, LBS middleware connects customers on mobile terminals and the Internet, third-party application providers, and network operators to offer one single location-based application portal, consisting of several individually customizable services. The middleware integrates with the network infrastructure, including location servers, WAP gateways, subscriber portal services, customer care, customer activation services, billing systems, accounting systems, and operational systems. An end-to-end system architecture, showing mobile users, network operator, third-party application providers, and several of the aforementioned subsystems is presented in Figure 4.1.

LBS middleware differ in the kind of services offered to the subscriber, the network operator, and the application provider. For subscribers, fine-grained control over their profiles and their location, as well as context,

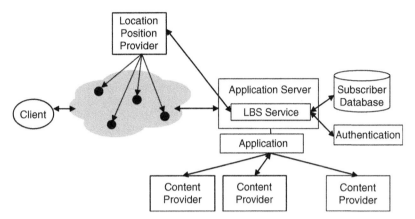

Figure 4.1 Overall system architecture.

are important features. It should be possible to disable and enable location information and profile on an individual application service basis (i.e., to select which of the offered applications should receive the user's location information at what time and in which context). Network operator and third-party application provider are supported with real-time billing, revenue-sharing schemes, and subscriber information access, to name just a few features.

Applications are layered on top of the middleware, without much concern for the lower-level services (i.e., fully transparent to application developer). A detailed logical architecture of LBS middleware is depicted in Figure 4.1, and an end-to-end invocation, originating from a mobile terminal, traversing the different middleware stacks and architecture components, is depicted in Figure 4.2.

LBS middleware are distinguished by the features they offer their users (i.e., mobile user, network operator, and application provider). Many different architectures exist in the marketplace, without one dominant player at this point in sight. Moreover, there is not one standard architectural reference model that uniquely describes the components of LBS middleware available to date.

By far the most interesting component of an LBS middleware system is the matching engine (aka, event correlator, filter engine, or matching kernel). The design of this module dictates the kinds of services that can be supported by the overall middleware. The next section is dedicated to understanding the different options. We term this the *middleware model* because it constrains the possible services and interaction scenarios that can be implemented with LBS middleware.

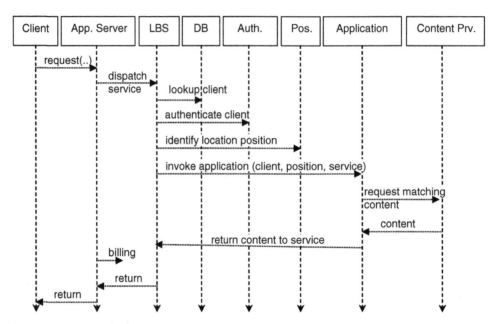

Figure 4.2   Sequence diagram: Typical stages in a location-based service request (client-initiated information pull).

4.6   MIDDLEWARE MODELS

In this section, we survey different middleware models that are at the core of an LBS, driving its main service functionality. The various models we review exhibit a wide spectrum of different characteristics, as discussed previously.

4.6.1   Publish/Subscribe

Applications that are based on the publish/subscribe middleware model are organized as a collection of cooperating components, consisting of producers, which interact by publishing events (often simply referred to as publications), and consumers, which subscribe to specific events they are interested in. A central component of the architecture, the event broker, is responsible for managing subscriptions and forwarding events to interested subscribers (i.e., subscribing consumers).

The last few years have witnessed the development of many publish/subscribe middleware systems differing along several dimensions. Among many others, two of these dimensions are usually considered fundamental: the expressiveness of the data model (subscription language and publication model) and the architecture of the event broker.

The data model of a publish/subscribe system is often distinguished by the expressiveness of the subscription language model, drawing a line between topic-based systems, content-based, type-based, and recently subject spaces [LeJa02, LeJa03]. In the topic-based model, subscriptions identify classes of events belonging to a given channel, a subject, or hierarchy, and publications are directly associated or tagged with a corresponding label. In the content-based model, subscriptions consist of predicates (often referred to as event filters or constraints) that give rise to sophisticated matching on the event content, and publications are lists or sets of attribute value pairs over which the predicates are defined. In the type-based model, subscriptions are procedure or method calls that register a subscriber's interest in a particular programming language type, and publications are instances of this type. The subject space model no longer distinguishes between subscriptions and publications, but treats them synonymously. Topic-based systems are simpler to implement but are less flexible and expressive. Type-based approaches are tightly integrated with a given programming paradigm and environment. Content-based publish/subscribe systems and subject spaces–based systems are the only models that can provide the required expressiveness to filter millions of publications for millions of users with potentially different, but possibly overlapping, interests [FJL+01b, ALJ02].

The architecture of the event broker can either be centralized or distributed. In the first case, a single component acts as broker, which potentially reduces system scalability and introduces a single point of failure, but may be sufficient for smaller-scale operations. In the second case, a network of event brokers, often realized as an overlay network, defines the publish/subscribe middleware. Publishers and subscribers may connect to any broker, and messages (publications and subscriptions) are routed through the whole network of brokers. The overall topology of the network of brokers and the strategies adopted to route subscriptions and events change from system to system.

The publish/subscribe middleware model is inherently (1) asynchronous, because information providers and information consumers operate asynchronously through the mediation of the broker; (2) multipoint, because publications are sent to all interested subscribers; (3) anonymous, because the publisher need not know the identity of subscribers, and vice versa; (4) implicit, because the set of event recipients is determined by the subscriptions, rather than being explicitly chosen by the sender; and (5) stateless, because events do not persist in the system, rather they are sent only to those components that have subscribed before the event was published.

Much research has gone into extending the expressiveness of publish/subscribe, such as for the management of uncertain information [LiJa02, LiJa04] (the Approximate Toronto Publish/Subscribe System [A-ToPSS]) or the management of semantic relationships between publications and subscriptions [PBJ03] (the Semantic Toronto Publish/Subscribe System [S-ToPSS]). Further research has developed schemes for efficiently supporting disconnected operations in networks of publish/subscribe brokers [BJD+04] (the Mobile Toronto Publish/Subscribe Systems [M-ToPSS]), and the layering of publish/subscribe on top of peer-to-peer networks to increase scalability has been explored [TAJ03].

The publish/subscribe paradigm is well suited for modeling selective information dissemination tasks, where data entities are matched according to a set of constraints. That is where publications are matched against subscriptions; however, to apply publish/subscribe for modeling LBS, the location information of publishers and subscribers, as well as the possible mobility of publishers and subscribers, has to be taken into account and added into the matching equation.

In [BJ03] an extension to publish/subscribe, the location-aware Toronto Publish/Subscribe System (L-ToPSS), is presented for the processing of location information in addition to publication and subscriptions. In this model, it is assumed that the system is periodically receiving location information about its users as (latitude, longitude, altitude) coordinates. The main component of the system is the publish/subscribe filtering engine that matches the publications against the subscriptions in the system (see Figure 4.4 for details). The publications describe real-life objects, such as books that, for example, can be characterized by title, author, and edition. This type of information can be represented by semi-structured data used in traditional publish/subscribe systems. In L-ToPSS, the publication is expressed as a list of attribute-value pairs. The formal representation of a publication is given by the following expression: $\{(a_1, val_1), (a_2, val_2), \ldots, (a_n, val_n)\}$. For the book example, the publication can be expressed as:

$\{$(title, *"Middleware for location-based services"*), (author, *"H.-A. Jacobsen"*)$\}$

The subscriptions describe user interests or user profiles. In L-ToPSS, subscriptions are represented as conjunctions of simple predicates. Each predicate expresses a value constraint for an attribute name. For example, the predicate (edition > *2000*) restricts the value of the attribute "edition" to a value greater than *2000*. In a formal description, a simple predicate is represented as (attribute-name **relational-operator** *value*) triple. A predicate (*a* **rel-op** *val*) is matched by an attribute-value pair (*a'*, *val'*) if and only if the attribute names are identical (*a* = *d'*) and the (*a* **rel-op** *val*) Boolean relation is true. In our system, a subscription *s* is matched by a publication *p* if and only if all its predicates are matched by some pair in *p*.

If either the publisher or the subscriber is stationary, we assume that the publication or the subscription, respectively, is associated with the fixed location of the corresponding entity. The location information is expressed as (*latitude, longitude, altitude*) coordinates. Similarly, when an entity is mobile, the information it produces contains the Mobile Identification Number (MIN), a unique identifier of the mobile device.

The system architecture is depicted in Figure 4.3. First, we explain how the system works for the stationary publisher–mobile subscriber case. Then, we argue that the mobile publisher–stationary subscriber scenario can be treated symmetrically. Finally, we present the mobile publisher–mobile subscriber case.

Both subscriptions and publications are sent to the filtering engine. When a subscription is matched by a publication, a *location constraint* that contains the MIN of the subscriber and the (*latitude, longitude, altitude*) coordinates of the publisher is sent to the location matching engine. This component stores the location constraints, as well as the associations with the subscriptions and the publications that have generated them.

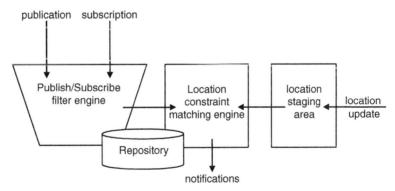

Figure 4.3   Publish/subscribe system model to support location-based services.

If the publication is a long-lived one, it is stored in a local repository. In this way, subscriptions entering the system will be matched against the existing publications in the repository. For each match, a location constraint is created in the same way as explained above and then it is sent to the location matching engine. The location constraint is kept in the location matching engine as long as the publication exists in the system. Conversely, if the publication is instantaneous, it is not stored in the system. The instantaneous publication and the location constraints that it produces are discarded after a period of time equal to the duration of a cycle of location updates (i.e., the time needed for receiving and processing the location updates for all connected clients). This means that in order to receive notifications about instantaneous publications, interested subscribers have to be in the area of the publisher at the moment when the publication is issued.

The system periodically receives updates of users' location. This information is processed in the location staging component. Each location information is represented as a (*user_MIN*, *current latitude*, *current longitude*, *current altitude*) triple. This triple is forwarded to the location matching engine, which matches it against the location constraints in the system. A triple (*user_MIN*, *current latitude*, *current_longitude*, *current altitude*) matches a location constraint (*MIN*, *latitude*, *longitude*, *altitude*) if and only if $MIN = user\_MIN$ and the distance (i.e., the distance can be expressed as a function defined by the subscriber) between the two points determined by (*current_latitude*, *current_longitude*, *current_altitude*) and (*latitude*, *longitude*, *altitude*) does not exceed a certain value. If a location constraint is matched, this means that the corresponding subscriber is close to a point of interest. Therefore, the system will send a notification to the user about the publication associated with the location constraint. The notification is sent to the mobile device identified by the *MIN*. After the notification is sent, the location constraint is deleted. In this way, the user will be notified at most once about a publication, avoiding sending the user the same piece of information again.

The mobile publisher–stationary subscriber case can be modeled symmetrically. In this case, the static location is associated with the subscription, while the *MIN* is contained in the publication. The system processes the information in the same way as in the previous case. In this scenario, the stationary subscriber will be notified when the publisher comes nearby.

For the mobile publisher–mobile subscriber case, each entity has associated an *MIN*: *MIN-pub* and *MIN-sub*. In this case, the location constraint contains only the (*MIN-pub, MIN-sub*) tuple, and it is associated with the corresponding publication and subscription. For each *MIN* that appears in the location constraints, the system stores the last location update and the timestamp when it was received. The location matching proceeds as follows. When a location update (MIN_1, *latitude, longitude, altitude*) enters the system, the corresponding location information and the timestamp are updated. Moreover, for all the location constraints (MIN_1, MIN_2), the system checks if the last location received for MIN_2 is close to that of MIN_1 and also if the timestamps are close in time. If this is the case, the appropriate subscriber is notified about the publication associated with the location constraint.

Both the publisher and the subscriber can retrieve their publication or subscription, respectively. When a publication or a subscription is deleted, all the corresponding location constraints have to be deleted.

4.6.2 Subject Spaces

The publish/subscribe model discussed is inherently stateless (i.e., neither subscription state nor publication state is maintained). A few exceptions were discussed earlier that extended the traditional publish/subscribe model. The subject spaces model, on the contrary, is a stateful model. Here, both subscriptions and publications involve state. The *subject spaces model* is a generic system model to express asynchronous interactions of decoupled entities. In that sense, it is similar to publish/subscribe-style interactions; however, existing publish/subscribe models do not generally retain subscription and publication state (i.e., they are not state persistent), which makes it difficult to implement stateful scenarios for LBS based on this model. The state of a subscription refers to whether the subscription is true or false with respect to a given publication. The relationships of all publications and subscriptions form the state of a publish/subscribe system.

The objective of subject spaces is to provide a precise description of the behavior of publish/subscribe systems. It is designed to retain the semantics of all current models and to overcome their limitations [LeJa02, LeJa03]. This section presents the subject spaces model in the context of LBS. Analogous to the topics in the topic-based model, subject spaces are used for categorizing publications and subscriptions. Under this model, information is structured by subject spaces, which are metadata of the system. Intuitively, subject spaces are multidimensional spaces, and data form regions in these spaces. Publications and subscriptions are declared as a correlation of the regions in the subject spaces.

A subject space is a grouping for related publications and subscriptions that can be described by the same set of properties, and each dimension represents a property. We define a publish/subscribe system to be a set of subject spaces $\Sigma = \{\sigma_1, \sigma_2, \ldots, \sigma_k\}$. The set of subject spaces is used to categorize information in a publish/subscribe system. Subject spaces are the metadata of a publish/subscribe system, and they help describe the values and relationships of publications and subscriptions.

Each subject space is defined as a tuple $\sigma = (D_\sigma, V_\sigma)$, where $D_\sigma = \{d_1, d_2, \ldots, d_n\}$ is the set of dimensions of the subject space and V_σ is the set of values allowed in this space. A subject space is a multidimensional space. Each dimension is defined as a tuple $d = (name, type)$, where *name* is the unique identifier of the dimension and *type* is a data type. Each dimension d has a domain of values, $dom(d)$, which is the set of all possible values that can be represented by *type*. This model allows each dimension of the multidimensional space to have a different domain. Examples of dimension data types include real numbers, integers, strings, Booleans, and enumerated values. User-defined data types that are subsets of these data types are also possible. The domain of a subject space is the Cartesian product of the domains of its dimensions:

$$V_\sigma = dom(d_1) \times dom(d_2) \times \cdots \times dom(d_n).$$

Example 1 Geographic coordinates can be represented by a subject space *location*, which has three dimensions: $D_{location} = \{(x, double), (y, double), (z, double)\}$.

Subject spaces are related by sharing dimensions. Define $\sqsubset$ as a relation on the set Σ of subject spaces. Specifically, $\sqsubset \subseteq \Sigma \times \Sigma \times \{1, p, 0\}$. In a tuple $(\sigma_1, \sigma_2, \delta) \in \sqsubset$, we refer to the value δ as the degree of containment. Given two subject spaces σ_1 and σ_2,

1. σ_1 fully contains σ_2, $(\sigma_1, \sigma_2, 1) \in \sqsubset_1$, or simply $\sigma_1 \sqsubset_{1 p}$, if $D_{\sigma 2} \subset D_{\sigma 1}$;

2. σ_1 partially contains σ_2, $(\sigma_1, \sigma_2, p) \in \sqsubset_p$, or simply $\sigma_1 \sqsubset_p \sigma_2$, if $D_{\sigma 1} \cap D_{\sigma 2} \neq \emptyset$ and $D_{\sigma 1} \cap D_{\sigma 2} \subset D_{\sigma 1}$ and $D_{\sigma 1} \cap D_{\sigma 2} \subset D_{\sigma 2}$;

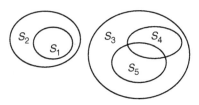

Figure 4.4   Relationship between subject spaces.

3. σ_1 and σ_2 are unrelated, $(\sigma_1, \sigma_2, 0) \in \sqsubseteq_0$, or simply $\sigma_1 \sqsubseteq_0 \sigma_2$, if $D_{\sigma_1} \cap D_{\sigma_2} = \emptyset$.

Example 2   This example illustrates the use of related subject spaces in LBS. The information about the user profiles can be represented in a user profile subject space $\sigma_{user\_profile}$ with the following structure: $D_{user\_profile} = \{(name, string), (age, integer), (profession, string)\}$. Suppose that one of the service providers in the system is a coffee shop that sells coffee and cakes. The information about its products is represented using the following three subject spaces: *product*, *coffee*, and *cake*. The product subject space stores general information common to both coffee and cakes. The *coffee* and *cake* subject spaces are supersets of the *product* subject space and store information about each item, respectively.

$$D_{product} = \{(SKU, string), (price, double), (discount, percentage)\}$$
$$D_{coffee} = \{(flavor, string)\} \cup D_{product}$$
$$D_{cake} = \{(type, string), (name, string)\} \cup D_{product}$$

With this subject space definition, we may conclude: $\sigma_{coffee} \sqsubseteq_1 \sigma_{product}$; $\sigma_{cake} \sqsubseteq_1 \sigma_{product}$; $\sigma_{user\_profile} \sqsubseteq_0 \sigma_{product}$; $\sigma_{cake} \sqsubseteq_p \sigma_{user\_profile}$.

Data exist in subject spaces in the form of *regions*. Intuitively, data or regions occupy some volume within a subject space. Formally, a region is defined as a tuple $r = (C_r, V_\sigma^r)$. $C_r = \{c_1, c_2, \ldots, c_j\}$ is the set of constraints of r. A constraint is a subset of the domain of a given dimension. The set of values of constraint c in dimension d is denoted as $dom(c_d)$, i.e., $dom(c_d) \subseteq dom(d)$. V_σ^r is the set of values of region r with respect to subject space σ. V_σ^r can also be interpreted as the spatial extension of region r with respect to σ. Denote the set of dimensions of C_r as D_{C_r}. Let $D_{C_r} \cap D_\sigma = \{d_{i_1}, d_{i_1}, \ldots, d_{i_p}\}$, and $D_\sigma \backslash D_{C_r} = \{d_{i_{p+1}}, d_{i_{p+2}}, \ldots, d_{i_n}\}$. If $D_{C_r} \cap D_\sigma \neq \emptyset$, then $V_\sigma^r = dom(c_{d_{i_1}}) \times \cdots \times dom(c_{d_{i_p}}) \times dom(d_{i_{p+1}}) \times \cdots \times dom(d_{i_n})$. Otherwise, $V_\sigma^r = \emptyset$. A region r is said to be *valid* in σ if $V_\sigma^r \neq \emptyset$. A region can be valid in multiple subject spaces.

Example 3   Location information for mobile users is represented as a point in the location subject space. For example, let the position of a mobile user be ℓ, where $C_\ell = \{x = 50, y = 20\}$. A point is a special case of a region that has no spatial extension. On the other hand, a building or a shop can be represented as a rectangle on a 2D map, such as $C_\ell = \{x = [30, 100], y = [50, 130]\}$.

There are two types of regions: *interest regions* and *object regions*. They have the same definitions as a region, but they have different semantics. An interest region represents the set of values within the subject spaces a subscriber is interested in. $\mathcal{I}$ denotes a set of interest regions, and i represents a particular interest region in $\mathcal{I}$. An object region represents values a publisher provides, the state of an entity that may be of interest to one or more subscribers. $\mathcal{O}$ denotes a set of object regions, and o represents a particular object region in $\mathcal{O}$.

Example 4   Using the subject space definitions in Example 2, two possible interest regions, i_{coffee} and i_{cake}, in the coffee and cake subject spaces are defined as follows:

$$C_{i_{coffee}} = \{\textit{flavor}=\text{"Irish Cream"}, \text{price} < 2\},$$
$$C_{i_{cake}} = \{\text{name} = \text{"black forest"}, \text{price} < 20\}.$$

Define m as a relation between regions r_1 and r_2 such that r_1 *matches* r_2. Regions are spatial extensions within the subject spaces. Intuitively, two regions match if they touch each other or they are "close" to each other to some extent. There are many possible matching semantics. The subject space data model does not restrict the meaning of matching and allows multiple matching semantics. Four representative matching semantics and their corresponding matching relations are defined as follows:

1. *Containment.* The containment semantics requires that for r_1 to match r_2, r_2 must be entirely "inside" r_1. $r_1 \; m_c \; r_2$ iff $V_\sigma^{r_1} \cap V_\sigma^{r_2} = V_\sigma^{r_2}$

2. *Enclosure.* The enclosure semantics requires that for r_1 to match r_2, r_1 must be entirely "inside" r_2. $r_1 \; m_e \; r_2$ iff $V_\sigma^{r_1} \cap V_\sigma^{r_2} = V_\sigma^{r_1}$

3. *Overlap.* Two regions *overlap* each other if they are touching each other in all dimensions. $r_1 \; m_o \; r_2$ iff $V_\sigma^{r_1} \cap V_\sigma^{r_2} \neq \emptyset$

4. *Nearest Neighbor.* The nearest neighbor matching semantics is the most general notion of a match. Under this definition, r_1 matches r_2 if r_2 is the closest region to r_1. The degree of closeness is defined by

a distance function. If a subject space can be represented as a multidimensional Euclidean space, then the distance between two regions can be defined as the Euclidean distance between the closest points between the two regions. In general, the distance function can be defined by using some metrics that indicate the relationships between two values. Let the distance function be *dist*, the definition of the nearest neighbor semantics is: $r_1 \text{ m}_n r_2$ iff $\forall r \notin \{r_1, r_2\}$, $dist(V_\sigma^{r_1}, V_\sigma^{r_2}) \leq dist(V_\sigma^{r_1}, V_\sigma^{r})$.

Example 5 Consider a one-dimensional space with the dimension d in the real number domain. Let constraints be defined as closed intervals of real numbers. Let there be four regions, r_1, r_2, r_3, and r_4.

$$C_{r_1} = \{2 < d < 3\}, \ C_{r_2} = \{1 < d < 5\}, \ C_{r_3} = \{4 < d < 6\}, \ C_{r_4} = \{7 < d < 8\}$$
$$r_2 \text{ m}_c r_1; \ r_1 \text{ m}_e r_2; \ r_2 \text{ m}_o r_1 \text{ and } r_2 \text{ m}_o r_3.$$

Let the distance function be defined as the minimum distance between two regions. Formally, define where p is a point, *lb* and *ub* are the lower and upper bounds of an interval.

Given the above distance function, $r_4 \text{ m}_n r_3$.

A filter is an integral part of both publications and subscriptions. The definition of a filter applies to both publications and subscriptions. A filter is expressed as $\{R \mid \exists \ r_1, r_2, \ldots, r_n \in R : P(r_1, r_2, \ldots, r_n)\}$. $R = \{r_1, r_2, \ldots, r_m\}$ is a set of regions and $P(r_1, r_2, \ldots, r_n)$ is a Boolean function that takes a number of regions as variables. The expression represents the set of R such that P is true.

A subscription specifies conditions for notifications. A subscription $\mathcal{S}$ is defined as a tuple $\mathcal{S} = (\mathcal{I}_S, f_S)$. $\mathcal{I}_S$ is a set of interest regions that represents the constraints of the subscription. These interest regions can be in different subject spaces. f_S is an expression that represents the set of object regions that satisfy the conditions indicated by the rule of the filter. $f_S = \{\mathcal{O} \mid \exists \ o_1, o_2, \ldots, o_n \in \mathcal{O} : P(o_1, o_2, \ldots, o_n)\}$.

Example 7 Let σ_{car} be a subject space that represents the attributes of a car. The dimensions of σ_{car} can be defined as: $D_{car} = \{(plate\_number, string), (fuel, percentage)\}$.

The user preference subject space σ_{pref} is for specifying preferred settings for various services. Among others, a dimension in σ_{pref} is *refuel_level*. If the level of fuel in the car falls within the range specified in refuel_level, the driver should receive a reminder to refuel. σ_{gas} is the subject space used by gas stations. σ_{gas} has a price dimension that indicates the current gas price per liter. Like in all LBS, the locations of cars and gas stations are represented as regions in the location subject space σ_{location}. If a driver would like to receive an alert when his car comes close to a gas station, and the gas price is cheap, he can express the subscription as follows:

Define $m_{1\,\text{km}}$ as a match relation between objects that are within 1 km with each other.

$\mathcal{I}_S = \{\ell_{car}, i_{car}, i_{pref}\}$, where ℓ_{car}, i_{car} and i_{pref} are interest regions in $\sigma_{\text{location}}, \sigma_{\text{car}}$ and σ_{pref}, respectively.

$C_{i_{car}} = \{\text{plate\_number} = ABC123, \text{fuel} = 60\%\},$

$= C_{i_{pref}} = \{\textit{refuel\_level} < 20\%\},$

$f_S = \{\mathcal{O} \mid \exists\ \ell_{\text{gas\_station}},\ o_{car},\ o_{pref} \in \mathcal{O}: \ell_{car}\ m_{1\,\text{km}}\ \ell_{\text{gas\_station}} \wedge o_{car}\ m_e\ i_{car} \wedge o_{pref}\ m_e\ i_{pref}\}$

A publication targets content to a subset of the subscribers. A publication π is defined as a tuple $\pi = (\mathcal{O}_P, f_P)$. $\mathcal{O}_P$ is a set of object regions that represents the constraints of the publication. These object regions can be in different subject spaces. f_P is an expression that represents the set of sets of interest regions that satisfy the conditions indicated by the rule of the filter. $f_P = \{\mathcal{I} \mid \exists i_1, i_2, \ldots, i_n \in \mathcal{I}: P(i_1, i_2, \ldots, i_n)\}$.

Example 8   A gas station may like to send advertisements to cars nearby whose fuel level is below 70%. This publication can be defined as:

$\mathcal{O}_P = \{\ell_{\text{gas\_station}}, o_{gas}, o_{car}\}$, where $\ell_{\text{gas\_station}}$ and o_{gas} are object regions in σ_{location} and σ_{gas}, respectively.

$C_{o_{car}} = \{\text{fuel} < 70\%\}, C_{o_{gas}} = \{\text{price} = 65\cancel{c}\}$

$f_P = \{\mathcal{I} \mid \exists \ell_{car}, i_{car} \in \mathcal{I}: (\ell_{\text{gas\_station}} m_{1\text{km}}\ \ell_{car}) \wedge i_{car}\ m_o\ o_{car}\},$

Define $\mathcal{M}$ as a relation between a publication π and a subscription $\mathcal{P}$, such that $\mathcal{P}$ matches $\mathcal{S}$.

$$(\mathcal{P}, \mathcal{S}) \in \mathcal{M} \text{ iff } \exists \mathcal{R} \subseteq \mathcal{I}_S: \mathcal{R} \in f_P \hat{\exists} \mathcal{R} \subseteq \mathcal{O}_P: \mathcal{R} \in f_S.$$

In order for a publication to match a subscription, some object regions of the publication must satisfy the subscription filter, *and* some interest regions of the subscription must satisfy the publication filter. If either of these two conditions is not met, this pair of publication and subscription is not a match. This demonstrates the symmetric property of publish/subscribe systems.

Example 9   Reconsider Examples 7 and 8. If the car described in Example 7 comes within 1 km of the gas station described in the example, the subscription would have satisfied the publication (i.e., $\mathcal{I}_S = \{\ell_{\text{car}}, i_{\text{car}}\} \in f_P$), because the car is within 1 km of the gas station and the fuel level of the car is below 70%; however, the publication does not satisfy the subscription because the fuel level is not below the threshold of 20% as indicated in the user preference. This example illustrates the symmetrical property of the subject spaces model. Drivers use subscriptions to filter out unwanted information. At the same time, gas stations use publications to target a subset of cars driving by.

The subject spaces model can also support the notion of time to express temporal correlation between events (for details, see [LeJa02, LeJa03]). In a state-persistent publish/subscribe system, a broker only sends notifications upon state transitions. In other words, the broker sends notifications to a subscription S if a publication-subscription pair (π, S) is added to or removed from $\mathcal{M}$. State transitions can take place in several situations, include adding a publication or subscription, updating a publication or subscription, and deleting a publication. Note that no notification needs to be sent if a subscription is deleted from the system. It can be shown that the four models described in the section on publish/subscribe can be mapped to the subject spaces model. (For further details, please refer to [LBJ03, LeJa02, LeJa03]).

4.6.3   Tuple Spaces

The inherently stateless traditional publish/subscribe model is well suited to support selective information dissemination applications. The state-persistent subject spaces model is able to track objects and detect critical conditions and correlations of these objects. The tuple space model's primary strength is its ability to coordinate many concurrent activities, including the stateful interaction among multiple activities.

The idea of coordinating concurrent activities via a tuple space originated in the parallel programming community in the 1980s [Gel85]. To this date, tuple spaces–based middleware models have been widely implemented (e.g., InfoSpaces, JavaSpaces, and TSpaces), and the model has found widespread applications, especially to coordinate activities in mobile environments [HICSS99, DWFB97].

Tuples are typed data elements, designated as *actuals,* if they contain data values, and as *formals,* if they do not contain data values, but simply specify a data type. Collections of tuples—possibly identical ones—exist in so-called tuple spaces. Tuples can be dynamically inserted, read, and removed from the tuple space, but they cannot be altered while in the space. Updates and changes to tuples can be effected by first removing the tuple from the space, updating it, and inserting it back into the space. Tuple spaces are shared among several processes that can all access it by inserting, removing, or reading tuples from the space. All communication is performed via the tuple space, also referred to as generative communication [Gel85]. Tuples are persisted in the tuple space, thus communication persists across time and space, while keeping the interacting entities decoupled and a priori anonymous. A coupled communication scheme (i.e., synchronous) between two processes may be achieved, if the sending process submits a designated tuple to the space and waits on a response tuple, which is generated by the receiving process in response to the message sent by the sender.

Originally, the tuple space concept was implemented as an extension to a host programming language. Current implementations are stand-alone middleware services, used by communicating application processes (e.g., JavaSpaces and TSpaces). Early implementations, namely the original Linda model, support four operations:

1. out(t). Inserts tuple *t* into the tuple space; *t* is a mix of actuals and formals and becomes visible to all processes with access to the tuple space.

2. in(t). Extracts a tuple-matching tuple template *t* from the tuple space. A match occurs if a tuple is found for which all actuals correspond in type and value to the data elements of *t* and all formals correspond in type. One matching tuple is nondeterministically extracted from the space, and actuals are bound to formals in the template. The operation blocks until such a match is established.

3. rd(t). Is syntactically and semantically equivalent to in(t), except that a matching tuple is copied and not removed from the tuple space.

4. eval(..). Generates active tuples that turn into (passive) tuples, as the associated computations terminate. An active tuple associates with each data element a separate process, which yields a data element upon completion.

Over the years, several extensions to this API have been realized, most notably the inp and rdp operations that constitute nonblocking versions of the in and rd operations, respectively. Moreover, multiple tuple spaces and distributed tuple spaces have been considered (see [DWFB97] for a more detailed list of extensions).

In a location-based application, information producer and information consumer interact via a tuple space by inserting and extracting tuples. The tuple space decouples the communication between producer and consumer. This interaction is a priori asynchronous; however, synchronous interaction styles can also be modeled on top of a tuple space. This model is therefore very flexible, which is currently actively applied to model mobile applications and other application scenarios [HICSS99].

4.6.4 DBMS-Based Model

The previously described middleware models primarily support coordination activities among a large number of decoupled and anonymous entities (e.g., mobile terminals and users). Some of the models realize a stateful interaction, whereas others are stateless; some support persistency, whereas others are inherently transient. Common to these models is their ability to coordinate activities among several concurrent entities and to support an event-based and push-driven interaction style (e.g., a server-initiated style of interaction).

This section briefly reviews a DBMS-based model as an underlying middleware and coordination model. Note, this does not refer to database technology as it is used in any LBS to store and manage subscriber profiles, registration data, accounting information, and billing records, but rather to database technology for enabling the core information service provided.

This model supports a pull-style interaction scheme (see Figures 4.1 and 4.2 for a detailed presentation of this model). A mobile terminal–initiated request is evaluated on a database, and any results are returned to the requester. Depending on the complexity of the application, a single request may first be processed in an application-server tier and then evaluated against one or more local or remote databases. Lookup services and information queries are implemented in this fashion. The application-server tier may be responsible for obtaining the location position information of the request-initiating mobile terminal, if this location information is not already part of the request. Location information and request are then passed on to a database to retrieve the relevant information. Database queries may be nearest neighbor queries, spatial queries, similarity queries, or conventional database queries. Many geographic information systems operate according to this scheme. The underlying database may support a range of spatial data and query-processing capabilities. This model enables the interaction between one mobile terminal and the database, which stores information relevant to the mobile terminal. Certainly, several concurrent requests from multiple independent mobile terminals can be processed, but the model does not support the coordination and correlation of multiple concurrent entities, as some of the models do.

4.7   CONCLUSION

The primary focus of this chapter has been the characterization of LBS applications and the discussion of middleware models that support these various characteristics. There are several fundamental differences in applications and models. First, several applications require the coordination and interaction of multiple users with location information correlated entities, whereas others are based on the model of one mobile entity interacting with a service provider. The former applications are supported by the publish/subscribe model, by the tuple space model, and by subject spaces, whereas the latter are supported by the database-based model.

Second, a key difference exists between push- and pull-driven applications and between push- and pull-enabling middleware models. In the push-based model, the service activity is initiated by the service entity and in the pull-based model, the service activity is initiated by the mobile entity. The inherently pull-based model discussed is the database-based model.

Finally, several applications require the maintenance of state across interactions and across interactions among different mobile entities, whereas others are inherently stateless. The tuple space model and subject spaces are inherently state-based, whereas traditional publish/subscribe is inherently stateless.

A middleware system for LBS supports many other functionalities, such as management of subscriber information, management of billing records and accounting, and enforcement of privacy. Furthermore, a middleware architecture supports the integration of these functionalities in an interoperable fashion, often enabled through an open services architecture and the support of open standards and interfaces. To date, no standard middleware for LBS exists; however, standard organizations are defining location positioning protocols that enable interoperability across mobile carriers and applications. By far the most challenging problem middleware for LBS has to address is the coordination and interaction problem discussed throughout this chapter. This problem includes filtering of information for mobile entities, correlation of information with location information, correlation of movements and movement patterns of mobile entities, and tracking of mobile entities.

ACKNOWLEDGMENTS

The subject spaces model was developed in the master thesis of Hubert Leung in the Middleware Systems Research Group at the University of Toronto. The L-ToPSS system was developed by Ioana Burcea as part of her master thesis in the Middleware Systems Research Group at the University of Toronto. The author is very grateful for support from the Bell University Laboratories and the fruitful collaboration with Tony Hui from Bell Mobility, who have inspired much of the discussion in this chapter.

References

[ALJ02]   G. Ashayer, H. Leung, and H.-A. Jacobsen. Predicate Matching and Subscription Matching in Publish/Subscribe Systems. In Proc. of *Distributed Event-Based Systems Workshop at ICDCS'02*, IEEE Computer Society, pages 539–546, 2002.

[BJ03]   I. Burcea and H.-A. Jacobsen. "L-ToPSS: Push-Oriented Location-Based Services." In Proc. of the 4th VLDB Workshop on Technologies for E-Services (TES'03), Lecture Notes in Computer Science No. 2819, Springer Verlag, Berlin/Heidelberg, 2003.

[BJD+04]   I. Burcea, H.-A. Jacobsen, E. DeLara, V. Muthusam, and M. Petrovic. "Disconnected Operations in Publish/Subscribe." *IEEE Mobile Data Management*, IEE Publication, pages 39–50, 2004.

[CJ02]   G. Cugola and H.-A. Jacobsen. "Using Publish/Subscribe Middleware for Mobile Systems." *ACM SIGMOBILE Mobile Computing and Communications Review* (MC2R) 6(4): 25–33, ACM Press, New York, October 2002.

[DRL01]   Durlacher Research Ltd., 2001, UMTS-Report (available from *http://www.durlacher.com*)

[DWFB97]   N. Davies, S. P. Wade, A. Friday, and G. S. Blair. "Limbo: A Tuple Space Based Platform for Adaptive Mobile Applications." In *Proceedings of the International Conference on Open Distributed Processing/Distributed Platforms (ICODP/ICDP)*, 1997.

[FJL+01a]   F. Fabret, H.-A. Jacobsen, F. Llirbat, J. Pereira, and D. Shasha. "WebFilter: A High-throughput XML-based Publish and Subscribe System." VLDB software demonstration proposal, Rome, Italy. In *Proceedings of the Very Large Database Conference (VLDB)*, 2001.

[FJL+01b]   F. Fabret, H.-A. Jacobsen, F. Llirbat, J. Pereira, K. Ross, and D. Shasha. "Filtering Algorithms and Implementation for Very Fast Publish/Subscribe Systems." In *Proceedings of the SIGMOD Conference*, ACM/SIGMOD, May 2001.

[Gel85]   D. Gelernter. "Generative communication in Linda ACM." *Transactions on Programming Languages and Systems* (TOPLAS), 7(1):80–112, January 1985, ACM Press, New York.

[HICSS99]   "TSpaces: The Next Wave." Hawaii International Conference on System Sciences (HICSS-32), January 1999.

[Jac01]   H.-A. Jacobsen. "Middleware Services for Selective and Location-based Information Dissemination in Mobile Wireless Networks." Advanced Topic Workshop on Middleware for Mobile Computing, November 12–16, 2001.

[LBJ03]   H. Leung, I. Burcea, and H.-A. Jacobsen. "Modeling Location-based Services With Subject Spaces." In *Proceedings of CASCON Conference*, pages 177–187, IBM Publisher, 2003.

[LeJa02]   H. Leung and H.-A. Jacobsen. "Subject Space: A State-Persistent Data Model for Publish/ Subscribe Systems." Computer Science Research Group, University of Toronto, CRSG, nb. 459, September 2002. (Appeared as student paper in CASCON 2002.)

[LeJa03]   H. Leung and H.-A. Jacobsen. "Efficient Matching for State-Persistent Publish/ Subscribe Systems." In *Proceedings of CASCON Conference*, pages 188–202, IBM Publisher, 2003.

[LiJa02]   H. Liu and H.-A. Jacobsen. "A-TOPSS: A Publish/Subscribe System Supporting Approximate Matching." VLDB Conference, August 2002, Humboldt University, Berlin, Germany.

[LiJa04]   H. Liu and H.-A. Jacobsen. "Modeling Uncertainties in Publish/Subscribe." IEEE International Conference on Data Engineering, 2004.

[MMJ00]   Mobile Media Japan, "More than 10 million i-mode subscribers," *http://www.mobilmediajapan.com*, August 6, 2000.

[OGC]   The OpenGIS Consortium, *http://www.opengis.org*

[PBJ03]   M. Petrovic, I. Burcea, and H.-A. Jacobsen. "S-ToPSS: Semantic Toronto Publish/Subscribe System." Very Large Databases Conference, September 2003, Humboldt University, Berlin, Germany.

[Sim02]   D. Sims. "Who will win the cell phone battle?" *The Standard.com*, May 24, 2002.

[ST03]   A. Sanchez del Campo and L. Telleria. "Business and legal issues in LBS," *http://www.vtt.fi/tte/rd/location-techniques/sanchez.pdf*. Accessed January 30, 2003.

[TAJ03]   T. Ye, H.-A. Jacobsen, and R. Katz. "Mobile Awareness in a Wide Area Wireless Network of Info-Stations." *ACM/IEEE International Conference on Mobile Computing and Networking* (MobiCom'98), pages 109–120, September 1998, Denver, Colorado.

[WHFG92]   R. Want, A. Hopper, V. Falcao, and J. Gibbons. "The Active Badge Location System." *ACM Transactions on Information Systems*, 10(1):91–102, January 1992.

[YJK98]   T. Ye, H.-A. Jacobsen, and R. Katz. "Mobile Awareness in a Wide Area Wireless Network of Info-Stations." *ACM/IEEE International Conference on Mobile Computing and Networking* (MobiCom'98), pages 109–120, September 1998, Denver, Colorado.

[ZGL03]   V. Zeimpekis, G. M. Giaglis, and G. Lekeko. "A Taxonomy of Indoor and Outdoor Positioning Techniques for Mobile Location Services," *SIGecom Exchanges*, 3–4:19, Winter 2003.

5

Database Aspects of Location-Based Services

Christian S. Jensen, Aalborg University

CONTENTS

Adopting a data management perspective on location-based services (LBS), this chapter explores central challenges to data management posed by LBS. Because service users typically travel in, and are constrained to, transportation infrastructures, such structures must be represented in the databases underlying high-quality services. Several integrated representations, which capture different aspects of the same infrastructure, are needed. Furthermore, all other content that can be related to geographic space must be integrated with the infrastructure representations.

The chapter describes the general concepts underlying one approach to data modeling for LBS. The chapter also covers techniques that are needed to keep a database for LBS up to date with the reality it models. As part of this, caching is touched on briefly. The notion of linear referencing plays an important role in the chapter's approach to data modeling. Thus, the chapter offers an overview of linear referencing concepts and describes the support for linear referencing in Oracle.

5.1   A CONTENT-CENTRIC VIEW

The delivery of LBS in practice depends on the existence of a well-functioning value chain. At a high level of abstraction, the value chain begins with *content providers* that supply various types of content that can be georeferenced to a content integrator. Examples of content include the following:

- Weather data
- Traffic condition data, including information about accidents and congestion
- Information about sights and attractions (e.g., for tourists)
- Information about hotel rooms, cottages, and the like available for booking
- Information about the current locations of a population of service users

The *content integrator* manages content received from multiple sources. This management includes several aspects. The content integrator must create and maintain a database and IT infrastructure that are capable of capturing the content received. The resulting database system must be able to absorb the content received, while making the content available to LBS offered by multiple *service providers*.

This (partial) value chain reflects the conventional wisdom that "content is king," in that it enables reuse of the same content across multiple services, and in that it places the content integrator at center stage. Another consequence of this arrangement is that it becomes possible to ensure that the different kinds of content received are truly integrated and mutually consistent. Put differently, it becomes possible to ensure high data quality. The result is a solid foundation for the deployment of collections of high-quality, integrated services. In addition, this arrangement provides a basis for the rapid development of new services. This will be important for certain types of services (e.g., games that merge virtual worlds with the physical world). The lifetime of a game may be short, and it may well be important for users to have access to the most advanced game currently available.

One may distinguish between two types of content: (1) the geographic infrastructure itself and (2) all of the other "real" content that may be given geographic references and that must reference the infrastructure. So-called point-of-interest (POI) data (e.g., [KK99]) is an example of real content.

The geographic infrastructure, or geocontent, concerns the geographic space itself, with hills, lakes, rivers, fjords, and so on. It also concerns the transportation infrastructure. We focus on the transportation infrastructure for cars, termed road networks, although different infrastructures also exist for pedestrians, trains, aircraft, and ships. The infrastructure for cars is of high interest because users may frequently be either constrained to, or at least using, this infrastructure.

Geocontent is essential to LBS. Users think of the real content as being located in a transportation infrastructure and access the content via the infrastructure. For example, a POI's location is typically given in terms of the road it is located on, and directions for how to reach the location are given in terms of the transportation infrastructure. Users are most often not interested in Euclidean distances, but in road distances.

All of the real content, also termed business data, encompasses any content that may reference, directly or indirectly, the geographic infrastructure. A museum, a store, or a movie theater may have both a set of coordinates and a location in the road network. This type of content is open-ended and extremely voluminous. For example, it may include listings of movies currently running in the movie theater, seat availability information for the different shows, and reviews of the movies. Most often, the real content has the primary interest of the users.

In current systems, geocontent and real content often live separate lives. Special-purpose geographic information system (GIS) software manages the geocontent, while a general-purpose relational database management system (RDBMS) manages the real content. In LBS, the special-purpose GIS world and the general-purpose relational data management world need to be integrated. In the remainder of this chapter, we assume that the geocontent moves in with the real content in the relational world.

5.2   CHALLENGES ABOUND

Several data management challenges exist in relation to LBS. These relate to the modeling and representation of content, the update of content, and the querying of content.

It is important to realize that assuming content to be static is problematic. Rather, content is generally dynamic. This applies to road networks, where road construction and accidents change the characteristics of the networks with varying degrees of permanence. It applies perhaps even more clearly to the other content, partly because of its open-endedness. Examples abound: New stores open and existing stores relocate or close. The opening hours of a facility may change. The program of a movie theater changes. The sales available in a store change. This dynamism of content implies that a representation of content must be designed to accommodate updates. It also implies that temporal data management techniques, which enable the management of multiple versions of content, play a role.

Content is more or less dynamic. The content that derives from the tracking of continuous processes belongs at the highly dynamic end of the spectrum. A prime example of such content in LBS is the locations of mobile users. Such content is obtained via some form of sampling. Capturing the present positions, and possibly the past as well as anticipated future positions, of a large population of mobile users requires special techniques.

Because of the dynamism of the content used in LBS, which increases as more content is included, and the availability of wireless communications, the current generation of largely offline, CD-ROM-based telematics systems fall short.

The need for multiple representations of the road infrastructure represents another type of data management challenge. This infrastructure plays a central role in the LBS we consider. As mentioned, user movement is generally constrained to the infrastructure, and all or most content is accessible via the infrastructure. We need representations of the infrastructure that support different uses, including the following:

♦ *Content capture.* Road infrastructures are equipped with systems of physical markers that enable the convenient positioning of content within the infrastructures. These systems must be captured. Other content (e.g., the positions of mobile users) is given by geographic coordinates. Thus the geographic coordinates of the road infrastructures must also be captured.

♦ *Content representation, update, and querying.* The association of content with the infrastructure must support updates as well as efficient querying.

♦ *Route planning and way finding.* Here, a graph representation is suitable.

♦ *Display.* In order to display a road infrastructure on maps at different scales, cartographic symbols must be associated with the elements of the infrastructure, and the infrastructure must be represented at different levels of generalization that correspond to the map scales.

♦ *Representation integration.* The different representations of a road infrastructure must be integrated so that it becomes possible to translate from one to the other.

In the following section, we consider the modeling and representation of content.

5.3   CONTENT MODELING

We consider the types of LBS that drivers and other mobile, outdoor individuals are expected to use. Such services rely on multiple representations of the physical space in which their users are embedded.

We proceed to describe a generic approach to the modeling of a transportation infrastructure in a relational setting. This approach is based on principles from a variety of approaches that aim at use in practice [DeBl93, DuBu98, DKSS02, HJP+03, KA02, OSM95,

VCSA97, Vig94]. For brevity and to maintain focus on principles, many details are omitted.

5.3.1 Multiple External Infrastructure Representations

To capture all aspects of the infrastructure, several representations are needed. We will describe three representations: a *road-centric representation based on kilometer posts*, a *graph representation*, and a *geo-representation*. These representations must be integrated, so that it is possible to switch between them.

The kilometer post representation is used in connection with the capture of some content that is closely related to the roads themselves, and it is used for road administration in general. It is common practice to specify the location of some geocontent relative to the nearest kilometer post on a specific road. For example, the entry to a new parking area may be indicated by a road, a kilometer post on that road, and an offset. The representation is used by administrative authorities. This representation is attractive because simple technological means suffice when entering data, rendering the representation cost effective and practical.

The graph representation describes a directed mathematical graph. The graph representation shows an abstract view of an infrastructure that ignores geographic detail but preserves its topology. It is used for connectivity-type queries, such as route guidance and way finding. A graph consists of a set of nodes and a set of directed links between pairs of nodes. A node generally represents a point in the infrastructure where traffic properties of the infrastructure change significantly. This occurs, for example, where a driver may choose to follow different roads (e.g., at an intersection). Links connect pairs of nodes and indicate that it is possible for a driver to move from the first node to the second. The links are weighted, and a weight may represent distance, travel time, or some other property associated with the link.

The geo-representation captures the geographic coordinates of the road infrastructure. With this representation, it is possible to map a location given in terms of geographic coordinates to a location in the infrastructure. Locations given in terms of geographic coordinates come from a variety of sources, including global positioning system (GPS) receivers and point-on-map-and-click interfaces.

5.3.2 Internal Infrastructure Representation

In order to integrate the three infrastructure representations just introduced, we define an internal infrastructure representation. By connecting the other, external representations to this representation, we obtain the desired integration among the external representations.

The internal representation is quite simple. An infrastructure is simply seen as a collection of so-called linear elements and a collection of connection points that connect linear elements and thus allow movement between the elements. A linear element is any kind of geographic feature for which it is meaningful to state the location of any point on the feature as a distance from some start point on the feature [Sca02]. This notion is quite general. Examples include roads, rivers, train tracks, footpaths, and so on.

The internal representation uses three tables. A table **element** records the linear elements. Each row in **element** identifies an element and has an **elementID** attribute as its primary key and an attribute **length** that indicates the length of the element. Next, a table **connection** captures connections. It has an attribute **connectionID** as its primary key. Additional attributes describe the connection. The last table, **elementConnection**, relates elements and connections. It has a row for each occurrence of an element meeting a connection point. This table has three attributes: **elementID**, **connectionID**, **distance**. The first two are foreign keys. A row indicates that the specified element intersects with the specified connection point at the specified distance from the start of the element.

When we describe the three external infrastructure representations in detail, we also connect these to the internal representation.

5.3.3 Kilometer Post Representation

The kilometer post representation may be described by two relational tables: a **road** table and a **kilometer-post** table. The **road** table identifies individual road parts. It thus has one row per road part and has a column **roadPartID** as its primary key. For each road part, this table may contain a description of the road part, information about which authority is in charge of maintaining the road part, and so on.

To illustrate, consider Figure 5.1, which contains an aerial photo from somewhere in Denmark. In particular, consider the road fragment that stretches from the bottom-left to the top-right. This fragment of the road,

Figure 5.1   Fragment of Road 337. DDO 1995, copyright COWI.

termed road 337, consists of five parts: Part 0 stretches from the bottom-left to the top-right. Assuming that movement is from bottom to top, a vehicle that exits the road will use the lower-right exit lane, termed Part 3, and a vehicle that enters the road will use the top-right access lane, termed Part 5. The corresponding lanes for movement in the opposite direction are termed Part 4 and Part 6, respectively.

The identification of roads and road parts for the kilometer post representation is defined by administrative procedures [DKSS02]. Specifically, the authorities in charge of road administration maintain guidelines on how to identify roads and road parts. Typically, the roads partition the infrastructure, and the road parts partition a single road. In addition, road parts typically represent separate engineering structures that constitute a single road in a physical sense.

The **kilometer-post** table simply captures the kilometer posts for each road part. A row in this table thus corresponds to a post and contains a reference to a row in the **road** table. The distance value specifies the location along the road of the post from a reference point on the road. The posts may be either physical or imaginary.

The road parts from the photo in Figure 5.1 are shown in Figure 5.2, which also illustrates kilometer posts and their relation to road parts. This figure indicates that kilometer post 47 appears five times in the **kilometer-post** table, once for each of the Parts 0, 3, 6, 4, and 5. The posts on the three first parts are physical, and the posts on the last two parts are imaginary.

The kilometer post representation is connected to the internal representation by means of two tables. A table **roadElement** relates road parts to elements. The idea is that an element is built from road parts.

A **roadPartID** attribute identifies a road part, and an **elementID** attribute identifies an element. Attributes **eStart** and **eEnd** describe the part of the element to which the road part corresponds. To illustrate, consider Figure 5.3. The fragment of road 337 we consider is modeled as three elements (numbered 893, 894, and 896). Table **roadElement** contains two rows for element 894. The first identifies Part 3 of road 337

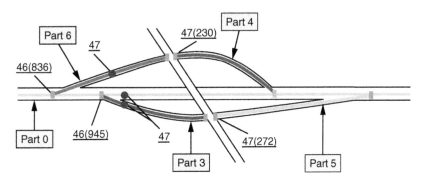

Figure 5.2 Road parts and kilometer posts.

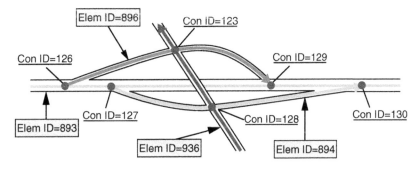

Figure 5.3 Elements and connections.

and has start value 0 and end value 338. The second identifies Part 5 of road 337 and has start value 338 and end value 724.

In a similar fashion, we may relate the **kilometer-post** table to the **element** table. This is the purpose of table **postElement**. This table contains a reference to an element and a section of the element, given by start and end values that refer to the beginning of the element. It also refers to a row in the **road** table (i.e., to a road part). Finally, it refers to a kilometer post with an offset. Let us consider some examples. An example row could be as follows: (893, 35064, 36069, 6068, 47, 0). Here, "6068" refers to Part 0 of road 337. This row states that element 893 from 35.064 to 36.069 corresponds to milepost 47 (with zero offset) on Part 0 of road 337. The rows for element 894 may look as follows, where "6071" and "6074" denote the third and fifth parts of road 337: (894, 0, 55, 6071, 46, 945), (894, 55, 327, 6071, 47, 0), (894, 327, 724, 6074, 47, 272). So the first 55 meters of element 894 is covered by the imaginary kilometer post on Part 3 of road 337 that is located 945 meters after physical kilometer post 46 (on Part 0 of road 337). The next part is covered by kilometer post 47 on Part 3 of road 337, and the last part is covered by the imaginary kilometer post on Part 5 of road 337 that is located 272 meters after the start of physical post 47 on Part 3. The reader may verify that this description is consistent with the information given in Figures 5.2 and 5.3.

Note that it is also possible to infer rows from tables **element**, **connection**, and **elementConnection** from Figure 5.3. For example, the last table contains the two rows (893, 127, 35009) and (894, 127, 0), which indicate that element 893 meets connection 127 after 35,009 meters and that element 894 meets the connection at 0 meters (i.e., it starts at connection 127).

5.3.4 Graph Representation

The graph representation of a road network is an abstraction that is ideally suited for the provisioning of routes and for the support of services to do with connectivity. In practice, we may need several graph representations of the same road infrastructure. For example, different graphs may be used to capture the road infrastructure at different resolutions. One may also use different graphs for different types of vehicles. Buses may use roads that are not accessible to other vehicles.

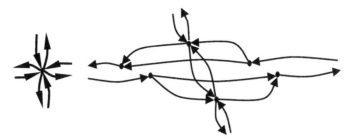

Figure 5.4 Alternative graph representations.

We can capture the graph representations by means of two tables: **node** and **link**. A row in the node table describes a node, and thus has a **nodeID** attribute and a **representationID** attribute. The same intersection may be part of several graph representations, but a **nodeID** value is unique within a representation. For efficiency, a single primary key attribute, **nID**, is introduced.

A row in the **link** table connects two rows in the **node** table that have different **nodeID** values and the same **representationID** value. In addition to **nIDbegin** and **nIDend** attributes, this table has an **lID** attribute, which is the primary key, and a **length** attribute, which indicates the length of the link. Figure 5.4 gives two graph representations for our example at two different levels of detail.

Finally, we create a table **linkElement** that relates links, and thus nodes, to elements. A row in this table identifies a link in the **link** table and an element in the **element** table. A link corresponds to only part of an element, so **eStart** and **eEnd** attributes are included as well.

5.3.5 Georeferences

A road network is not just a collection of roads with intersections and kilometer posts or a graph. Rather, the geographic coordinates of the roads and the road intersections are important as well.

The geographic coordinates of the infrastructure are captured by attaching geographic coordinates to the internal linear elements. Specifically, we associate polylines with the elements. A polyline is a sequence of connected line segments, and a line segment is given by a start and an end coordinate. A linear element is then represented by a collection of polylines. More than one polyline may be necessary because the linear elements can have gaps.

Furthermore, just as we could have different graph representations of the same infrastructure, we can have different geographic representations of the same linear element. These representations differ with respect to how accurate they are: the more accurate a representation is, the more line segments are used in its description.

A table **coordinates** is used to capture the geographic coordinates of elements. A row in this table references a linear element and represents a single line segment located on that element. For each line segment, it is also indicated how far into the element it starts and ends. Thus the attributes of this table include **elementID**, **eStart**, **eEnd**, **xStart**, **yStart**, **xEnd**, and **yEnd**. An additional attribute, **accuracy**, is used to capture the accuracy of the geographic description. The attributes **elementID**, **eStart**, and **accuracy** are a key for this table.

5.3.6 Summary of Infrastructure Representations

Figure 5.5 summarizes the schema described throughout Section 5.3.

5.3.7 Content Modeling

Having modeled different aspects of a transportation infrastructure, we need to relate real content, or business data (e.g., POI data) to the infrastructure, and the content needs graphical coordinates. The latter may be obtained by ensuring the former. The idea is simply to relate

element = (*elementID*, length)

connection = (*elementID (fk)*, *descriptive attributes*)

elementConnection = (*elementID (fk)*, *connectionID (fk)*, *distance*)

road = (*roadPartID*, roadID, partID)

kilometer-post = (*roadPartID (fk)*, post)

roadElement = (*roadPartID (fk)*, *elementID (fk)* , eStart, eEnd)

postElement = (*elementID (fk)*, eStart, eEnd, *roadPartID (fk)*, *post (fk)*, offset)

node = (*nID*, nodeID, representationID)

link = (*lID*, nIDbegin (fk), nIDend (fk), length)

linkElement = (*lID (fk)*, *elementID (fk)*, eStart, eEnd)

coordinates = (*elementID (fk)*, eStart, eEnd, xStart, yStart, xEnd, yEnd, *accuracy*)

Figure 5.5 Database schema.

content to linear elements. Because elements are related to everything else, so is the content.

Different kinds of content may be envisioned. For example, we may record the locations of tourist attractions. One attraction may be mapped to one or more points on one or more elements. A point on an element is simply given as a distance from the start of the element. Several points may be used if the attraction has several access points. Other attractions may be mapped to one or more intervals for one or more elements. This may be reasonable if the attraction is a sight. An interval of an element then indicates that the sight is visible during that interval. Other kinds of content are stores, private residences, speed limits, and accidents.

5.4 UPDATE MANAGEMENT

A database that models a dynamic reality or that must support changing applications typically needs to support updates. The need to support updates is not to be taken lightly. For example, an important rationale for the relational, dependency-based normalization theory was exactly to ensure that updates could be performed efficiently, primarily by ensuring that the same data are not represented multiple times.

In our context of LBS, updates come in two guises. The first relates to discrete change and is the conventional type of update. Here, we need to be able to modify the database when changes occur in the modeled reality. We focus on updates caused by changes in the transportation infrastructure. The second relates to aspects that change continuously. Specifically, we may want to capture the continuously changing positions of moving users.

5.4.1 Update Caused by Discrete Change

In a conventional database, the primary and foreign keys are the glue that ties all of the data together. It is generally recommended that so-called dumb keys be used as primary keys. Dumb keys carry no meaning in the modeled reality, and their values need not (indeed, should not!) be seen by any applications. In these senses, they are opposites of social security numbers, employee IDs, and so on. One important attraction of dumb keys is that they render the database robust when certain changes occur in the modeled reality. For example, if dumb keys are used, a change in a social security number is handled by an update of a single row.

In contrast, many updates would be needed if the social security number were used as a primary key: one for the primary key table and one for each foreign key table.

In the model of transportation infrastructures presented in the previous section, the internal element-based representation plays the role of dumb keys. This representation ties the external representations together. Two external representations are interrelated by independent mappings to the internal representation. This arrangement isolates the impact on the database of changes to the infrastructure in comparison to the predominant alternative, where a representation based on the external route numbering of roads is used to interrelate different representations. For example, if the authority of a road is transferred (e.g., from county to state or from one county to another), the new authority is likely to alter the representation of the road. The resulting changes have global impact on the database.

Another aspect is the update of content, particularly content that maps to intervals on linear elements (e.g., speed limits). If linear elements are relatively short, the same speed limit may have to be associated with multiple elements. Thus one important criterion when partitioning the infrastructure into elements is to obtain long elements. This results in the smallest possible replication of interval content, which yields a compact representation that is efficient to update.

5.4.2 Update Caused by Continuous Change

In the context of mobile services, it may be of interest to track the positions of some service users. This is one aspect of the general notion of context awareness, and it may be used to deliver better services to the users.

The problem is one of maintaining an adequately accurate record of the past, current, and anticipated future position of a service user. It is realistic to assume that a GPS receiver attached to the user delivers position samples. Because GPS readings are imprecise and because we rely on sampling, we are unable to maintain a precise record of a user's location. Furthermore, there is a cost related to each update of a user's location, so it is preferable to perform as few updates as possible. We therefore look to the services that need tracking for their functioning in order to determine a required accuracy. For example, if we are to provide up-to-date weather information, low-accuracy tracking will suffice.

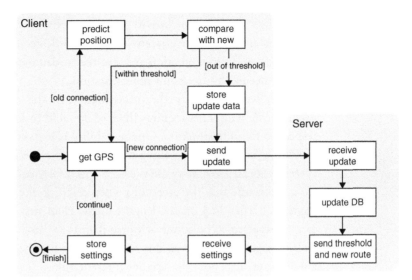

Figure 5.6 Position tracking.

In contrast, much higher accuracy is needed if we want to maintain, for each service user, a list of the closest and friendly service users.

We may now envision a scenario in which the central server maintains a representation of a user's movement and where the local client (e.g., the mobile phone) is aware of the server-side representation. The client frequently compares its GPS position with the server-side position, and when the two differ by a threshold slightly smaller than the required accuracy, an update is issued to the server, which then revises its representation and sends its new representation to the client. This scenario is illustrated in Figure 5.6.

Different representations of a user's movement result in different rates of update. We consider several possible representations in turn. First, we may represent the movement of a user as a constant function (i.e., as a point). With this representation, an update is needed every time the user has moved a (Euclidean) distance equal to the threshold away from the previous position. This is a simple representation, and it may be useful when the user is barely moving or is moving erratically within an area that is small in comparison to the area given by the threshold used.

Second, we may represent the movement by a linear function (i.e., by a vector). When the user exceeds the threshold, the user sends the current GPS location and the current speed and direction (also provided by the GPS receiver) to the server. The server then uses this information to predict the user's to-be-current positions. Experiments with real data from cars traveling in a city environment indicate that, for a range of thresholds, this representation reduces the updates needed to one-third of those needed by the point representation.

Third, we may utilize the infrastructure in the representation of a user's movement. This requires that we are able to locate the user with respect to the infrastructure. One possibility is to assume that the user is moving at constant speed along the linear element on which the user is currently located. We may use the GPS speed for the constant speed, and we may assume that the user stops when reaching the end of the current segment. Depending on the lengths of the elements, this representation can be expected to be better or worse than the vector representation. For realistic segments, however, this representation has the potential for using less updates than does the vector representation.

Next, we may use the route of the user in place of the segments. Folklore has it that 80% to 90% of humans who move have a known destination. Most often, we do not move around aimlessly. Furthermore, being creatures of habit and perhaps for maximum efficiency, we tend to follow routes we have previously followed. Therefore, it is a good assumption that we are frequently able to predict correctly the route on which a service user travels. Using the correct route in place of a segment means that the number of updates needed to maintain the user's position with the desired accuracy decreases further. Updates occur only because of incorrectly predicted speeds; no updates are caused by incorrectly predicted "locations." It should also be observed that if a route is predicted incorrectly (e.g., because the user makes a turn), this does not lead to a breakdown. Rather, this simply forces an update and a new prediction.

5.4.3   Client-Side Caching

In this section, we have so far discussed updates of the server-side database, to ensure that it adequately reflects the relevant, changing reality. When a client-side mobile user is using a service based on the server-side database, content is extracted from the database and is sent to the client. Prime examples of such content include the locations of stationary and moving points of interests, as well as other content concerning these points of interest. Furthermore, when points of interest are displayed on the user's screen, they must be displayed with a map as background because simply displaying points on an otherwise blank screen is generally not useful. Such map data may be obtained in raster format (e.g., JPEG format) from a separate map server. Given a rectangular area and a resolution, the map server returns the requested fragment of the appropriate map.

An example service to a family on holidays might continuously display all nearby hotels, within a certain price range and with rooms available, as the family drives along. With this type of scenario and assuming that current wireless technology (e.g., GPRS) is used for the communication between the client and the server, it turns out that client-side caching of map data is the prime concern.

As our sample family moves along, new map fragments need to be displayed. An initial approach is to request a new rectangular map fragment when the family approaches the boundary of the map data currently available on the client. The fragment to request may be chosen so that it extends in the direction of the anticipated movement of the client. This may well reduce somewhat the amount of map data to request.

A simpler and more effective approach is possible, however [ACK03]. With this approach, the underlying map is partitioned by means of a grid into small cells, and it is no longer possible to request arbitrary rectangular fragments. Instead, the unit of map data is that of a cell, meaning that one or more entire cells are requested.

With this approach, when new map data needs to be displayed, the cells needed are first calculated. Then the client's cache is inspected to see if the needed cells are available there. Only those cells not found are requested from the map server. Cells received from the server are placed in the cache, which may use a standard cache replacement policy, such as least recent used, or a customized policy. The cache hit rate depends on the movement pattern of the client and on the cache size. Replacement policies for outdated cache content are not a main concern because maps are quite static.

It is reasonable to assume that caching occurs in not only the mobile clients, but also elsewhere on the path from the map server's database to the client. The recommended approach works well with such caching. In contrast, the initial approach does not easily benefit from such caching because two map fragments that overlap almost completely will be perceived as completely separate, and there is no reuse from one to the other.

An important issue is the choice of cell size. To shed light on this subject, we proceed to review a possible concrete design that has been used in prototype services. We assume that the client is a Nokia 7650 or 3650, which have a screen size of 176×208 pixels. A cell size of 256×256 pixels is chosen. A cell is then slightly larger than what can be displayed on the screen, which means that parts of at most four cells can be displayed at the same time. A cell corresponds to an area of 2000×2000 meters.

JPEG format is used for the cells, and depending on which compression is used, the size in bytes of a cell varies from approximately 8 to 100 kilobytes. A compression that yields a cell of approximately 11 kilobytes is reasonable. With such cells and a GPRS connection, this translates into a typical download time of 15 to 20 seconds per cell. This corresponds to a downstream bandwidth that is well below the "possible" bandwidth. As bandwidth continues to improve, the download time will continue to decrease.

A simple policy for requesting cells from the map server (or cache) works as follows. Assume that the screen on the mobile device is placed on top of four neighboring cells (covering 512×512 pixels), which are available for display. Imagine further that each cell is partitioned into four 128×128 pixel subcells. At any point in time, the center of the screen is then located in a subcell of one of the four cells. Depending on which subcell the center is in, different actions are taken. For example, assume that the center is located in the bottom-left subcell of the top-right cell. Then no action is taken. Next, assume that the center of the screen enters the top-left subcell. Now, the two cells on top of our four cells are requested. More advanced policies take into account download times of cells, the geographic coverage of a cell, and movement patterns of the clients (e.g., their speeds).

5.5 LINEAR REFERENCING

Linear referencing is a fundamental technique for modeling transportation infrastructures. This section first describes the general concept of linear referencing, followed by a description of the support for linear referencing in Oracle Spatial, which is the only database management system with built-in support for linear referencing. Oracle's support for linear referencing makes it an attractive platform for the management of data structured according to the type of model described earlier in this chapter.

5.5.1 Linear Referencing Concepts

We proceed to describe the basic concepts in linear referencing [ANSI03, TRB97, Sca02]: linear elements, point and linear events, and so-called linear referencing methods.

- *Linear elements.* Locations are specified along these objects. Any geometric feature that can be given a meaningful start point and where all points on the feature can be given by a distance from the start point can be considered a linear element. The class of so-called curvilinear objects meets these requirements. Roads, footpaths, rivers, train tracks, and so on may be modeled as linear elements. Figure 5.7 illustrates a small road network consisting of three routes, each of which can be considered a linear element.

- *Events: point, linear.* Events occur along linear elements. The location of an event is specified in terms of the linear element(s) along which it occurs. A point event occurs at a single point, and it is specified as a distance from the start of a linear element. Examples are traffic accidents and roadside emergency phones. In contrast to a point event, a linear event has an extent, and it is given by a pair of distances from the start of a linear element. Examples include pavement types and speed limits. Figure 5.8 illustrates point and linear events along Route 1. Assume that the length of Route 1 is 400 units. On position 270, there is a record of an accident. In addition, there is information that the speed limit for the interval 0 to 180 is 60 km/h;

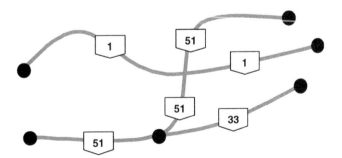

Figure 5.7 Linear elements example—routes.

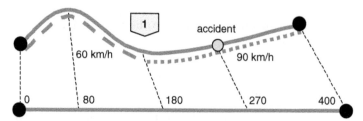

Figure 5.8 Point and linear events example—accidents and speed limits.

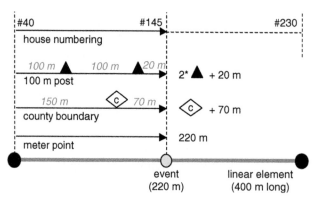

Figure 5.9 Linear referencing methods.

for the rest of the element (the interval from 180 to 400), the speed limit is 90 km/h.

♦ *Linear referencing method.* A linear referencing method describes how a location along or beside a linear element is measured. A location along an element is given by some sort of distance value, and a location beside a linear element also has a displacement. Examples of different linear referencing methods are shown in Figure 5.9. On the 400-unit-long linear element, there is a point event at position 220 from the start of the element. The figure depicts the event's linear location using four different methods. The most immediate of these is probably the one that gives the locations as the distance from the start point. Next, two relative methods are illustrated. One gives the distance from the most recent county boundary. This means that locations in one county need not be updated if changes occur in another county. An example could be that an intersection along a linear feature is replaced by a rotary, which increases the length of the linear element slightly. This change affects only (some of) the events in the county where the rotary is being built. The other relative method specifies location in terms of meter posts and the distance to the most recent post. The last method is more specialized. It gives a distance in terms of a house number.

5.5.2 Linear Referencing in Oracle

We proceed to describe the particular realization of linear referencing in Oracle. No other object-relational database management system offers built-in support for linear referencing. We first describe some of Oracle's linear referencing concepts. Then elements of Oracle Spatial are introduced that are subsequently used to illustrate Oracle's support for linear referencing. Finally, query examples are given.

ORACLE-SPECIFIC LINEAR REFERENCING CONCEPTS AND TERMS
The central concept is that of a *geometric segment* (termed an *LRS segment*). It is one of the following:

- *Line string.* An ordered, nonbranching, continuous geometry (e.g., a simple road)
- *Multiline string.* Unconnected line strings (e.g., a highway with a gap)
- *Polygon.* A line string that starts and ends at the same point (e.g., a racetrack)

Figure 5.10 depicts an example of a geometric segment (a simple line string) along with several other concepts, to be discussed in the sequel.

When constructing a geometric segment, a sequence of *shape points* is specified. Each shape point is assigned measure information and coordinates. The *measure* is the linear distance (in the measure

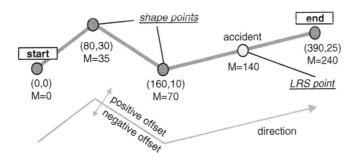

Figure 5.10 Oracle linear referencing system.

dimension) from one of the two end points of the geometric segment to the shape point. The *coordinates* give the geographic location of the shape point. The figure has four shape points.

In addition, points with only linear measure information along the geometric segment are allowed. These are called *LRS points*. Unlike the shape points, the LRS points are created as separate objects of what is called SDO_GEOMETRY type (more on this shortly). The figure has one LRS point.

A *linear feature* is a spatial object that can be described as a logical set of linear segments. A linear feature in Oracle Spatial thus corresponds to the linear element in the general linear referencing terminology introduced earlier.

The *direction* of a geometric segment is defined to be positive from the start to the end point of the segment. The start and end points are determined according to the order of the shape points in the definition of the segment. Next, the perpendicular distance between a point and the geometric segment is called the *offset* of the point. Offsets are positive for points to the left of the segment and negative for points to the right when traversing the segment in the positive direction.

We proceed to introduce the parts of Oracle Spatial to be used for linear referencing.

SDO_GEOMETRY OBJECT TYPE

The object type SDO_GEOMETRY is used in Oracle for describing spatial objects. The definition of this object type is as follows:

```
CREATE TYPE sdo_geometry AS OBJECT (
SDO_GTYPE NUMBER,
SDO_SRID NUMBER,
SDO_POINT SDO_POINT_TYPE,
SDO_ELEM_INFO MDSYS.SDO_ELEM_INFO_ARRAY,
SDO_ORDINATES MDSYS.SDO_ORDINATE_ARRAY);
```

The first attribute of SDO_GEOMETRY, the SDO_GTYPE, indicates the geometry type. The format of the values of this attribute is four digits, *dltt*, where d specifies the number of dimensions (2, 3, or 4, where 4 can be used for linear referencing only), l specifies the dimension of the linear referencing measure value (3 or 4; for nonlinear reference uses, $l = 0$), and *tt* specifies the type of the geometry. Valid values of SDO_GTYPE are shown in Table 5.1.

Table 5.1 Valid SDO_GTYPE values.

Value	Geometry Type	Description
dl00	UNKNOWN_GEOMETRY	spatial ignores this geometry
dl01	POINT	one point
dl02	LINE or CURVE	one line or curve
dl03	POLYGON	one polygon with/without holes
dl04	COLLECTION	heterogeneous collection of elements
dl05	MULTIPOINT	multiple points
dl06	MULTILINE or MULTICURVE	multiple lines or/and curves
dl07	MULTIPOLYGON	multiple, disjoint polygons (more than one exterior boundary)

The next attribute of the SDO_GTYPE is SDO_SRID, which identifies the spatial reference system that is used for specifying the geometry (i.e., coordinates of shape points are specified using the identified coordinate system).

The third attribute is SDO_POINT, which is used if the geometry is a nonlinear referencing point. A linear referencing point is defined using the SDO_ELEM_INFO and SDO_ORDINATES attributes.

The information about ordinates of a spatial object is provided in the attribute SDO_ELEM_INFO. The ordinates are captured by the attribute called SDO_ORDINATES. Each element of SDO_ELEM_INFO contains three numbers:

1. SDO_STARTING_OFFSET: indicates the starting ordinate within the SDO_ORDINATES array for this element

2. SDO_ETYPE: the type of the element

3. SDO_INTERPRETATION: interpretation

Possible combinations of values for SDO_ELEM_INFO elements are listed in Table 5.2.

The following examples illustrate the differences between defining a two-dimensional point and defining a linear referencing point. The definition of a two-dimensional point with coordinates (33,102) is as follows:

```
point2d := MDSYS.SDO_GEOMETRY(
2001,   NULL,   MDSYS.SDO_POINT_TYPE(33,102,NULL),
NULL, NULL);
```

Table 5.2 Values in SDO_ELEM_INFO.

SDO_ETYPE	SDO_INTERPRETATION	Meaning
0	any numeric value	For geometry types not supported by Oracle Spatial
1	1	Point type
1	n > 1	Point cluster with n points
2	1	Line string whose vertices are connected by straight line segments
2	2	Line string made up of a connected sequence of circular arcs
1003 or 2003	1	Simple polygon whose vertices are connected by straight line segments
1003 or 2003	2	Polygon made up of a connected sequence of circular arcs that closes on itself
1003 or 2003	3	Rectangle type (sometimes called optimized rectangle)
1003 or 2003	4	Circle type
4	n > 1	Compound line string with some vertices connected by straight line segments and some by circular arcs
1005 or 2005	n > 1	Compound polygon with some vertices connected by straight line segments and some by circular arcs

On the other hand, the definition of the linear referencing point at coordinates (33,102) is:

```
pointLRS := MDSYS.SDO_GEOMETRY(
3301, NULL, NULL,
MDSYS.SDO_ELEM_INFO_ARRAY(1,1,1),
MDSYS.SDO_ORDINATE_ARRAY(33,102,NULL));
```

METADATA

All metadata related to spatial tables must be inserted by the user into the USER_SDO_GEOM_METADATA view. The schema of the view is given next:

```
( TABLE_NAME VARCHAR2(32),      - layer name
COLUMN_NAME VARCHAR2(32),       - geometry column name
DIMINFO MDSYS.SDO_DIM_ARRAY,    - dimension informa-
                                  tion
SRID NUMBER);  - spatial reference system ID
```

The dimension information DIMINFO column is defined as follows:

```
CREATE   TYPE  sdo_dim_array   AS   VARRAY(4)   of
SDO_DIM_ELEMENT;
```

Furthermore, each element of the SDO_DIM_ARRAY array is defined in the following way:

```
CREATE TYPE sdo_dim_element AS OBJECT (
SDO_DIMNAME VARCHAR2(64),   – dimension name
SDO_LB NUMBER,              – lower bound
SDO_UB NUMBER,              – upper bound
SDO_TOLERANCE NUMBER        – tolerance
);
```

The example next gives dimension information metadata for three linear referencing dimensions (X, Y, and M, where M is the measure dimension):

```
diminfo := MDSYS.SDO_DIM_ARRAY (
MDSYS.SDO_DIM_ELEMENT('X', 0, 500, 0.005),
MDSYS.SDO_DIM_ELEMENT('Y', 0, 500, 0.005),
MDSYS.SDO_DIM_ELEMENT('M', 0, 500, 0.005)  – measure
dimension
);
```

Having now given the necessary background for creating and working with linear referencing objects in Oracle, the next section offers examples of how to create, register, and use geometric segments.

ORACLE LINEAR REFERENCING

Assume that we have a simple route defined by four coordinate sets and named Route 1. The first example shows how to define a route geometry based on this data:

```
route_geo := MDSYS.SDO_GEOMETRY(
3302,NULL,NULL,
MDSYS.SDO_ELEM_INFO_ARRAY(1,2,1),
MDSYS.SDO_ORDINATE_ARRAY(0,0,0,80,30,NULL,
160,10,70, 390,25,240)));
```

The type of the geometry "3302" indicates that this is a 3D LRS object containing one line string. The fourth attribute of the

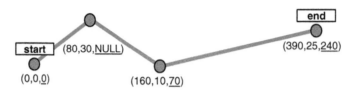

Figure 5.11   Route geometry.

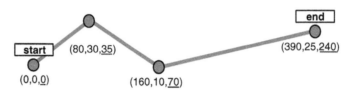

Figure 5.12   Route geometry after measures have been populated.

SDO_GEOMETRY states that all of the ordinates will form a single line string. As seen in the fifth attribute, for all (X,Y,M) coordinates, except the second, a measure value is provided. Figure 5.11 depicts the route geometry from this example.

In order to be able to perform linear referencing operations on the geometric segment, it must be registered as such:

```
MDSYS.SDO_LRS.DEFINE_GEOM_SEGMENT(route_geo,
diminfo);
```

When a geometric segment is registered, NULL measure values are populated according to the known measure values. Figure 5.12 depicts the measure values of the shape points after measures have been populated. We see that the measure of the second shape point has been populated according to the measure values of the first and third shape points.

Next, we create a table of routes:

```
CREATE TABLE lrs_routes (
route_id NUMBER PRIMARY KEY,
route_name VARCHAR2(32),
route_geometry MDSYS.SDO_GEOMETRY);
```

In this table, the "route_geometry" column contains spatial data, namely, SDO_GEOMETRY objects. The metadata about this column should be inserted into the USER_SDO_GEOM_METADATA view:

```
INSERT INTO user_sdo_geom_metadata VALUES(
'lrs_routes',                    - layer name
'route_geometry',                - geometry column name
diminfo,                         - dimension information
NULL);
```

As we have the geometry for Route 1, route_geo, we can now insert this route into the table of routes:

```
INSERT INTO lrs_routes VALUES (1, 'Route 1', route_
geo);
```

Next, we turn to the recording of content. Specifically, we create a table for storing data about accidents (i.e., point events) that happen on routes recorded in the "lrs_routes" table:

```
CREATE TABLE accidents (
accident_id NUMBER PRIMARY KEY,
route_id NUMBER,
description VARCHAR2(1000),
accident_geometry MDSYS.SDO_GEOMETRY);
```

An "accident_geometry" value contains a linear referencing point that corresponds to the accident's location along the geometric segment (i.e., the route). We will insert an accident with ID #101 that happened on measure value 140 along Route 1 on March 3, 2003:

```
INSERT INTO accidents VALUES(
101, 1, 'happened on 03/03/2003',
SDO_LRS.LOCATE_PT(route_geo, diminfo, 140));
```

The function SDO_LRS.LOCATE_PT returns the linear referencing point that is located at the specified distance from the start of the segment.

As an illustration of the capture of linear events, the following table records information about speed limits on routes recorded in the "lrs_routes" table:

```
CREATE TABLE speed_limit (
route_id NUMBER,
speed_value NUMBER,
speed_geometry MDSYS.SDO_GEOMETRY);
```

The "speed_geometry" column contains geometric segments that correspond to speed limit information on different linear parts of routes.

We proceed to insert a "60 km/h" speed limit from the start of Route 1 until measure value 70 inclusive, and a "90 km/h" speed limit for the rest of the route:

```
INSERT INTO speed_limit VALUES (
1,    '60',    SDO_LRS.CLIP_GEOM_SEGMENT(route_geo,
diminfo, 0, 70));
INSERT INTO speed_limit VALUES (
1,    '90',    SDO_LRS.CLIP_GEOM_SEGMENT(route_geo,
diminfo, 70, 240));
```

The SDO_LRS.CLIP_GEOM_SEGMENT function returns the geometry object resulting from a clip operation on the route_geo geometric segment.

As was mentioned in the brief introduction to the elements of Oracle Spatial, metadata about the spatial tables should be provided:

```
INSERT INTO user_sdo_geom_metadata VALUES (
'accidents', 'accident_geometry', diminfo, NULL);
INSERT INTO user_sdo_geom_metadata VALUES (
'speed_limit', 'speed_geometry', diminfo, NULL);
```

Next, before discussing querying, we describe how to create a spatial index.

SPATIAL INDEXING

A spatial index may improve the efficiency of window queries (that find objects within a certain data space) as well as spatial joins (finding pairs of objects that somehow interact, e.g., intersect, spatially with each other). Oracle Spatial supports R-trees and quadtrees, and both of these indexing methods can be used in the context of linear referencing objects. The measure dimension is not indexed. If linear referencing data contains 3D objects, the quadtree is used on the (X, Y) coordinates. For 4D linear referencing objects, the (X, Y, Z) coordinates are indexed with an R-tree.

An example of creating a spatial index on the "route_geometry" column in the "lrs_routes" table follows:

```
CREATE INDEX lrs_routes_idx ON lrs_routes(route_geo-
metry)
INDEXTYPE IS MDSYS.SPATIAL_INDEX;
```

QUERIES

We conclude the description of linear referencing in Oracle by considering queries.

For example, to retrieve all accidents on Route 1 between measure values 80 and 200, we perform the following query:

```
SELECT a.accident_id, a.description, a.accident_-
geometry

FROM accidents a, lrs_routes r

WHERE r.route_name = 'Route 1'

AND SDO_LRS.FIND_MEASURE(r.route_geometry,

a.accident_geometry) BETWEEN 80 AND 200;
```

Here, the SDO_LRS.FIND_MEASURE function returns the measure value along the geometric segment (along the route) for the accident geometry.

If we were instead interested in information about speed limits on all of Route 1, the following query would give us the result:

```
SELECT

SDO_LRS.GEOM_SEGMENT_START_MEASURE(s.speed_geome-
try),

SDO_LRS.GEOM_SEGMENT_END_MEASURE(s.speed_geometr-
y),

s.speed_value

FROM speed_limit s, lrs_routes r

WHERE s.route_id = r.route_id AND r.route_name =
'Route 1';
```

The functions SDO_LRS.GEOM_SEGMENT_START_MEASURE and SDO_LRS.GEOM_SEGMENT_END_MEASURE return the start and end measure of a linear event, respectively.

5.6 CONCLUSION

Adopting a data management–centric view of LBS, this chapter views the modeling of select aspects of reality as the foundation for the delivery of integrated, high-quality LBS. Specifically, by capturing relevant aspects of the modeled reality in appropriate structures that enable efficient update and querying, an ideal foundation for the delivery of services and the rapid development of new services is obtained.

Because mobile users typically travel in, and are confined to, a transportation infrastructure such as a road network, it is essential to capture these in the underlying data model. Many relevant services can either not be supported adequately or cannot be supported at all without this. This chapter presents an approach to the modeling of transportation infrastructures that supports multiple, integrated representations of the same infrastructure. Externally accessible graph representations, a known-marker representation, and geographic representations are integrated through an internal representation. The different representations serve different purposes. Points of interest and other content are also related to the infrastructure representations through the internal representation.

Relational data management technology is utilized for modeling. In particular, the concept of linear referencing is utilized. With linear referencing, a transportation infrastructure is modeled as a set of linear elements, and content is mapped to these. The location of a piece of content is then given by an element, a distance from the start of the element, and possibly a signed displacement from the point on the element identified by the distance. With linear referencing, two-dimensional computations may be reduced to one-dimensional computations that are more efficient. We thus describe general linear referencing concepts as well as the support for linear referencing in Oracle.

This chapter leaves many important aspects of data management uncovered, including caching, transactions, concurrency control, recovery, and access control. This chapter also did not delve into the architectural embedding (e.g., in a modern n-tier architecture) of data management.

Many research activities are ongoing in the area of data management techniques for LBS, which may affect practice in the medium or longer term. In this chapter, we have described the currently readily applicable techniques that the research contributions must seek to complement or outperform.

ACKNOWLEDGMENTS

This chapter is based in large part on concepts and ideas explored in collaborations with the author's colleagues in ongoing projects at Aalborg University, including the DBGlobe project, sponsored by the European

Commission; the M-Track project, sponsored by ETRI; and the LBS project, sponsored by CIT. Special thanks go to Kristian V. B. Andersen, Michael Cheng, Christian Hage, Augustas Kligys, Torben Bach Pedersen, Laurynas Speicys, and Igor Timko.

Permission to use the photo in Figure 5.1 was given by COWI, who hold the rights to the photo.

References

[ACK03]   K. V. B. Andersen, M. Cheng, R. Klitgaard-Nielsen. "Online Aalborg Guide: Development of a Location-Based Service." Student Report, 102 pages, Aalborg University, 2003.

[ANSI03]   American National Standards Institute. "Geographic Information Framework, Data Content Standards for Transportation: Roads (Part XXX)," draft standards document, 48 pages, 2003.

[DeBl93]   R. A. Deighton and D. G. Blake. "Improvements to Utah's Location Referencing System to Allow Data Integration," 16 pages, 1993, *http://www.deighton.com/library/paper2.pdf.* Accessed on February 16, 2003.

[DKSS02]   O. Djernæs, O. Knudsen, E. Sørensen, and S. Schrøder. "VIS-brugerhåndbog: Vejledning i opmåling og inddatering." VISudvalget. 58 pages, 2002. (In Danish.)

[DuBu98]   K. Dueker and J. A. Butler. "GIS-T Enterprise Data Model with Suggested Implementation Choices," *Journal of the Urban and Regional Information Systems Association*, 10(1):12–36, 1998.

[HJP+03]   C. Hage, C. S. Jensen, T. B. Pedersen, L. Speicys, and I. Timko. "Integrated Data Management for Mobile Services in the Real World." In *Proc. of Very Large Data Bases Conference*, pages 1019–1031, 2003.

[KK99]   H. Kanemitsu and T. Kamada (Eds.). "POIX: Point Of Interest eXchange Language Specification." W3C Note, *http://www.w3.org/TR/poix.* Accessed June 24, 1999.

[KA02]   N. Koncz and T. M. Adams. "A Data Model for Multi-Dimensional Transportation Location Referencing Systems." *Journal of the Urban and*

Regional Information Systems Association, 14(2):27–41, 2002.

[Mur02]   C. Murray. "Oracle Spatial User Guide and Reference." Release 9.2, Oracle Corporation, 486 pages, 2002.

[TRB97]   Transportation Research Board. "A Generic Data Model for Linear Referencing Systems." Washington, DC, 28 pages, 1997.

[OSM95]   P. Okunieff, D. Siegel, and Q. Miao. "Location Referencing Methods for Intelligent Transportation Systems (ITS) User Services: Recommended Approach." In *Proc. GIS-T Conference*, pages 57–75, 1995.

[Sca02]   P. Scarponcini. "Generalized Model for Linear Referencing in Transportation." *GeoInformatica*, 6(1):35–55, 2002.

[VCSA97]   A. Vonderohe, C. L. Chou, F. Sun, and T. Adams. "A Generic Data Model for Linear Referencing Systems." NCHRP Research Results Digest #218, Transportation Research Board, Washington, DC, 1997.

[Vig94]   Viggen Corporation. "Location Referencing Systems: Analysis of Current Methods Applied to IVHS User Services." 1994.

6

LBS
Interoperability
Through Standards

Lance McKee, Open GIS Consortium, Inc. (OGC)

CONTENTS

6.1   INTRODUCTION

Information and communications technology standards are critically important to the commercial rollout of location-based services (LBS) and to the fulfilment of their potential.

6.1.1   Standards are Important to LBS Users

Although the market has taken longer to materialize than many predicted a few years ago, individuals and corporate customers are now beginning to purchase location-based emergency services, location-based advertising, location-aware games, location-responsive instant-messaging systems, and other location-based services. They look to their telecommunications carrier companies to provide timely, personalized information delivery in ways that afford new efficiencies, conveniences, safety measures, and work flows. They expect LBS to accompany them when they cross cell phone roaming boundaries, as in Figure 6.1. They expect billing for LBS to be integrated into their current billing format as just another set of phone charges. They expect services such as friend finder and mobile gaming to work even if their friends use a wireless carrier that is different from their own.

6.1.2   Standards are Important to LBS Providers

Carriers want cost control, predictability, rapid rollout, and easy migration. They want all of their service offerings to be well integrated with their management information systems for billing, accounting,

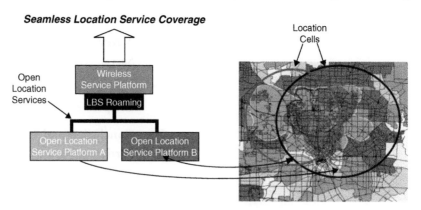

Figure 6.1   Open service and information framework enables roaming between location cells (Diagram courtesy of OGC).

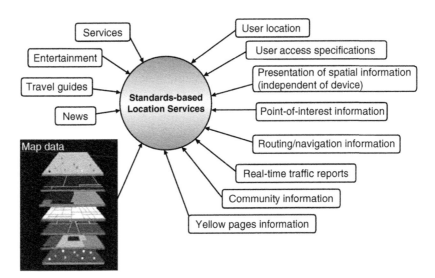

Figure 6.2   With open interfaces, applications can access many sources of content and services. (Diagram courtesy of OGC.)

customer service, maintenance, and so on. They want to be able to pick and choose from a broad field of platforms, applications, integration services, devices, and content, as in Figure 6.2. Providers of these products and services in the value chain want to succeed by focusing on their strengths and by "building one and selling it many times," rather than building everything differently for every customer.

The first three chapters of this book present the basics of LBS applications and the technologies that make these applications possible. Chapters 4 and 5 describe the issues of LBS data management and software. This chapter focuses on interoperability and standards. It reviews the layers in the technology stack that support LBS and shows how standards are essential for each layer. It explains both the technical context and the business context in which LBS standards are evolving. It shows how an understanding of standards and participation in the standards process can help organizations plan for the future. The relevant standards consortia and de jure standards organizations are described.

6.2   STANDARDS SUPPORT LBS BUSINESS MODELS

When we use a location service, we are depending on technologies that can do the following:

◆ Provide us with wireless communications.

◆ Provide us with position determination.
◆ Store, serve, and apply georeferenced (location-related) data in response to queries.

All of the service technologies and data could be provided by a single provider, just as AT&T once provided all of the equipment and services for telephony in the United States. If this were the case, the necessary interfaces between all of these technologies could be totally proprietary, and there would be no need for this chapter. But today's reality is quite different. Despite telecom industry mergers and acquisitions, the number of carriers, service providers, application providers, and content providers is growing. Companies are focusing on their core strengths and turning to vendors and other partners to provide complementary strengths. The ecosystem metaphor is appearing in discussions of Information and Communications Technology. The trend is toward diverse technology, service, and content providers providing only one or two links in value chains that grow longer and more detailed as the industry evolves. At each link, multiple companies compete.

Carriers want LBS platforms that provide application programming interfaces (APIs) that can connect multiple devices to their choice of accurate, up-to-date, and comprehensive map content, reliable Location Engines, and other services. The best applications will use the best, most accurate data and the fastest, most reliable routing and mapping algorithms, and they will meet needs that have broad consumer appeal. Carriers and others in the value chain have discovered that it is not feasible, without standards, to maintain integration among even a target subset of the possible permutations of devices, Location Engines, service providers, and content providers.

In addition to this set of reasons for interoperability, governments have moved in the direction of requiring carriers to become common carriers, opening their wires, fibers, and spectrum to other service providers. So, the growing requirement for open interfaces comes from a need to compete more effectively in the marketplace, from a proliferation of different devices, and from a government mandate to open up a corporate proprietary resource to enable other companies to compete more freely. The compound effect of these demands weighs overwhelmingly in favor of a comprehensive framework of open interoperability interfaces.

Early implementers of LBS recognized the need to provide interfaces against which third-party GIS companies and other technology providers could build applications [Spi03]. But these proprietary interfaces, shared with close partners, did not protect carrier/operators from having to invest heavily in integration and customization for each LBS application. The applications' requirements were too dissimilar to be accommodated by these prestandard interfaces. The problem was complicated by the simultaneous need for the LBS applications to be connected to the carrier/operators' central IS frameworks to support billing, customer service, and maintenance functions. In today's enterprise integration terms, there was a need for service layering and chaining, and a need to support different platforms and devices. In LBS, as in many enterprise computing domains, these needs are driving sophisticated technology users to demand standards.

Standards are important in LBS for the same reason they are important in other markets: They help providers deliver usable products and services while saving time and money and reducing business risks. In almost every market, providers add value and make money by offering proprietary implementations based on nonproprietary standards infrastructure. These standards range from staple sizes, chemical formulas, safety specifications, and plug configurations to container volumes.

LBS standards benefit providers in the LBS value chain by enabling the following:

◆ *Increased billable utilization of carrier's spectrum and wireless network.* By introducing desirable new services, carriers can potentially reduce the rate of customer turnover and increase average revenue per user (ARPU). New products and services roll out in stages, capturing new customers and generating new sales from existing customers. In some cases, new applications increase the return on accounts and devices already sold. In other cases, old accounts buy new devices, and in others, the new applications attract new accounts. All new business increases the return on the carriers' investments in spectrum, towers, transmitters, and so on. New services build on existing services, and existing services can be reused in a market supported by open interfaces.

◆ *Niches for providers with special products and services.* As described previously, the value chains are differentiating. If multiple carriers, for example, are using the same basic platform, there exists a business case for service companies to provide those carriers with pieces of the LBS platform. The carriers save time and money and reduce risk through outsourcing to these service companies.

◆ *A business case for different content providers.* Most carriers prefer not to be in the content development business, just as they prefer not to be in the printed phone directory business. Yet they want to be able to provide accurate, up-to-date local content to a mobile user as the user roams about. This means that the LBS framework the consumer is tied into needs to be able to seamlessly access and use content from multiple providers as the consumer travels down a major highway or goes from country to country. When content providers can sell content to multiple carrier/providers, they will be able to invest more in their content offerings, which will potentially improve their customers' (the carriers') service offerings. As this opportunity yields multiple content providers, the carriers' content choices expand. An important characteristic of location-based information is that the richest and most accurate content is local (i.e., specific to a given region, city, or county); therefore, much of it is best maintained locally. The more local content providers there are, the more important it is to have open, standard interfaces by which they can publish and others can access their content. In Europe, INSPIRE (INfrastructure for SPatial InfoRmation in Europe) aims to provide this kind of seamless access to distributed local (and regional and national) data sources for a variety of purposes. (The first domain INSPIRE focuses on is environmental data, but this will expand to include many other classes of data themes, leading to a coherent European Spatial Data Infrastructure. Ideally, the standards platform for LBS will be consistent with the standards that provide interoperability in the larger European Spatial Data Infrastructure.)

◆ *Expansion of LBS from a niche service to a mass market service.* The GSM Association suggests that:

Operators should seriously consider the question of provision of services that can be accessed and used by customers of other networks in the same market...A similar example of how this approach has been successful in the recent past is SMS (Short Message Service) where the usage increased dramatically in markets where operators allowed inter-working with other networks in their market. [GSM03]

The growing need for pluggable resources is being addressed by standards consortia that develop and gain industry consensus on open interfaces, protocols, and schemas. These software connectors are codified in publicly available specifications that enable both Developer A and

Developer B to build a device, program, or service that will work with Developer C's device, program, or service. A set of open interface layers is being established that enables one provider of technology, service, or content to serve many carriers, as long as the provider has the same interface as the carrier. For carriers, this reduces the cost and time of application development. Developed in technical committees made up of experts from many companies, these specifications tend to serve also as implementation guides, containing lessons learned and industry consensus on a detailed framework for developing specific interoperable components.

Ultimately, the value chains will become more complex and weblike. "These standards will be the road map for the definition of an industry and its customer-driven deployment of mass market services and content by carriers and Internet service suppliers like AOL, Microsoft, and even member organizations such as AAA [American Automobile Association]," wrote Jim VanderMeer, in an article in *Directions* magazine [Van02]. Maporama, locationbox, Webraska, LocationNet, and Mapflow are European examples.

Because several technologies and industries are involved, the standards picture is complex. The specifications come from many standards-setting organizations (see next section), and they mesh well only when effective coordination exists among these standards groups. Location-based services (like other services such as caller-ID and directory services) depend on the underlying wireless communication technology, which is still fragmented from vendor to vendor and country to country.

The standards picture is also complex because location determination technologies often reside both in the carrier's network and out of that network. Standards for LBS need to address the fact that the carrier's network is usually not the Internet network, and Hypertext Markup Language (HTML) is not the ideal protocol for implementing LBS. Two sets of important relationships need to be addressed by interoperability interfaces: (1) the set of relationships that are mediated across the Internet, such as those involving Web-based content providers; and (2) the set of relationships inside the carrier between the LBS operations and other parts of the organization, relationships served by the carrier's huge internal network. Inside a company such as Hutchinson, for example, all services are tied together on an enterprise integration application platform for the whole company, not just for customers, but also for internal use. Knowledge of the customer has to be accessible throughout the enterprise for billing, customer service, marketing, and so on, not just for LBS.

6.3   MULTIPLE CONSORTIA PROVIDE LBS STANDARDS

The key standards organizations providing LBS standards are the Open Mobile Alliance (OMA) (*http://www.openmobilealliance.org*) and the Open GIS Consortium, Inc. (OGC) (*http://www.opengis.org*). But several other standards organizations also provide important elements of the LBS standards infrastructure.

The Location Interoperability Forum (LIF), now merged with OMA, was founded in September 2000 by Motorola, Ericsson, and Nokia with the purpose of developing and promoting industry common solutions for LBS. They addressed the early and obvious problems related to the multiplicity of methods for location determination. Mobile device location can be provided by multiple technologies, hybrid technologies, and service strategies that may even include user-entered location information. These companies managed to get basic agreement among other mobile device makers and wireless transmission technology providers regarding technical means for communicating the geographic location of wireless terminals and devices. That is, they agreed on the network interface for delivering the geographic locations of wireless terminals and devices independent of the location determination technology. Their interface abstracts secure access methods and hardware-based location technologies such as Cell-ID[1] and Timing Advance,[2] E-OTD (GSM), AFLT (IS-95),[3] and MS-Based Assisted GPS (Geo-Positioning System)[4] [RMR03]. The LIF and OGC reached a basic

---

1. Each cellular phone "cell" is the region served by a cellular communications transmitter. Each transmitter has an identification number (ID). This cell-ID can be included in data sent to both sending and receiving phones. Accuracy is several kilometers.
2. "Timing advance" technologies measure the time it takes a signal to travel between a cell phone and a transmitter, to calculate rough distance. Accuracy is about 1 kilometer.
3. E-OTD (GSM) and AFLT (IS-95) use *trilateration* (i.e., comparison of distances from three or more transmitters) to calculate a location more accurately than can be calculated with information about distance from only one transmitter.
4. The mobile includes a GPS receiver. In an emergency call, GPS position is sent back to the network, which provides information to the GPS to help it make a determination. Accuracy is between 10 and 100 meters.

agreement on sharing information where overlap occurs between the LIF and OGC domains of interest.

LIF's Mobile Location Protocol (MLP) enables location applications to interoperate with the wireless networks irrespective of their underlying air interfaces and positioning methods [Lif02]. MLP defines a common interface that facilitates the exchange of location information between location-based applications and the wireless networks represented by location servers. MLP supports privacy and authentication to ensure that users' whereabouts are protected and are only provided to those who are authorized. OGC's OpenLS Services [OCG03] equate with LIF's Advanced MLP Services, but they provide additional benefits related to the fact that they are part of a larger and more comprehensive geospatial framework (see Figure 6.3).

The Wireless Application Protocol (WAP) Forum is also now part of OMA. WAP is a worldwide standard for providing wireless Internet communications and advanced telephony services on digital mobile phones, pagers, PDAs, and other wireless terminals. OMA addresses all key elements of the wireless value chain, now including those related to LBS and addressed by LIF, and contributes to the timely and efficient introduction of services and applications [OMA02]. OMA works in conjunction with other existing standards organizations and groups.

OGC's main area of interest in the wireless industry is LBS. Most of OGC's work involves a broad and complex set of geospatial software interoperability issues at a level in the communications technology stack that is in most respects above the level addressed by OMA. From OMA's

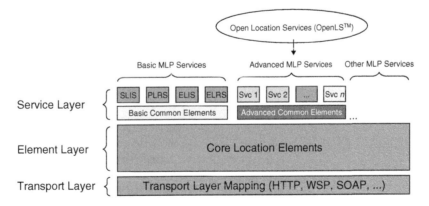

Figure 6.3   OpenLS and Location Interoperability Forum (LIF) Mobile Location Protocol (MLP). (Diagram courtesy of OGC.)

viewpoint, OGC focuses at the application interface level. Part of OGC's challenge was to show the telecommunications industry that geospatial interoperability issues such as coordinate transformation, Web mapping, and XML encoding of spatial information are relevant in LBS. As a result of OGC's efforts and the efforts of MapInfo, Vodaphone, and others, LIF, and now OMA, have adopted a strategy and work program that is harmonized with OGC's strategy and work program to ensure that both organizations' specifications meet the low-level requirements of advanced location services. To provide their customers with services that take advantage of Internet content, the companies in OMA are paying attention to this level in the stack above IP, the level that involves Web services, including OGC Web services for geoprocessing.

By accommodating OGC's spatial standards platform, OMA enables the growth of LBS value chains and enables applications to work with roaming. Consistency with OGC's broader set of specifications also establishes the hooks to tie mobile devices into complex geospatial applications familiar to GIS, facilities management, navigation, cartography, sensor web, geospatial fusion, and remote sensing experts.[5]

It is important to note that OMA and OGC are also in close touch with the Internet Engineering Task Force (IETF) and the World Wide Web Consortium (W3C), the principal Internet and World Wide Web standards bodies, and with the Organization for the Advancement of Structured Information Standards (OASIS), an important Web services standards organization. IETF, W3C, and OASIS recognize that all standards related in any way to spatial information and services need to be developed by OGC and OMA or in consultation with them.

To mesh spatial standards with communication standards (i.e., to weave LBS into the Internet, the Web, and wireless), OGC works closely not only with OMA, IETF, W3C, and OASIS, but also with the MAGIC Services Forum (MAGIC was originally known as Mobile/Automotive Geographic Information Core Services), International Organization for

5. GIS involves combination and analysis of thematic map layers. Facilities management involves spatial information about indoor and outdoor built environments (useful in LBS for multimodal navigation, e.g., across a campus and through a building's corridors and elevators). Navigation involves route determination and other transportation information functions. Sensor webs are sets of Web-connected, location-aware sensors and imaging devices with Web services for data acquisition and control. Geospatial fusion refers to automated methods for linking and finding place-related audio, video, text, and photo data. Remote sensing refers to analysis of data from airborne and spaceborne imaging devices.

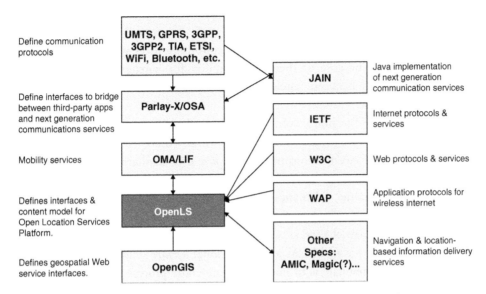

Figure 6.4   The LBS Standards Framework. (Diagram courtesy of OGC.)

Standardization (ISO) Technical Committees (TC211) and 2(TC204), WAP Forum, and the Automotive Multimedia Interface Collaboration (AMI-C). Specifications emerging from OGC's work must also cohere with those from telecommunications standards groups connecting wired and wireless voice systems and the Internet, such as Parlay, Third Generation Partnership Project (3GPP), 3GPP2, European Telecommunications Standards Institute (ETSI), and the Telecommunications Industry Association (TIA). See Figure 6.4.

Other standards organizations with a role in LBS include the following:

♦ The Parlay Group's Open Services Architecture provides secure portal elements, open interfaces, and integrated media control capabilities that free operators to open up content and services development to a broad range of partners without compromising their network security, service integrity, or control over subscriber. APIs for OSA/Parlay[6] facilitate service implementations within existing fixed and mobile telecommunications networks. This architecture can complement the GeoMobility Server described in the next section.

---

6. Parlay (*http://www.parlay.org/specs/index.asp*) is a consortium developing open APIs based on their Open Systems Architecture (OSA) for mobile networks, containing functionality for authentication, authorization, and access to network services.

◆ The Cellular Telecommunications & Internet Association (CTIA) (WOW-COM) have occasional communication with LBS standards groups because of their responsibility for wireless technologies and the ties between wireless and the copper/fiber/microwave physical network.

◆ Two ISO technical committees are working in the spatial technologies domain. ISO TC/211 Geomatics works closely with OGC to channel OGC's specifications into the *de jure* ISO standards process. TC/211 has a working group devoted to LBS. ISO TC/204 Road Transport and Traffic Telematics tends to focus on automobile navigation services based on hard media rather than Web services, although this focus may change as wireless access to navigation data and services becomes available. As an international *de jure* standards organization, ISO's mandate is to manage a democratic process in which countries (rather than the specific agencies, nongovernmental organizations, and companies in a consortium) vote on standards. OGC and ISO work diligently to coordinate their efforts.

◆ The Parlay/OSA specifications and APIs relate to the opening of the telecom network to external access. Such access must address authentication, identity of applications, use of service level agreements, and so on. In addition, the Parlay Group is providing a set of specifications for Web services that make it easier to build deployable products that use the telecom network.

◆ The Third Generation Partnership Project 2 (3GPP2), the Wi-Fi Alliance, and the Bluetooth SIG become involved in sorting out the multimodal communications protocols used in some LBS applications.

◆ The Automotive Multimedia Interface Consortium (AMIC) is a group of automobile manufacturers facilitating the development of standards for in-car navigation systems, cell phones, pagers, video systems, CD players, PDAs, and automotive PCs. They have defined Java specifications for an "offboard navigation API" that are derived from OGC's OpenLS specifications.

6.4 A KEY STANDARD: THE GEOMOBILITY SERVER (GMS)

OGC members have cooperatively developed the GeoMobility Server (GMS), which is essentially a set of specifications for open interfaces for

LBS middleware [OGC02].[7] The standard is freely available to the public at *http://www.opengis.org/specs* as OGC Project Document 03-006r3, "XML for Location Services (XLS): The OpenLS Platform".

GeoMobility Server is a good name, in that *mobility* has two meanings in this context. *Mobility* refers to mobile devices, of course, but it also refers to mobile (i.e., transportable, migrateable, interoperable) software components. This interoperability enables LBS platform providers and content providers to provide their software and data to multiple carriers.

Telcos think in terms of the set of capabilities that can be handled on a server. Customer relationship management (CRM) applications, for example, are built on a CRM server platform, just as LBS applications are built on a GMS server platform. Companies in the value chain, such as geotechnology providers like CubeWerx, ESRI, Intelliwhere, Ionic, MapInfo, Navigation Technologies, Oracle, and Webraska understand how to hook up to the GMS to provide their pieces of applications such as emergency response (e.g., E-911), personal navigator, traffic information service, proximity service, location recall, mobile field service, travel directions, restaurant finder, corporate asset locator, concierge, routing, vector map portrayal and interaction, friend finder, and geography voice-graphics.

The GeoMobility Server is an open service platform comprising the Core Services developed under the OGC OpenLS initiatives. The goal is to enable communication of location (and time), route, types of service, and so on across diverse technology platforms, application domains, classes of products, carrier networks, and national regions. It was developed as a set of prototype interfaces and schemas in OGC's Open Location Services (OpenLS Testbed Initiative, *http://www.openls.org*), which culminated in a demonstration on October 30, 2002. In June 2003, OGC members voted to adopt the OpenGIS Location Services (OpenLS[T]) Implementation Specification, which includes most of the interfaces that enable the operations described in Figure 6.5 [Bis03]. The current specification provides a set of recipes for rapid development of key elements of LBS offerings. Additional OpenLS specifications are under review in OGC, and others may be proposed in the future.

The primary objective of OpenLS is to define access to the Core Services and Abstract Data Types (ADTs) that comprise the GeoMobility Server.

---

7. Some sentences in this section of the chapter are borrowed verbatim from [OGC02].

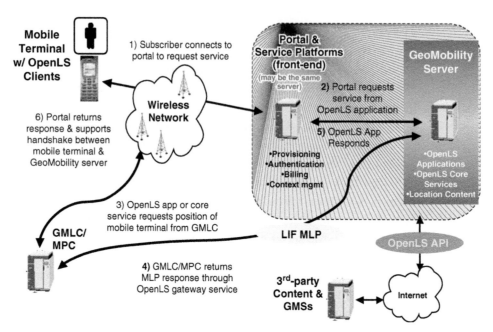

Figure 6.5 A typical service/request response via the GeoMobility Server. (Diagram courtesy of OGC.)

In Figure 6.6, the portal above the blue line is the front end that manages communication between the carrier's customers and third-party systems that typically provide data and services not directly provided by the carrier. APIs based on the Parlay/OSA specifications enable this communication, providing a standard way to handle authentication, identity of applications, use of service level agreements, and so on. In addition, the Parlay Group is providing a set of specifications for Web services that make it easier to build deployable products that use the telecom network.

Underneath the blue line, OGC's GeoMobility Server provides open interfaces to core services for LBS, including the following:

♦ *Route determination.* Determine route and navigation information between locations.
♦ *Location utility.* Geocoder (get <x,y> coordinates from street address) and reverse geocoder (get street address, intersection, place name, or postal code from position, that is from the <x,y> coordinates).
♦ *Presentation.* Create display information showing map, route, point of interest (POI), and/or route instructions.

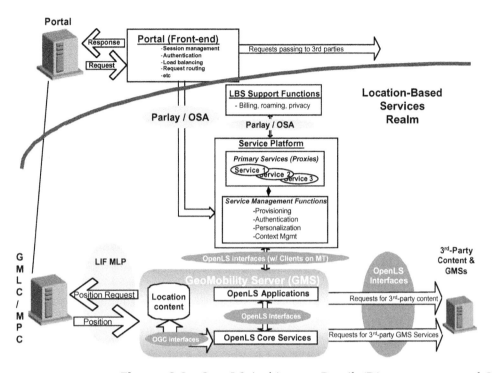

Figure 6.6   OpenLS Architecture Detail. (Diagram courtesy of OGC.)

◆ *Gateway.* Get position of a mobile terminal "from the network."
◆ *Directory Service.* Search for POIs. [OGC02]

To define these interfaces, OGC's OpenLS Working Group began by agreeing on a set of use cases that illustrate the range of functions the specifications would address. For example, the Location utility/geocoding use cases are as follows:

USE CASE 1

Given an address, find a position. A company has a database with a list of its customers and addresses. They employ an application that calls a Geocoder Service to geocode their database and have a geometry (Point) associated with the addresses. This will then be used to display customers on a mobile device.

USE CASE 2

Drive to an address (position). A motorist wishes to drive from home to an address in Regent Street, London. The address is geocoded, and its location is used as a destination within a routing application.

USE CASE 3

Given a place, find its position and display it on a map. Since his baby has left him, Elvis Presley wants a map to her new dwelling place. He only knows part of the address: "Heartbreak Hotel", "Lonely Street" and enters it into a form on his cell phone. The result is a map showing him the location of the matched address.

USE CASE 4

Given a jurisdiction, find all addresses and their positions. Postman Pat is using a GPS-enabled mobile device to plan his delivery route. He uses a Geocoder Service to find the location of all the addresses in Greendale.

Once a Geocoder Service determines a location, then the pertinent information element becomes a location-based resource that can be readily exploited by another service, such as Directory or Route Determination.

The OpenLS Specification sets forth a list of requirements for each of these services. The geocoder service, for example, should support the following:

- Given an Address ADT, use an address-matching geocoding algorithm to determine position.
- Handle one or more addresses in a single geocoding request.
- Be capable of performing geocoding using a partial address and return the completed (normalized) address information.
- Indicate the number of matches in the response (possibly zero) for a particular geocoding request.
- Provide information on the quality of the result using a "match code."

In addition to defining core services for LBS, the OpenLS Specification defines the OpenLS ADTs. An ADT is the basic information construct used by the GeoMobility Server and associated Core Services. It consists of well-known data types and structures for location information. ADTs are defined as application schemas that are encoded in XML for Location Services (XLS). They are encoded in a compact form to avoid the overhead of unnecessary encoding, decoding, and feature construction/deconstruction complexity for users of OpenLS services; and they are extensible.

The OpenLS ADTs are as follows:

- *Route.* Metadata pertaining to a route. The Route ADT is actually two ADTs: Route Summary and Route Geometry. Route Summary contains the route's overall characteristics, such as its start point, waypoints, end point, transportation type, total distance, travel time, and bounding box. Route Geometry contains a list of geographic positions along the route, ordered in the sequence of planned travel, starting with the position of the route's origin and ending with the position of the route's destination. The geometry includes the positions of all nodes along the route, including waypoints. The geometry also includes intermediate points needed to describe the geometric shape of the route segments between each node in the route. These two ADTs are generated by the Route Service and presented to a subscriber as routing information (e.g., as a route displayed over a map), via the Presentation Service, or they are used directly by an application to guide a mobile subscriber to his or her destination.

◆ *Route Instructions List.* Provides turn-by-turn navigation instructions for a route. The Route Instructions List ADT contains a list of travel instructions consisting of turn-by-turn directions and advisories along the route, ordered in sequence of their occurrence and formatted for presentation to the user. The Route Instructions List ADT is generated by the Route Service and presented to a subscriber via the Presentation Service.

◆ *Location.* A location (e.g., position, address, or POI). The Location ADT is the extensible, abstract type for all expressions of location that can be used by OpenLS application and services to specify the location of a target or a subscriber. Location is the root of a semantic tree that includes a Point, Position ADT, Address ADT, and POI ADT as its subtypes.

◆ *Position.* The Position ADT contains any observed or calculated position, in the broad semantic context of the use of the term. It primarily contains a geographic position and quality of position. Position is the primary output from a Gateway Service. Position maps to the semantics of the *Location, Shape,* and *Quality of Position* elements, as defined in the Mobile Location Protocol (MLP) Specification (Version 3.0, LIF). Thus, it contains the full definition of a position of a mobile terminal (Standard Location Immediate Service). Position may also be used by an OpenLS application to represent any position of interest. Position is distinguished from POI, which is a well-known place with a position, name, address, and so on.

- *Area of Interest.* This ADT contains an Area of Interest as defined by a named circle, bounding box, or polygon. It is used as a search parameter and can be displayed for a subscriber (e.g., Hot Zone).
- *Point of Interest.* The location where someone can find a place, product, or service. The POI ADT is a place or entity with a fixed position that may be used as a reference point or a target in an OpenLS service. The POI is the primary output from a Directory Service, and thus is also the place where one might obtain a product or service. It contains name, type, category, address, phone number, and other directory information about the place, product, and/or service.
- *Address.* The Address ADT contains address information for a geographic place. Addresses reference and uniquely identify particular points of interest and can serve as the basis for aggregating data for that location. The Address ADT consists of a street address (or intersection), place name (e.g., country, municipality), postal code, street locator, building locator, and supplemental address information. As used here, addresses are the means of referencing primarily residences and buildings (of all types, where a subscriber may conduct business).
- *Map.* The portrayal of maps and feature overlays (routes and POI). The Map ADT contains a rendered map that results from the Map Portrayal Operation of the Presentation Service. It can then be used as input to other Presentation Services. The Map ADT consists of content information (format, width, and height) and context information (bounding box, center point, and scale).

The following example, provided in the specification, illustrates how a Position ADT might be used. (This solution is not the only solution.)

The use case is as follows:

Joe User wants to see where his house is located on a map. To satisfy this use case, the Presentation Service needs to show a base map with the position of Joe's house overlaid onto it.

In order to satisfy this use case, the application must acquire a Position ADT for the location of Joe's home. One way to do this is to have the Geocoder Service geocode his address, thus determining a Position ADT.

In this example, we are asking for:

- 640 × 480 image in PNG format

- At a scale of 1:20,000
- In WGS 84 / UTM zone 11N (EPSG : 32611) projection
- With a north orientation
- Centered on Joe's house
- Base map will consist of all layers (using default style) made available by the implementation.
- The location of Joe's home will be shown using the default style provided by the implementation.

The request takes this form:

```
<?xml version="1.0" encoding="UTF-8"?>
<PortrayMapRequest>
   <Output width="640" height="480" format="image/png">
     <gml:Envelope>
        <gml:pos>-114.342 50.234 -114.123 50.031 </gml:pos>
     </ gml:Envelope >
   </Output>
   <!—Ask the impl to exclude no layers (thus, create the base map
with all your layers) –>
   <Basemap filter="Exclude" />
   <Overlay>
     <Position>
        <!– This ADT contains the lat/lon of Joe's House –>
     </Position>
   </Overlay>
</ PortrayMapRequest >
```

And the response takes this form:

```
<?xml version="1.0" encoding="UTF-8"?>

<PortrayMapResponse>
   <!– There is an OutputResponse for each Output request (in the
same order as requested) –>
     <Map>
       <Content width="640" height="480" format="image/png">
        <URL>                    http://www.mapseter.com/lbs/maps/
hgtr837468.png </URL>
       </Content>
     <gml:Envelope>
```

```
        <gml:pos>-114.342 50.234 -114.123 50.031 </gml:pos>
    </ gml:Envelope >
  </Map>
</PortrayMapResponse>
```

The next section discusses generally how standards could apply in the use case presented in Chapter 2.

6.5   STANDARDS AT WORK IN THE CHAPTER 2 USE CASE

The use case provided in Chapter 2 involves a Find Friend application developed by Kivera for AT&T. Because the application was developed before most of the LBS standards described had been developed, Kivera could not take advantage of those specifications. For that reason, we can only discuss how the standards might be applied in such an application. Following is the list of the core LBS functions required in the use case, as listed in Chapter 2, Section 2.3.2, with comments in italics describing how the open specifications could today be employed to achieve the benefits described, in many cases, to reduce the software development and integration time.

Geocoding/Reverse Geocoding. The application must receive latitude/ longitude coordinates pinpointing the location of a user's mobile phone and resolve these positions to an address or cross street, city, and state. In AT&T's case, these positions come from a Nortel GMLC, which looks up the position of a cell tower location. (Further friend finder applications could achieve even more precise accuracy by obtaining the latitude and longitude from GPS chips embedded in mobile phone hardware.)

The subscriber would connect to the carrier's portal to request service. The request might come in a proprietary form, but the portal's front end would transmit the request to the GeoMobility Server (GMS) through an interface implementing the OpenLS specification. The GMS would use the LIF MLP API to get the subscriber's coordinates from the GMLC/MPC.

Phone Location Display. Once a phone's location has been reverse geocoded, it will display a description of the mobile phone position, including city and state. It will also display neighborhood information if found within a certain number of miles from the phone location. Distance criteria is to be a system set parameter.

The reverse geocoding to provide a street address would be performed by a reverse geocoding service that might or might not be running on the same computer or cluster or local network as the OpenLS GMS. The reverse geocoding service might be from a content provider on the Web (or other network) that specializes in this service. The carrier's options are open if the OpenLS reverse geocoding interface has been implemented by the content provider.

The content provider would probably have the reverse geocoder set up to send map display data (including neighborhood information) in OGC's Geography Markup Language (GML), a standard XML encoding scheme for spatial information that separates content from presentation. This enables programmable presentation choices (e.g., colors, line widths, font size, graphic or audio) to accommodate different display devices and different application requirements.

Driving Directions. A Find Friend user should be able to retrieve driving directions from the origin address or the mobile phone position to the destination address, and potentially provide a route map to email to an end user. A WAP interface for Driving Directions is provided, as well as interfaces for setting route origin and destination. Screens for route results, including trip summary and step-by-step narrative, are developed.

Through a WAP interface or through the OpenLS route determination interface, the GLS would communicate with a route determination server (again, hosted locally or out on the Web or other network) to submit origin and destination parameters and retrieve driving directions. As with the reverse geocoding service, if the route determination service returns displayable driving directions data, it would probably return the data encoded in GML.

Point-of-Interest (POI) Search by Proximity. A user must be able to search for stores, restaurants, and other points-of-interest near his current location, near his friend's location, or at a point between him and his friend. These POIs should be arranged in categories. Features include sort results by proximity and return a maximum of 18 results. POI information should include name, street address, phone number, and category. To access this functionality, WAP interfaces for selecting a POI category and setting radius for search are provided. Screens for POI results and individual POI records are developed. The POI results list includes name and distance in miles. An individual record screen includes name, distance, address, and phone number.

The OpenLS directory service specification makes the POI search something that multiple content providers could offer. This POI gazetteer data is one kind of data that will need frequent, perhaps constant, updating, and the updates will depend on local knowledge. Different kinds of gazetteer and directory services might be the proprietary value-added service that gets built on top of the standards.

Neighborhood search by proximity. This functionality would allow the phone user to search for neighborhood point data by proximity, allowing the user to know the neighborhood in which his friend is located, and provide driving directions from the phone's location to a given neighborhood.

See "Driving directions" above.

Determine city/neighborhood between two positions. This functionality allows two mobile phone users to get directions to a point between them. The application provides for a single function call that identifies a middle point between two coordinate positions and searches for the closest neighborhood (or, for example the closest NavTech city point) in proximity to that point. Features include a maximum of five results, an algorithm for setting the radius for a proximity search based on the distance, a return code for positions with an exact match, and a return code for straight-line distances greater than a system set parameter.

See "Driving directions" above.

Search for all friends. This function allows a user to locate the whereabouts of everyone in his friend list, allowing the user to, for instance, determine what night club to go to or where to find a party of friends. This application function call calculates the straight-line distance between mobile phone position and an array of mobile phone positions. Features include distance returned in miles, a description of mobile phone location for each position, and a return code for positions with an exact match.

See "Driving directions" above. This application is built on top of the basic functionality provided by the standard services.

6.6   CONCLUSION AND CALL FOR PARTICIPATION

The rollout of LBS depends on the existence of a standards platform that will support the growth of multivendor value chains. That platform is complete enough now to enable today's carriers to begin using it. There is still plenty of work to do, but the necessary standards foundation has been established. Business, government, and consumer applications will roll out in the next few years, driven by emerging technologies in the Internet and in devices, by falling costs, and by the benefits of an increasingly coherent set of standards at the intersection of wireless, Internet, and spatial technologies.

There is a need for continued standards group harmonization and also stakeholder participation in OGC and the other standards organization processes. Providers and users of LBS share an interest in early deployment of services that conform to standards and that meet application requirements. The best way to ensure progress, and to help shape it, is to participate in industry standards consortia. There are many other business benefits (e.g., network contacts, reduced time and cost of development, strategic influence over technology direction, technology risk reduction) for both users and providers.

References

[Bis03]   Y. Bishr. "ETS-1 Location-Based Services Gateway Service." *http://www.openls. org/dvd1/ets1/Gateway.ppt*. Image Matters LLC, 2003.

[GSM03]   GSM Association. Permanent Reference Document SE.23, "Location Based Services." *http://www.gsmworld.com/documents/lbs/se23310.pdf*, January 2003.

[LIF02]   Location Interoperability Forum. "Mobile Location Protocol, LIF TS 101 Specification Version 3.0.0." *http://www.openmobilealliance.org/lifdownload. html*. Accessed June 6, 2002.

[OGC02]   OGC OpenLS Working Group. "Open GIS Consortium's OpenLS Initiative: Event, Architecture and Spec Overview." Presented at the September OGC Technical Committee Meeting, September 10, 2002.

[OGC03]   Open GIS Consortium. OGC Request 17: "OpenGIS Location Services (OpenLS^{TM}) Implementation Specification." OGC Location Services Working Group, A Request for Comments. *http://www.opengis.org/info/techno/rfc17in-fo.htm*, 2003.

[OMA02]   Open Mobile Alliance. "Short Paper." *http://www.openmobilealliance.org/ overview.html*, 2002.

[RMR03]   Roke Manor Research, *http://www.roke.co.uk/download/datasheets/Location_ Technology.pdf*, 2003.

[Spi03]   J. Spinney. "A Brief History of LBS and How OpenLS Fits Into the New Value Chain." *www.jlocationservices.com*, *Directions*, *www.directionsmag.com*, July 30, 2003.

[Van02]   VanderMeer, J. "Ubiquitous Wireless Location Interoperability." *Directions*, *http://www.directionsmag.com*, July 23, 2002.

Part 3

Aspects of
Communication in LBS

Data Collection

Jörg Roth, University of Hagen

CONTENTS

Location-based services (LBS) must be able to detect the location of a mobile user. In this chapter, we present the mechanisms to collect location data for LBS. After introducing the basic mechanisms and techniques, we discuss some positioning systems.

7.1   INTRODUCTION

Positioning and navigation have a long history. As long as people move across the earth's surface, they want to determine their current location. Especially seafarers need precise location information for long journeys. In the past, they used stars and lighthouses to find out their position; now they rely on electronic systems, especially satellite navigation systems.

Several positioning systems have specific advantages and disadvantages, but currently, no single positioning system fulfills all of the needs of any LBS. Satellite-based positioning systems such as GPS achieve high coverage and precision, but they fail in indoor environments. Indoor positioning systems require cost-intensive installations and are restricted to buildings or even some rooms inside a building.

Positioning is an important function for many areas, such as land surveying, aviation, aeronautic, robotic, or virtual and augmented reality. In this section, we limit the large area of positioning to systems and techniques that are appropriate for LBS. We do not discuss positioning systems that use space-consuming equipment (e.g., inside planes) or that are restricted to small spaces (e.g., in virtual reality environments). Positioning systems for LBS need to provide considerable coverage and to allow the location of mobile users with small mobile devices or badges.

7.1.1   Properties of Location Data

Different positioning systems provide location data with different characteristics. A positioning system has to meet the specific requirements of the LBS. We can identify the following properties of location data:

◆ *Coordinate system.* Coordinate systems that describe a 3D worldwide unique location can be divided into two classes: (1) Latitude, Longitude, and Altitude systems (LLA) use two angles and a height to specify a location in three dimensions; (2) Earth Centered, Earth Fixed (ECEF) systems use Cartesian coordinates with the zero point in the earth's center of gravity. Models of the earth's surface, usually an ellipsoid, serve as reference frames for coordinate systems. A popular model, WGS 84 (World Geodetic Survey 1984) [EURO98], forms the basis for GPS computations. Many coordinate systems make 2D mappings of the 3D surface of the earth using cylindrical or spherical projections. It depends on the specific task or data to choose an appropriate coordination system.

◆ *Scope.* A positioning system has a certain scope and defines an area of potential coordinates. A location can be worldwide unique or only valid in a small area (e.g., a building). Indoor positioning systems often provide local locations, relative to, for example, a certain corner of the building.

◆ *Coverage.* The actual coverage of a location system may be smaller than the area of potential locations specified by the scope. For example, the scope of an indoor positioning system may be an entire building; however, some rooms are not equipped and therefore outside the coverage.

◆ *Precision.* Capturing a location, a positioning system produces certain measurement errors. This inaccuracy sometimes is not a result of the used mechanism, but depends on environmental conditions (e.g., temperature, atmospheric conditions). Therefore, a certain position measuring can lead to different values at the same place depending on the time of day. Users and services that access location data must be aware of inaccuracy.

◆ *Geographic vs. semantic locations.* Users of LBS are often interested in the meaning of a location rather than in the geographic coordinates. Semantic locations [Prad00] are a powerful representation for a great amount of LBS. For example, instead of the geographic coordinates N51°22.579/E007°29.615/169 m, it may be more meaningful to use the term "University of Hagen, building IZ, back door." Some positioning systems already provide semantic locations.

◆ *Additional spatial data.* Besides the location, more spatial information sometimes is required. For navigation or map services, for example, it is useful to know the user's orientation. We specify the orientation in space by the so-called three angles: *roll, pitch,* and *yaw.* If we only need the direction on the horizontal plane, the yaw angle is sufficient. Unfortunately, most positioning systems cannot determine the orientation directly, but calculate the direction when the user moves. Electronic compasses are able to roughly determine the yaw angle. Further data is speed. If the positioning system cannot determine the speed directly (e.g., with the help of the Doppler effect), it can use two deferred position measurements.

7.1.2   Basic Location Techniques

Systems that determine the location of a mobile user can be divided into two categories: tracking and positioning.

We talk about *tracking*, if a sensor network determines the location. The user has to wear a specific tag or badge that allows the sensor network to track the user's position. The location information is first available in the sensor network. If the mobile user needs his or her location data, the sensor network has to transfer this information to the user by wireless communication.

If the mobile system determines the location itself, we use the term *positioning*. A system of transmitters or beacons sends out radio, infrared, or ultrasound signals. Location information is directly available at the mobile system and does not have to be transferred wirelessly. In addition, location information is not readable for other users, thus the positioning system does not have to consider privacy issues.

Systems using tracking as well as positioning are based on the following various basic techniques, often used in combination:

◆ *Cell of Origin* (*COO*). This technique is used if the positioning system has a cellular structure. Wireless transmitting technologies have a restricted range (i.e., a radiated signal is available only in a certain area, the *cell*). If the cell has a certain identification, it can be used to determine a location.

◆ *Time of Arrival* (*TOA*), *Time Difference of Arrival* (*TDOA*). Electromagnetic signals move with light speed. Because this speed is very high (approximately 300,000 km/s), the corresponding runtimes are very short. If we assume a nearly constant light speed, we can use the time difference between sending and receiving a signal to compute the spatial distance of transmitter and receiver. A similar principle can be used with ultrasound. The signals take a longer time, thus measurement is simpler, but ultrasound can only reach low distances. If we measure the time difference between two signals, we use the term TDOA. In GSM networks, the term Enhanced Observed Time Difference (E-OTD) is often used instead of TDOA.

◆ *Angle of Arrival* (*AOA*). If we use antennas with direction characteristics, we can find out from which direction a certain signal arrives. Given two or more directions from fixed positions to the same object, we can compute the location of the object. Because it is too difficult to constantly turn an antenna for measuring, receivers use a set of antennas that are lined up with a certain angle difference in all directions.

◆ *Measuring the signal strength.* The intensity of electromagnetic signals decreases even in vacuum with the square of the distance from their source. Given a specific signal strength, we can compute the distance to the sender. Unfortunately, obstacles such as walls or trees additionally reduce the signal strength, thus this method is inaccurate.

◆ *Processing video data.* Using video cameras, we can look for significant patterns in a video data stream to determine the user's location. If users wear badges with conspicuous labels, they can be detected in video images. For this, positioning systems use techniques from image processing to detect and interpret image data. In principle, video positioning systems are based on the AOA technique: a specific pixel in an image represents a certain angle relative to the camera's optical axis; however, video data can transport color information, which can be used to transfer additional information (e.g., the user's identification).

7.1.3   *Triangulation, Trilateration, and Traversing*

Precise positioning methods have their roots in land surveying, where geometric approaches are used to determine locations with the help of angles and distances. Any positioning system that provides geographic coordinates is still based on these geometric principles. Figure 7.1 shows how to compute the coordinates of a location u.

◆ *Triangulation* (Figure 7.1a) needs two fixed positions (p_1 and p_2). From each position, we measure the angle to the location u. Geometrically speaking, we get u if we intersect two lines. With the help of trigonometric functions, we can calculate the coordinates of u.

◆ *Trilateration* (Figure 7.1b) also needs two fixed positions, but uses two distances to the unknown location. We get the location u if we intersect two circles. Usually, there exist two intersection points, thus we have to eliminate one point with the help of additional information. In contrast to triangulation, trilateration leads to nonlinear equation systems, which have no closed solution for 3D

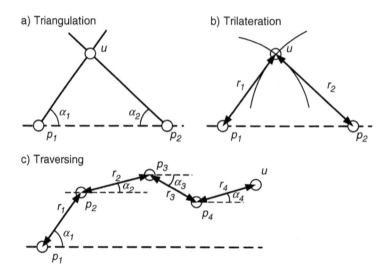

Figure 7.1   Triangulation, trilateration, and traversing.

positioning. To get a solution, we have to solve equations with the help of numeric methods (see Section 7.2.1).

- *Traversing* (Figure 7.1c) uses several distance–angle pairs. We start with a known point p_1 and measure the distance and direction to another point p_2. After a few steps, we reach the unknown point u. Note that in principle we could use a single step from a known point to the unknown point.

Even though the term *triangulation* originally has the meaning shown previously, it is often used for any kind of geometric approaches for location.

Note that in Figure 7.1, we assume a positioning in two dimensions. For 3D positioning, we can use similar mechanisms, but we need three values (either angles or distances) to calculate 3D coordinates.

In the following sections, we present several systems and techniques in more detail. We divide positioning systems into three classes: satellite positioning systems, indoor positioning systems, and systems that use an existing network infrastructure.

7.2   SATELLITE POSITIONING SYSTEMS

The idea of using satellites for positioning goes back to the 1960s. Using satellites for positioning has important advantages, such as the following:

- Positioning can in principle be carried out everywhere on the earth.
- Environmental conditions, such as the weather, have only minimal influence on the positioning process.
- A high precision is obtained.

Among other things, these advantages make satellite navigation interesting for use by the armed forces, but a variety of applications is also conceivable for civilian purposes.

Satellite navigation also has some disadvantages, such as the following:

- Considerable costs arise for launching and supervising the satellites.
- The positioning only works if the user receives a sufficient number of satellites. Particularly, positioning inside buildings is not possible.

The most prominent example of a satellite navigation system is the Global Positioning System (GPS). Before we describe GPS, we present the basic mechanisms of satellite navigation.

7.2.1 Basic Principles

A user who wants to determine a position with the help of satellites needs the exact positions of the satellites (s_i) as well as the exact distances to the satellites (r_i). Figure 7-2a shows this principle.

If the user determined the values s_i and r_i, his or her position is restricted to the spherical surfaces around each satellite. We need at least three satellites to determine the user's location u in three dimensions (Figure 7.2a).

Taken exactly, the cut of three spherical surfaces normally leads to two intersection points (Figure 7.2b). The second intersection point lies far in

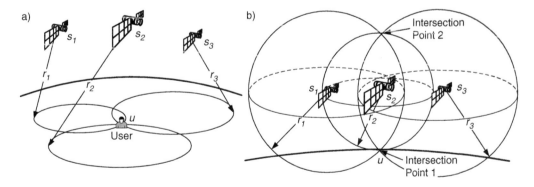

Figure 7.2 Principle of satellite positioning. Adapted from *Mobile Computing* by Jörg Roth, dpunkt-Verlag (May 2002).

the space; therefore, it can simply be filtered out for a user within the earth's atmosphere.

Satellites move on fixed orbits, thus a mobile user can easily compute his or her exact position at a certain time. A so-called almanac contains a list of all working satellites and their orbits. The almanac is frequently downloaded to the mobile user's receiver. It is also updated when satellites are shut down or new satellites start their work in new orbits. Note that the precision of the values s_i directly influences the precision of the location u.

To compute the distances r_i, every satellite sends a signal, which exactly specifies the current satellite time. A receiver compares this time with its internal clock. The distance r can be determined from the time difference Δt with the formula $r = c \cdot \Delta t$. Here, c denotes the speed of light, which is approximately 300,000 km/s.

The time measurement is the critical point at this procedure. Because the light velocity is very high, the time measurement must be carried out exactly. An error of only $1\,\mu$s, for example, leads to a difference of 300 meters in the position calculation. Every satellite is therefore equipped with an atomic clock, which allows an exact time measurement. The exact time of the entire navigation system is called the *system time*.

A mobile device cannot be equipped with an atomic clock because of the high cost and space requirements. Without synchronized clocks, it is not possible to achieve the necessary precision. Unfortunately, synchronization directly with the clocks of the satellites is not possible because the time information can only be transmitted with the speed of light. As a solution to this dilemma, a fourth satellite is included for position calculation. For the following explanations, we introduce some variables:

t_s denotes the system time at which a signal is sent out by a satellite
t_u denotes the system time at which the user receives a signal
$\tilde{t}_s = t_s + \delta t_s$ denotes the local satellite time at which the signal is sent out; δt_s denotes the offset to the system time
$\tilde{t}_u = t_u + \delta t_u$ denotes the local user's time at which the signal is received; δt_u denotes the offset to the system time
$\Delta t = t_u - t_s$ denotes the exact runtime of the signal
$\Delta \tilde{t} = \tilde{t}_u - \tilde{t}_s$ denotes the measured runtime of the signal
c denotes the speed of light

If the clocks were exact, the distance could be computed exactly with the formula $r = c \cdot \Delta t = c \cdot (t_u - t_s)$. The measured distance that the receiver determines is called *pseudo range*, denoted by p:

$$
\begin{aligned}
p &= c \cdot \Delta \tilde{t} \\
&= c \cdot (\tilde{t}_u - \tilde{t}_s) \\
&= c \cdot ((t_u + \delta t_u) - (t_s + \delta t_s)) \\
&= c \cdot (t_u - t_s) + c \cdot (\delta t_u - \delta t_s) \\
&= r + c \cdot (\delta t_u - \delta t_s)
\end{aligned}
$$

In the following, we assume that the satellite time corresponds exactly to the system time (i.e., $\delta t_s = 0$). Permanently supervising and synchronizing the satellite clocks can achieve this correlation.

As a next step, we express r by the coordinates of the satellite and the user. To do this, we use an arbitrary Cartesian coordinate system, which has, for example, the zero point in the center of gravity of the earth. We get:

$$
\begin{aligned}
p &= r + c \cdot \delta t_u \\
&= \sqrt{(s_x - u_x)^2 + (s_y - u_y)^2 + (s_z - u_z)^2} + c \cdot \delta t_u
\end{aligned}
$$

This equation contains four unknown variables: u_x, u_y, u_z, and δt_u. We need four equations and thus four satellite signals to determine their values. Unfortunately, the resulting system of equations is nonlinear. To solve this problem, we can use algebraic solutions [Ban85], solutions with Kalman filters [Kap96], or iterative solutions. At this point, we briefly outline the iterative approximation with Taylor series.

The iterative approximation is based on an estimation to solve the system of equations. The difference between estimation and exact value is then expressed as a *linear* system of equations. The solution of this system leads to a more exact set of values, which are represented as follows:

$$
\begin{aligned}
u_x &= \hat{u}_x + \Delta u_x \\
u_y &= \hat{u}_y + \Delta u_y \\
u_z &= \hat{u}_z + \Delta u_z \\
\delta t_u &= \delta \hat{t}_u + \Delta t_u
\end{aligned}
$$

Here $\hat{u}_x$, $\hat{u}_y$, $\hat{u}_z$, and $\delta\hat{t}_u$ denote the estimations. If we get good approximations for the delta values, we can get a more exact estimation in the next step. The estimated pseudo ranges can be computed as follows:

$$\hat{p}_i = \sqrt{\left(s_{xi} - \hat{u}_x\right)^2 + \left(s_{yi} - \hat{u}_y\right)^2 + \left(s_{zi} - \hat{u}_z\right)^2} + c \cdot \delta\hat{t}_u$$

With the help of linearization techniques (i.e., by defining suitable functions for the four variables and the corresponding Taylor series and removing nonlinear terms), we get a linear system of equations. For a satellite $i \in \{1, \ldots, 4\}$, we get:

$$\hat{p}_i - p_i = a_{xi} \cdot \Delta u_x + a_{yi} \cdot \Delta u_y + a_{zi} \cdot \Delta u_z - c \cdot \Delta t_u$$

where

$$a_{xi} = \frac{s_{xi} - \hat{u}_x}{\hat{r}_i}, \quad a_{yi} = \frac{s_{yi} - \hat{u}_y}{\hat{r}_i}, \quad a_{zi} = \frac{s_{zi} - \hat{u}_z}{\hat{r}_i},$$

$$\hat{r}_i = \sqrt{\left(s_{xi} - \hat{u}_x\right)^2 + \left(s_{yi} - \hat{u}_y\right)^2 + \left(s_{zi} - \hat{u}_z\right)^2}.$$

This results in the following system of equations for four satellites:

$$\begin{bmatrix} \hat{p}_1 - p_1 \\ \hat{p}_2 - p_2 \\ \hat{p}_3 - p_3 \\ \hat{p}_4 - p_4 \end{bmatrix} = \begin{bmatrix} a_{x1} & a_{y1} & a_{z1} & -c \\ a_{x2} & a_{y2} & a_{z2} & -c \\ a_{x3} & a_{y3} & a_{z3} & -c \\ a_{x4} & a_{y4} & a_{z4} & -c \end{bmatrix} \cdot \begin{bmatrix} \Delta u_x \\ \Delta u_y \\ \Delta u_z \\ \Delta t_u \end{bmatrix}$$

The solutions Δu_x, Δu_y, Δu_z, and Δt_u of this system are added to the estimated values to get a better approximation. The procedure can be repeated until we achieve the desired precision.

The signals of the satellites are often interfered. With the help of more than four satellites, the resulting error can be minimized. This mathematically results, however, in a system of equations that is no longer solvable, but with the help of the least square methods, we can compute an appropriate position. Generally, the more satellite signals are taken into account, the more precise is the resulting position.

7.2.2   GPS

Different American organizations, especially the Department of Defense (DoD), the Department of Transportation (DoT), and the National

Aeronautics and Space Administration (NASA), were interested in a satellite-based positioning system until the early 1960s. When older navigation systems did not meet the requirements anymore, the DoD conceived a system in 1970 with the name NAVSTAR GPS (Navigation System with Timing and Ranging—Global Positioning System), in the following called GPS. In 1974, the first system tests were begun. In 1984, the first GPS satellites were launched. Until 1990, 12 satellites were working. A first operational status (initial operation capability, IOC) was achieved with 21 system satellites and three reserve satellites on December 8, 1993. The full operation capability (FOC) was declared on July 17, 1995.

The GPS system is divided into three segments: the user segment, the space segment, and the control segment (Figure 7.3).

◆ The *user segment* contains the devices of the mobile users (i.e., the GPS receivers). GPS receivers are subject to permanent miniaturization and price reduction. They are often the size of a mobile telephone. GPS receivers can be plug-in cards or separate devices with a serial interface connection.

◆ The *space segment* consists of the satellites. Every satellite weighs between 1.5 and 2 tons and has an autonomous energy supply with solar cells. The central computer of a satellite has a 16-MHz CPU.

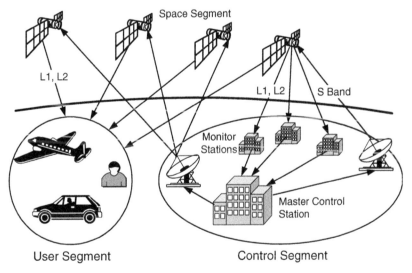

Figure 7.3 GPS segments. Adapted from *Mobile Computing* by Jörg Roth, dpunkt-Verlag (2002).

The satellites were programmed in Ada. The operating system of a satellite consists of approximately 25,000 lines of code.

◆ The *control segment* is necessary for administration of the satellites as well as for correction of the satellite internal data (system time and orbits). Several monitor stations permanently receive the satellite signals. They have a precisely known, fixed position and atomic clocks that are synchronized with the system time; thus, the monitor stations can calculate the correction data. They are passed on to the Master Control Station (MCS), which is located in Colorado Springs, Colorado.

In order to achieve global coverage from the equator to the poles, 24 satellites move on six different orbits with four satellites per orbit (Figure 7.4). Every satellite orbits the earth at the distance of approximately 20,200 km. A satellite needs 12 hours for a complete orbit. The satellites move in a way that at least five and at most 11 satellites are mostly visible over the horizon from every point on the earth's surface. The number of satellites that can actually be received can be lower because of shadowing by, for example, buildings or landscape formations. As represented in the last section, four satellites are necessary for a positioning in three dimensions.

A satellite has an expected lifetime of 7.5 years. In order for the GPS to remain operable after satellite failures, more than 24 satellites are in orbit. The number was sometimes increased up to 28. Currently, an operator needs 60 days to launch a new satellite into orbit after the failure of a

Figure 7.4   GPS satellite orbits. Reprinted with permission from *Mobile Computing* by Jörg Roth, dpunkt-Verlag (May 2002).

satellite. It is planned for reasons of cost to shorten the time for launching to 10 days. With this change, the number of satellites could be reduced to 25.

A user who wants to determine a position with the help of GPS does not have to register, but can use the GPS signals free of charge. The mechanism is based on one-way communication of the satellites to the user. Two GPS services exist:

♦ *Precise Positioning Service* (*PPS*). This service allows positioning with a precision of 22 m in the horizontal and 27.7 m in the vertical. Over a period of 24 hours, 95% of the measuring is within the given precision. PPS (formerly called P-Code or Precision Code) is encrypted and can only be decoded by the armed forces of the United States and members of the North Atlantic Treaty Organization (NATO). This service is not accessible to civilian users.

♦ *Standard Positioning Service* (*SPS*). This service (formerly called C/A-Code or Coarse/Acquisition Code) is available for civilian users. Until April 30, 2000, it had a precision of 100 m in the horizontal and 156 m in the vertical.

The satellites send out a continuous signal with approximately 20 W. They use two frequencies: *L1* (1575.42 MHz) for PPS and SPS, and *L2* (1227.6 MHz) exclusively for PPS.

Because all satellites send signals at the same frequencies, a receiver must have the ability to assign the signals to the respective satellites. GPS uses Code Division Multiple Access (CDMA) for this purpose: every satellite uses a unique code called the Pseudo Random Noise (PRN). The receiver knows all of the codes and can filter out the corresponding sequence from the superimposed signals of all satellites. The PRNs do not disturb themselves mutually (they are designed to be orthogonal). With the help of the satellite signal, the receiver can measure the time difference of the involved clocks and compute the pseudo range. As a second function, the signal transfers data with a data rate of 50 bits/s. These data contain the position of the satellite, the system time, and the orbits of other satellites.

The entire GPS system is subject to the following distorting effects, which influence the precision [HLC01]:

♦ *Clock errors.* Although the clocks in the satellites work exactly, clocks cause an error of 1.5 m in the position calculation.

Table 7.1 Precision of GPS services.

Service	Horizontal Precision	Vertical Precision
PPS	22 m	27.7 m
SPS with SA	100 m	156 m
SPS without SA	25 m	43 m

♦ *Fluctuations of the orbits.* The satellites do not move as exactly as calculated in their orbits. For example, the gravitational forces of the sun and moon disturb the orbits. Fluctuations cause an error of 2.5 m.

♦ *Disturbances of the atmosphere.* Atmospheric pressure and weather conditions affect the signal spreading and cause an error of 0.5 m.

♦ *Disturbances of the ionosphere.* The loaded particles of the ionosphere disrupt the signal spreading and cause an error of 5.0 m.

♦ *Multipath error.* Reflected signals in the environment of the receiver cause an error of 0.6 m.

In addition to these effects, the SPS signal was artificially distorted until the year 2000 to prevent a more exact measuring. This mechanism, called Selective Availability (SA), randomly dithered the time sent by the satellites. In addition, the orbit information was distorted. Through this system, an exact positioning was no longer possible. The background of SA was that the U.S. army did not want to enable too exact positioning for other forces. SA was switched off on May 1, 2000 [DOD01] for economic reasons. SPS now provides a precision of 25 m in the horizontal and 43 m in the vertical (with 95%). Table 7.1 summarizes the precisions of the different GPS services.

Future developments are planned to improve the precision of SPS, especially to correct ionospheric distortion. The new services will be deployed with satellite launches scheduled between 2003 and 2012, and with full operational capability expected in 2014.

7.2.3 DGPS and WAAS

The precision of GPS is often insufficient. With Differential GPS (DGPS), the precision can be improved significantly with the help of base stations on the earth's surface. These *reference* or *base receivers* have a fixed, precisely known position (Figure 7.5).

The base receiver executes a positioning with GPS. Because the positioning has errors, a difference to the exact position results. The

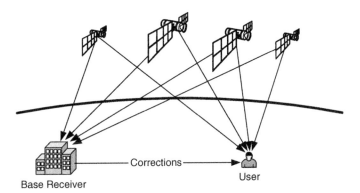

Figure 7.5 DGPS principle. Adapted from *Mobile Computing* by Jörg Roth, dpunkt-Verlag (2002).

base receiver contemporarily broadcasts correction data based on these differences to the users. This mechanism is based on the assumption that users in the nearer area of the base receivers get similar errors. The errors, therefore, almost are compensated with the correction data.

We can describe a first, naive approach of DGPS as follows:

◆ The base station permanently measures its own position (b_x, b_y, b_z) with GPS.

◆ It subtracts this position from the precise position $(b_{xex}, b_{yex}, b_{zex})$ and transmits the difference $(b_{xex} - b_x, b_{yex} - b_y, b_{zex} - b_z)$ to the users.

◆ A user, who determined his own position (u_x, u_y, u_z), adds the correction and gets a more precise position $(u_x + b_{xex} - b_x, u_y + b_{yex} - b_y, u_z + b_{zex} - b_z)$.

This procedure is simple but has a major disadvantage: It works satisfactorily only when the base receiver and the user choose the same satellites for positioning because only then do the errors fully compensate. As a solution, the base receiver could execute measurements with different combinations of satellites and provide the correction data with the used satellite combination. Obviously, this procedure fails because of the huge set of possible combinations. If too many satellites can be received at the same time, the number of combinations explodes. Note that the base receiver cannot ask a user for his satellite combination because only one-way communication is possible. Therefore, another mechanism based on pseudo ranges is used in DGPS. It works as follows:

◆ The base receiver measures the pseudo range p_{bi} to every satellite i with $p_{bi} = r_{bi} + E_{bi} + c \cdot \delta_{bi}$, where r_{bi} is the exact distance,

E_{bi} the measurement error, and $c \cdot \delta_{bi}$ is the distance offset, which results from the clock difference of the base receiver and system time.

◆ The base station sends a correction $\Delta p_{bi} = p_{bi} - r_{bi} = E_{bi} + c \cdot \delta_{bi}$ for every satellite to the user. Note that r_{bi} is a known value for the base receiver.

◆ A user who determined his own pseudo range p_{ui} subtracts the correction value and gets a corrected pseudo range $p_{ucorr} = p_{ui} - \Delta p_{bi} = r_{ui} + E_{ui} + c \cdot \delta_{ui} - E_{bi} - c \cdot \delta_{bi}$. Because the errors E_{ui} and E_{bi} arise from measuring with the same satellites, they almost compensate (i.e., $E_{ui} - E_{bi} \approx 0$). We get $p_{ucorr} \approx r_{ui} + c \cdot \delta_{ui} - c \cdot \delta_{bi} = r_{ui} + c \cdot \delta_{total}$. The user can establish and solve a system of equations from this as presented in Section 7.2.1.

The format for correction data from the base receivers is standardized under the name RTCM 104. With DGPS, we get a precision of approximately 1 to 3 m. The distance between user and base receivers has an important influence on the precision.

The Wide Area Augmentation System (WAAS) follows a principle similar to that of DGPS (Figure 7.6). With the help of base receivers, correction data are computed. Unlike DGPS, the transmitting is not

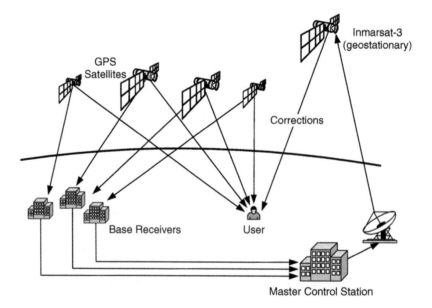

Figure 7.6 WAAS principle. Adapted from *Mobile Computing* by Jörg Roth, dpunkt-Verlag (2002).

executed with the help of terrestrial transmitters, but rather with the help of geostationary satellites. In the United States, approximately 30 base receivers operate at present. The correction values are passed to a master control station that then forwards them to an Inmarsat-3 satellite, which sends the correction data to users. Because the satellite is on a geostationary orbit (unlike the GPS satellites), correction data are always transmitted to the same geographic area. This is intended because the correction data consist of the base receivers of the covered area. For transmitting the correction data to users, the Inmarsat-3 satellite sends at the L1 frequency and uses a free PRN code.

7.2.4 Other Satellite Systems

Other satellite navigation systems exist besides GPS. The Russian counterpart to GPS is GLONASS (Globalnaya Navigationnaya Sputnikovaya Sistema), which began operation in 1996. It uses two frequencies similar to GPS, where one is reserved for the armed forces. GLONASS does not know encryption of the precise service or mechanism such as Selective Availability. A civilian user achieves a precision of 26 m in the horizontal and 45 m in the vertical.

Although GLONASS had the same availability with 24 satellites as GPS at the start time, more satellites failed because of the shorter lifetime of the GLONASS satellites (3 to 4 years). Moreover, GLONASS had financing problems. In 2000, only 10 satellites were still active, so global coverage could not be achieved anymore. In February 2004, only 9 satellites were operational.

In Europe, plans exist for a new satellite navigation system. In the first step, a system such as the American WAAS is planned, which provides satellite-based correction data to GPS and GLONASS. It is called EGNOS (European Geostationary Navigation Overlay System) and will start its service by 2004.

The second step of a European navigation system is an autonomous system like GPS or GLONASS. In 1999, the European Union ministerial committee decided to set up this system with the name GALILEO. In 2006, the first of 30 satellites will be launched; full operability is planned for 2008. GALILEO will offer three services: a free service, a service that can only be used by governmental organizations, and a further encoded service for which users will be charged.

7.3 INDOOR POSITIONING SYSTEMS

Satellite navigation provides comfortable, precise, and, from the end user's point of view, economical positioning. Unfortunately, these systems can only be used outside of buildings because the radio signals employed cannot penetrate solid walls. For positioning in buildings, additional installations (e.g., sensor networks) are required. Depending on the mechanisms and techniques, considerable costs arise for the stationary and mobile devices.

Although the mechanisms of the satellite navigation systems are very similar, indoor positioning systems are very different concerning the basic mechanisms, precision, and costs. Currently, many systems have been developed as research projects. Only in rare cases have indoor positioning systems reached a product state. In the following sections, we present some indoor positioning systems examples. We classify these systems by the measuring technique based on infrared, radio, ultrasound, and video.

7.3.1 Infrared Beacons

A class of indoor positioning systems uses infrared beacons. Infrared devices are highly available and cheap, thus this idea was realized in many projects. A very early project based on infrared beacons, called the Active Badge system [WHFG92], was developed by Olivetti (Figure 7.7a).

Every user visibly carries a small infrared transmitter, the Active Badge. It has a size of approximately 55 mm by 55 mm by 7 mm and weight of 40 g. Every 15 seconds, it sends an infrared signal of approximately 0.1 s. This signal transports a code that specifies the user's identity. Infrared sensors installed inside the building receive the signals and pass the information to a computer in the building.

The mechanism is based on the fact that infrared signals normally are limited to a single room. Inside a room, walls reflect the infrared signal, thus a sensor can even receive a signal if it has no direct sight to the user. The pulse duration of 0.1 s is very short compared to the waiting time, which has the following two advantages:

1. Because the infrared light pulse consumes the most energy, an Active Badge can work very long without battery changes. Active Badges work for approximately one year with a single battery.

2. More Active Badges in the same room only rarely produce colliding infrared light pulses. By low differences in the period duration of 15 s,

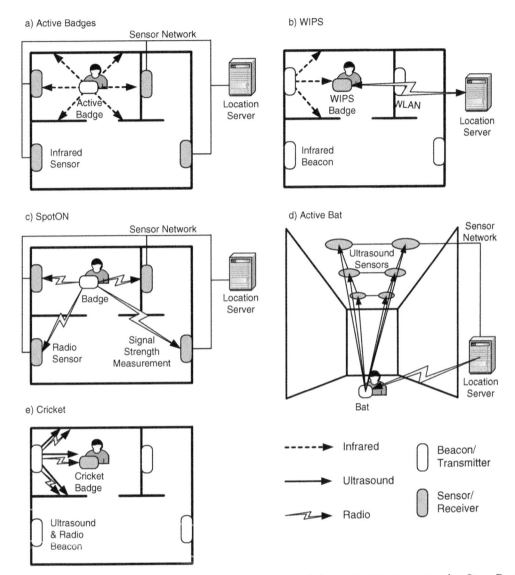

Figure 7.7 Indoor positioning systems. Adapted from *Mobile Computing* by Jörg Roth, dpunkt-Verlag (2002).

it is unlikely that two badges permanently sent signals at the same time. Note that the system even works if some of the transmissions are lost because of collisions.

In the first project stage, infrared sensors were connected to the server via a serial four-wire connection. In a second stage, an Ethernet network is used for communication.

The server collects all sensor information and offers it to other applications. Client applications can ask, for example, which persons are currently inside or outside the building or in which room a specific person currently resides.

One goal of the first Active Badges was to have low-cost equipment with a long battery lifetime. As a result, the first Active Badges were not able to receive information from the sensor network; however, the request for two-way communication arose for the following reasons:

◆ A person could easily duplicate a badge that emits the same infrared signal. Thus an unauthorized person could imitate the signal of another person. In some cases, location information could be critical (e.g., when location data are used to measure the working time of employees). A further development, so-called Authenticated Badges, use a secret cryptographic key, which is proofed according to the challenge-response mechanism, which needs two-way-communication.

◆ The Active Badge can also be used to display information. For this, two little lights and a loudspeaker were attached in an extended version of the Active Badges. They provide simple visual and acoustic signals.

To save battery power, a badge waits after its own transmission only for a very short time to receive a message. In order to receive messages, further computers became necessary. In the latest project stage, the system had the following servers:

◆ The *Location server* collects the information of the sensors.
◆ The *Name server* manages a database of all system users with the corresponding badge addresses.
◆ The *Message server* coordinates the passing of messages directed to the Active Badges.
◆ *Exchange servers* can combine different systems hierarchically to a larger system.

One objective of the Active Badge system was to keep the mobile devices as simple as possible. In 1992, the start of the Active Badge project, it was difficult to create small and computational powerful mobile devices with low energy consumption. As a major drawback, the location data are directly only available at the location server and not at the end user's device. As a result of the miniaturization of devices in the

following years, it was possible to exchange the roles of beacons and
sensors. The Wireless Indoor Positioning system (WIPS) [WIPS00]
realizes this idea (Figure 7.7b) and has the following characteristics:

- The infrared transmitters are no longer mobile, but form the fixed
  installation. They do not have to be connected to each other.
- The badges receive the signal of the beacons and pass the
  corresponding location information to the location server via a
  wireless LAN network (see Chapter 8).
- The location data are then processed by the location server and replied
  to the mobile device (again via wireless LAN).

The concept of WIPS allows the creation of more complex location-
based applications. The mobile devices are full computers and are
connected to the location servers, thus demanding services can be
executed. The beacons, on the other hand, can be built up very simply
because they only need to periodically send out a fixed signal, and they do
not require any network connection.

The cost-intensive parts of these systems are the end-user devices,
which need to be real computers with wireless LAN support. In the area
of LBS where users request demanding services via their mobile device,
this is no real disadvantage.

7.3.2 Radio Beacons

Because infrared signals usually flood whole areas such as rooms, they do
not allow exact position measurements. They are useful for positioning
systems, which provide semantic location information. Radio signals,
in contrast, can penetrate walls. If more than one radio transmitter is
in reach, a physical location can be determined with the help of signals.
If transmitters are attached in several height levels, a 3D positioning is
possible. Positioning systems can use signal strengths as well as TOA
to compute a location. In principle, positioning similarly to satellite
navigation could be installed indoor, with several fixed radio beacons
instead of satellites. TOA-based indoor systems based on radio are,
however, not widely available.

A project that uses signal strengths to determine a location is SpotON
[HBW00]. Figure 7.7c shows this principle. As in the Active Badge
system, the mobile user sends out a signal. Radio sensors in the building
receive the signal and transmit the signal strengths to a server. The

evaluation of these data is more complex than in the infrared case. The server has to find a location that matches all measured signal strengths. Therefore, it is assumed that the strength of an electromagnetic signal decreases with the square of the distance. Unfortunately, the signal strength depends on other factors (e.g., obstacles, disturbances, or variations in the transmitting power). As a result, it is not possible to get a precise measurement. SpotON tries to compensate for these errors by taking into account many sensor values. The system achieves a precision of 3 m.

Radio Frequency Identification (RFID) transponders are a variant of radio beacons. Passive RFID transponders are small systems with a processor, memory, and antenna but without a power supply. They take the necessary energy for work from the received radio signals. A signal addressed to a transponder can be an instruction to either load new data into the memory or reply data from the memory as an answer. The transmitter and the transponder normally have a maximum distance of 1 meter. RFID transponders are frequently used to track objects during the transportation process in a production. The exact 3D positioning is not in the foreground. RFID transponders can be used to find out if a certain object has already passed a waypoint on, for example, a conveyer belt.

7.3.3 Ultrasound Systems

Systems based on ultrasound can achieve considerably high precision. The time an ultrasound signal needs from transmitter to receiver is approximately proportional to the corresponding distance. Because the speed of sound (330 m/s) is low compared to radio signals, it is easier to get an exact measurement without high technical efforts. The ultrasound positioning system Active Bat [WJH97] obtained a precision of 10 cm. Figure 7.7d shows the principle of Active Bat.

A user carries a device, the so-called Bat, which sends a short ultrasound impulse upon a request to the server. The server transmits the send request by radio. The server always selects one specific Bat for positioning; therefore, ultrasound signals from different Bats cannot collide. Receivers that are assembled at the ceiling receive the ultrasound signal. The receivers are attached in a raster of 1.2 m. When they receive a signal, they immediately pass this information to the location server via a wired network.

The server has all of the necessary information about the positioning of the corresponding user. It can create and solve a system of equations using the runtimes of the ultrasound signals. The corresponding calculations are very similar to the calculations of satellite positioning (i.e., a nonlinear system of equations has to be solved; see Section 7.2.1). The calculation simplifies because the radio signals have very short runtimes compared to the ultrasound signals. Because they can be neglected, we have a common time basis. For positioning in three dimensions, the input of at least three sensors is required.

The Cricket system [PCB00] switches the roles of transmitter and receiver. Fixed installed beacons send ultrasound signals received by mobile badges. To measure the time, the beacons send a radio signal at the same time (Figure 7.7e). With the Cricket system, mobile users can determine their locations without a server. In this project, the exact 3D positioning is not in the foreground. When users enter a room, they get information about available network services (e.g., print services).

7.3.4   Video-Based Systems

Another class of positioning systems is based on the evaluation of video data. Processing video is generally computing intensive. With the help of special colored badges, the evaluation can be simplified significantly. Visual tags [SMR+97] have patterns that can be recognized easily and have, for example, red and green squares. The position of the squares in relation to each other can carry, similar to bar codes, simple information such as the user's identity. Because the size of the badges is fixed, the distance to the camera and the orientation in the room can be roughly detected. Sample visual tags are presented in Figure 7.8a and b.

Detecting a user's location can be done in two ways. First, the building can be equipped with cameras, which look for the visual tags (Figure 7.8c) in their image data stream. If at least two cameras detect the same tag, they can determine the corresponding angles under which the tag is visible. Because the positions of the cameras are known, they can compute the user's location by triangulation.

A second approach is presented in [RA00]: the mobile user is equipped with a small camera, mounted, for example, on the head. Visual tags are attached on walls inside the building. In this case, the visual tags have fixed positions. If the mobile camera detects two or more tags, it can find out its own position.

a) Visual tag [RA00]   c) Detecting a location with cameras

b) Visual tag [MERL01]

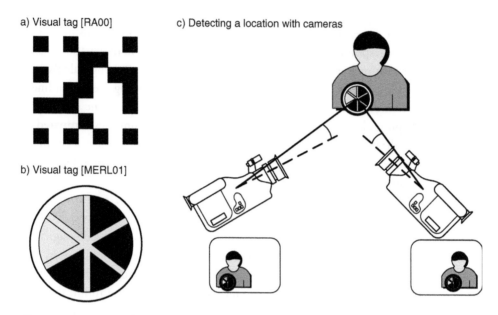

Figure 7.8   Visual tags and video positioning.

7.4   NETWORK-BASED POSITIONING

Installing positioning systems is often a significant investment. To reduce the costs, existing wireless networks can be used for positioning services. Particularly cellular networks are suitable for this purpose because the cell identification already transports a rough location (COO). Additional mechanisms such as runtime measurement (TOA) or angle measurement (AOA) allow a more exact delimitation of the position.

In the following sections, two systems that use a wireless network to determine positioning are introduced.

7.4.1   GSM

Cellular phone networks are highly available, cover a large geographic area, and reach a high number of mobile users. Cellular phone infrastructures are often viewed as the most promising platforms for LBS. In 2003, more than 1.2 billion people in the world used cellular phones.

A popular standard for cellular phone service is the Global System for Mobile communication (GSM), because it is used in more than 190 countries in the world. Without any further installations, a simple positioning is possible within the GSM network, which knows exactly in which cell which mobile telephone is registered. Any participant who enters a specific area is recorded by a decentralized database called the Visitor Location Register (VLR). This information is then passed to the central database, the Home Location Register (HLR), where it is retrievable. Each cell phone operator has its own HLRs. With this database, simple services can be offered, which are able to locate mobile users with the precision of a cell size.

The mobile participant can also access location-related data via the radio signals from the base stations. A base station can broadcast such data via so-called Cell Broadcast Channels (CBCHs), a logical data channel in the GSM data stream. A mobile phone has to listen for specific frames where small pieces of data, such as locations about the emergency phones, hotels, hospitals, gas station, and so on, can be transferred.

The resolution of the position is too inaccurate for some services. The cell radius varies from less than 1 km in city centers up to 35 km in the countryside. If a mobile user stays in a small cell, the position is relatively exact. The 35 km as a maximum are, however, far too large for most services.

Ericsson developed a system called the Mobile Positioning System (MPS) [MPS01], which makes more exact positioning possible in large cells. MPS cooperates with standard GSM systems and needs only minimal modifications for installation at the communication infrastructure. The mobile terminals (i.e., the cell phones) do not have to be modified. This point is particularly important because customers do not accept cost-intensive modifications of the terminals. The precision by MPS can optionally be improved by GPS, but this is not a mandatory prerequisite.

Among other things, the following applications are conceivable with MPS:

◆ The mobile participant can query (much more exactly than with standard GSM) for location-dependent data (e.g., the location of the nearest restaurant).
◆ Users can supervise the location of other mobile users. A GSM terminal can be installed into a vehicle, for example, so an owner can locate a stolen vehicle. Similarly, repair or rescue services can be guided to accident locations.

- It is important for transportation companies to supervise the locations of available vehicles. So, a cab enterprise can query for the position of all cabs, for example.
- An application for route planning in vehicles can calculate an optimal route to a target and permanently supervise the route used based on the position data.

To compute the positions, MPS uses several mechanisms (Figure 7.9):

- *Cell of Global Identity* (*CGI*) (Figure 7.9a). This mechanism uses the identification of a cell to roughly determine the position of the mobile participant. This inaccurate method is only used if more precise procedures are not available.
- *Segment antennas* (Figure 7.9b). Base stations often have antennas, which divide the 360 degrees into (usually two, three, or four) segments. Thus, a base station can limit the location of a mobile user to an angular segment of 180, 120, or 90 degrees.
- *Timing Advance* (*TA*) (Figure 7.9c). Base stations and mobile terminals use certain time slots for communication. Because the timing must be exact, the mechanism takes into account the signal runtime between terminal and base station. A mobile terminal sends a data burst earlier when the distance to the base station increases. With this mechanism, a burst always arrives at the base station exactly within a time slot. This information can be used to determine the position within a cell more exactly. The distance to the base station is measured in steps of

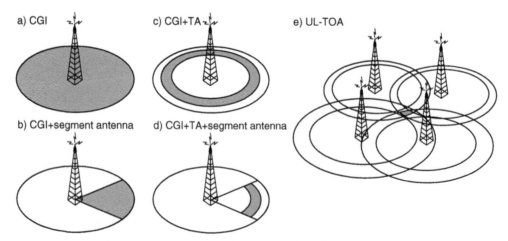

Figure 7.9 Positioning with GSM networks. Adapted from *Mobile Computing* by Jörg Roth, dpunkt-Verlag (2002).

approximately 555 m. Timing advance can be combined with segment antennas to increase precision (Figure 7.9d).

◆ *Uplink Time of Arrival (UL-TOA)* (Figure 7.9e). An even better positioning is possible if a mobile participant is in the reach of at least four base stations. By measuring the signal runtimes from a mobile terminal to the base stations, the position can be determined with a precision of 50 to − 150 m. A similar computation is used as in the case of satellite navigation.

The location data determined by the different procedures are transmitted to the Mobile Positioning Center (MPC). All data are processed and stored temporarily here. If required, other users can access these data (e.g., via the Internet).

Position data often have a personal character. Although position monitoring is desired for certain applications, most mobile participants want to publish their position data only reluctantly. MPS is fundamentally different on this point from GPS, in which only the user gets access to his or her own position data. Especially if position data become accessible over the Internet, a provider must think about access protection, authentication, and data encryption. MPS, therefore, allows access to position data only after authentication via a password.

7.4.2   Wireless LAN

Another positioning system uses an available wireless LAN infrastructure. Inside a building equipped with wireless LAN access points, a mobile user can find out his or her location by measuring the signal strengths of all access points. The idea was prototypically realized by Microsoft [BP99] and very similarly by the Nibble system [Nib01].

Before such a system can be used for positioning, it must be trained. For that purpose, a user visits several locations inside the covered area. For every location, the user makes measurements and stores them in a table using the following method:

◆ The user first has to enter the coordinates (x, y) as well as the orientation (d). Experiments have shown that different orientations lead to different signal strengths. During the training, a user has to execute measurements looking at different directions for a single location. The coordinate system may use a specific corner of the building as (0.0) and an orientation of 0 degrees parallel to a specific wall.

Table 7.2 Sample signal strength measurements.

x/m	y/m	d/°	SS$_1$/dBm	SS$_2$/dBm	SS$_3$/dBm	SS$_4$/dBm
1.0	3.5	0	20	10	18	25
2.0	3.5	90	25	15	17	25
2.5	3.0	90	15	18	16	16
2.5	1.5	180	6	35	18	20
2.0	2.5	0	12	10	22	14

◆ For each way point and orientation, the system measures the signal strengths of all available wireless LAN access points (SS$_i$), which can be identified by their network address. They are particularly differentiated from other wireless LAN transmitters (e.g., from other mobile computers).

A table such as Table 7.2 is built up during the training phase. If a user now wants to know his or her location, the system measures the current signal strengths SS$_i$. The system then looks up a set of signal strengths in the list that are most similar to the real measurement. To look up an appropriate entry, different algorithms are conceivable. The implementation of Microsoft searches the table linearly and finds the data set with the lowest Euclidean distance to the current measuring. In an experiment with a covered area of approximately 43 m by 22 m, a precision of 2 to −3 m was obtained with 70 way points.

If a building is only sparsely equipped with wireless LAN access points, a user often receives only one or two signals. This causes frequent jumps of the location output, even if the user moves only slightly. Another disadvantage of the procedure is the time-consuming training phase, which must be executed for every area in which position measuring shall later take place. Moreover, the training phase must always be executed again if the environmental conditions change (e.g., if new access points were installed).

To avoid the training phase, a program could generate signal strength values with the help of a physical model of the building. The access points, walls, ceilings, and so on must be entered into a program that carries out a physical simulation of the signal spreading. The program can then go through a grid of test points and write down the simulated signal strengths to the table. In experiments, this approach achieved a precision of approximately 4 m.

7.5   CONCLUSION AND OPEN ISSUES

In this chapter, we presented the basic mechanisms, techniques, and systems to capture location data of mobile users. Table 7.3 provides an overview of the presented systems.

Many LBS use GPS to determine the current location. GPS receivers are inexpensive, and the corresponding location output is accurate; thus GPS is widely accepted. GPS has a disadvantage, however: It only works outdoors because the receiver must have a direct view to at least four GPS satellites.

Indoor positioning systems are cost-intensive and require extensive installations. They have a small coverage (e.g., a single building) and provide moderate precision. A compromise between precision and costs may be a system that uses an existing network infrastructure for positioning purposes.

These issues have serious consequences for LBS. Currently, no positioning system is accessible everywhere. If a service wants to have high coverage, it has to rely on several positioning systems. Developers of LBS currently cannot deal with the positioning system as a black box, but rather they have to consider the specific system properties such as precision or coverage.

Table 7.3   Comparison of positioning systems.

Name	Category	Tracking/ Positioning	Mechanism	Medium	Precision
GPS	Satellite	Positioning	TOA	Radio	25 m
DGPS	Satellite	Positioning	TOA	Radio	3 m
WAAS	Satellite	Positioning	TOA	Radio	3 m
Active Badge	Indoor	Tracking	COO	Infrared	Cell
WIPS	Indoor	Positioning	COO	Infrared	Cell
SpotON	Indoor	Tracking	Signal Strength	Radio	3 m
Active Bat	Indoor	Tracking	TOA	Ultrasound/Radio	0.1 m
Cricket	Indoor	Positioning	TOA	Ultrasound/Radio	0.3 m
RFID	Indoor	Tracking	COO	Radio	Cell
Visual Tags	Indoor	Both	Video	Optical	Depends on camera resolution
GSM	Network	Both	COO, AOA, TOA	Radio	Cell, distance in 555 m steps
MPS	Network	Both	COO, AOA, TOA	Radio	150 m
Nibble	Network	Positioning	Signal Strength	Radio	3 m

References

[Ban85]   S. Bancroft. "An Algebraic Solution of the GPS Equations." *IEEE Trans. Aerospace and Electronic Systems*, AES-21(7):56–59, January 1985.

[BP99]   P. Bahl and V. N. Padmanabhan. "User Location and Tracking in an In-Building Radio Network." Microsoft Research Technical Report, MSR-TR-99-12, February 1999.

[DOD01]   Department of Defense. "Global Positioning System: Standard Positioning Service Performance Standard," October 2001.

[EURO98]   EUROCONTROL, European Organization for the Safety of Air Navigation. "WGS 84: Implementation Manual." Brussels, Belgium, February 1998.

[HBW00]   J. Hightower, G. Boriello, and R. Want. "SpotON: An Indoor 3D Location Sensing Technology Based on RF Signal Strength." Technical Report #2000-02-02, University of Washington, February 2000.

[HLC01]   B. Hofmann-Wellenhof, H. Lichtenegger, and J. Collins. *GPS: Theory and Practice*, 5th ed., Springer Verlag, New York, 2001.

[Kap96]   E. D. Kaplan. (Ed.). *Understanding GPS*. Artech House, Boston, 1996.

[MERL01]   Mitsubishi Electric Research Laboratory, *http://www.merl.com/projects/visual-tags*, 2001

[MPS01]   Ericsson, Mobile Positioning, *http://www.ericsson.com/developerszone*

[Nib01]   The Nibble Location System, *http://mmsl.cs.ucla.edu/nibble*

[PCB00]   N. B. Priyantha, A. Chakraborty, and H. Balakrishnan. "The Cricket Location-Support System." In *Proc. 6th Ann. Intl. Conf. on Mobile Computing and Networking*, Boston, Aug. 6–11, 2000.

[Prad00]   S. Pradhan. "Semantic Locations." *Personal Technologies*, 4(4):213–216, 2000.

[RA00]   J. Rekimoto and Y. Ayatsuka. "CyberCode: Designing Augmented Reality Environments with Visual Tags," In *Proc. DARE 2000*, 2000.

[SMR+97]   T. Starner, S. Mann, B. Rhodes, J. Levine, J. Healey, D. Kirsch, R. Picard, and A. Pentland. "Augmented Reality Through Wearable Computing." *Presence*, Special Issue on Augmented Reality, 6(4):386–398, 1997.

[WJH97]   A. Ward, A. Jones, and A. Hopper. "A New Location Technique for the Active Office." *IEEE Personal Communications*, 4(5):42–47, October 1997.

[WHFG92]   R. Want, A. Hopper, V. Falcao, and J. Gibbson. "The Active Badge Location System." *ACM Transactions on Information Systems*, 10(1):91–102, January 1992.

[WIPS00]   Royal Institute of Technology. WIPS Technical Documentation, Schweden, *http://2g1319.ssvl.kth.se/2000/group12/technical.html*

Data Transmission
in Mobile
Communication
Systems

Holger Karl, Technical University Berlin

CONTENTS

8.1 INTRODUCTION

The very concept of location-based services rests on the ability to communicate while being mobile. In traditional tethered communication systems, the need for LBS has never been keenly felt; it only became necessary to consider this concept as communication in a mobile environment became possible. Such mobile communication is enabled by wireless transmission.

On top of wireless transmission, mobile communication systems can be constructed in many different ways, serving many different purposes: Is the goal to provide a large number of (highly) mobile users with a constant quality of the transmission service at moderate data rates (e.g., mobile telephony systems)? Or is the goal to provide high data rates to few, stationary users? Different requirements lead to different types of architectures for mobile communication systems.

LBS can be built on top of many different system architectures. Their common task is to provide communication among different entities, whether they are mobile or fixed, and LBS use this facility to communicate (e.g., position information between a mobile terminal and a distant service provider). But the differences in system architectures will affect what type of communication support LBS can expect (e.g., with regard to the speed and cost of updating location information).

This chapter introduces the basics of the most common architectures of mobile communication systems and examines what functionality they can offer to the realization of LBS. This functionality is neither how location can be determined nor how location information can be used in a meaningful way—both points have been discussed elsewhere in this book—but how to communicate information between two entities that are involved in an LBS interaction.

To put this discussion into context, several design decisions have to be made for a mobile communications system. The most important decisions are the transmission medium to be used, the infrastructure support to be used (if any), and the type of mobility that should be supported. In addition, two large families of system architectures can be distinguished: one has its roots in telecommunication systems, the other in data communication.

The exposition in this chapter will be a rather high-level one, with many simplifications and without going into too many details; the interested reader can find more specific discussions in, for example, [Rapp02], [Schi03], [Stal01], [Stoj02], or [Toh01].

8.1.1 Choice of Transmission Medium

In order to build a wireless communication system, a transmission medium is required that can transport information without requiring a tethered connection between two communicating peers. In principle, different wireless media, such as ultrasound, infrared light, or electromagnetic waves in the radio spectrum, can be used. Each of these media has its specific advantages and disadvantages; however, for the purposes of LBS considered in this book, radio wave communication is the appropriate choice because it can support sufficiently high data rates (between a few kilobits per second up to some tens of megabits per second) over acceptable distances (ranging from a few meters to hundreds of meters or even kilometers) even when the participants are moving about. These properties, however, cannot all be simultaneously maximized; there are some inherent tradeoffs between them, which are discussed in Section 8.2. In brief, the larger the distance or the higher the speed, the lower the possible data rate.

8.1.2 Available Infrastructure

No matter how the tradeoff between data rates, mobility, and range is cast, wireless communication does have a limited range: It is not possible for two arbitrarily distant partners to communicate with each other. Hence, provisions have to be made by a mobile communication system to enable such long-range communication. Essentially, three different approaches can be taken: (1) infrastructure-based systems, (2) ad-hoc multihop systems, and (3) hybrid systems.

INFRASTRUCTURE-BASED SYSTEMS
To overcome the limited range of wireless communication, a wired infrastructure is introduced. A mobile terminal communicates wirelessly with a device, commonly called a base station or an access point, that is connected to a fixed, wired network. Such a base station receives the mobile terminal's wireless communication and sends the data toward its actual destination, which could be another mobile terminal

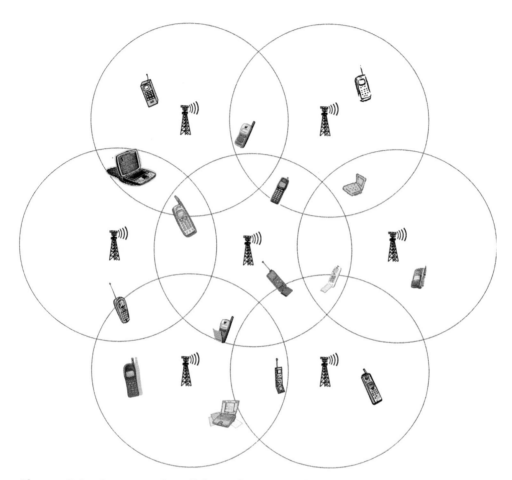

Figure 8.1   Structure of a cellular, infrastructure-based communication system.

communicating with another base station or a device directly located to a tethered network.

The typical structure of such a communication system is shown in Figure 8.1. Each base station covers a certain area (indicated by the dotted circles); for each terminal in this area, the base station ensures that data can be transmitted to and from the wired network. Because these areas are usually called *cells*, this type of system is also often called a *cellular system*.

AD-HOC/MULTIHOP SYSTEMS

An infrastructure is nice if faraway terminals want to communicate with each other. In some scenarios, however, all terminals could talk directly to

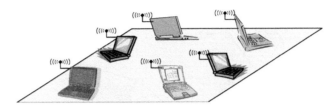

Figure 8.2 A direct-communication ad-hoc network.

each other as they are in their immediate vicinity; think of some laptops in a conference room, exchanging files via a wireless medium. In such a situation, infrastructure is neither necessary nor useful; it is conceptually much simpler to spontaneously set a network between these terminals in an ad-hoc (i.e., "for a specific purpose," "improvised") fashion. Figure 8.2 shows such an ad-hoc network where all terminals communicate directly with each other.

Such ad-hoc networks are even conceivable when the terminals are not all in mutual communication range of each other. A terminal in the middle can then act as a relayer for data coming from one terminal and forward the message toward its destination: a message travels over several radio hops, whereas in an infrastructure-based network, only one or two radio hops (if both sender and receiver are mobile) are used. Typical scenarios for such *multihop ad-hoc* networks are disaster relief operations (e.g., firefighters communicating wirelessly after an earthquake has disrupted existing infrastructure), construction sites or mining operations where setting up infrastructure is not possible, or cars informing each other of the traffic situation ahead (so-called vehicular networks). Figure 8.3 shows an example of such multihop ad-hoc networks; the lines indicate which members of this network can directly communicate with which other members.

A common characteristic of both single and multihop ad-hoc networks is the need to be self-organized in setting up and maintaining the network, without relying on additional outside infrastructure, even though members of the network are moving.

HYBRID SYSTEMS

In some situations, the advantages of infrastructure-based and ad-hoc/ multihop networks can be combined. One problem in cellular systems is illustrated by the terminal in the upper right-hand corner of Figure 8.1: It is unable to communicate with the fixed network because it is too

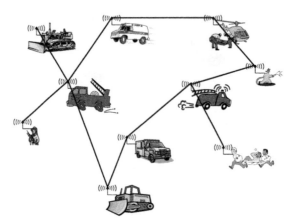

Figure 8.3   A multihop ad-hoc network.

far away even from the nearest base station; however, it could easily communicate with the terminal located between itself and the base station. Adding such multihop communication to cellular networks is a powerful way to widen the coverage area of base stations or to increase the capacity of a single cell.

8.1.3   Types of Wireless Communication and Mobility

The simplest case for wireless communication is to replace cabling: Installing network cabling for a communication network in an old office building can be expensive, but desktop computers still have to be able to access file or email servers. This setup can be realized by wireless communication. Here, the support of mobility is only a secondary concern, but wireless communication can give additional freedom and save costs compared to wireline communication. This scenario is simply called *cable replacement.*

When users of a communication system are mobile, they can require different types of support. The simplest case is that a user does not move while his device is switched on; think of somebody traveling with a laptop, which is switched off during the journey. After having reached his goal, the user's laptop is switched on and he tries to connect to an infrastructure-based or ad-hoc network, reconfiguring the laptop to reflect its change in location. Although in such a scenario it is simple to enable the mobile device to communicate with its environment, the challenge lies in ensuring that other devices can connect to such a mobile device using a well-known identity, irrespective of its current location. This type of mobility support is usually called *nomadic mobility*.

Nomadic mobility becomes truly useful when an additional requirement is made: The terminal should be allowed to stay switched on while moving, and ongoing communication sessions should occur without being disturbed by the mobile device's changing from one base station to another. The best-known example of this situation is telephony calls in cellular communication systems, which go on seamlessly even while the mobile user is moving. This most important type of mobility support is referred to as *true mobility*.

8.1.4   *Architecture Families*

Using radio-frequency-based wireless communication to support mobile devices has been pursued by the telecommunication industry and the data communication industry, resulting in somewhat different system architectures.

The telecommunication industry extended its fixed-network telephony systems to the wireless case to support mobile telephony users. Hence, the developed system architecture is an infrastructure-based system that guarantees—as far as possible—a quality of service that is appropriate for phone calls, supports a large number of users, provides full coverage to large geographic areas, and contains mechanisms for accounting, charging, authorization, and so on. Several generations of these systems have been standardized, including specifications for both the wireless communication as such and for the architecture of the infrastructure and for the management of mobility. These systems include the well-known GSM and UMTS systems, described in more detail in Section 8.3.

The data communication industry, on the other hand, focused on developing a wireless extension to the Internet. One concern is the wireless communication itself: Wireless counterparts to wireline local area networks have been developed, providing support for a small number of users in a small geographic area with only modest quality-of-service guarantees (if any at all), but at data rates much higher than the telephony-based systems and at much lower infrastructure costs. These wireless local area networks (WLANs) are described in detail in Section 8.4. This approach integrates easily into the existing Internet network; however, it provides only limited mobility support. Separate mechanisms for mobility support have been developed and are explained in Section 8.5.

Besides these infrastructure-based, wireless Internet developments, the concept of ad-hoc networks has found a much broader echo in the data communication community than within the telecommunication community. Hence, most ad-hoc developments are today driven by an Internet way of thinking; some basic ideas are described in Section 8.6.

For all of these three architecture families, the following sections describe their basic mode of operation. The primary goal is to point out what characteristics of these networks are relevant for LBS by answering the following questions:

- What are the consequences of a particular architecture for the generation of location information?
- Where is that information available?
- How can it be accessed and how long does it take?
- What type of communication service (in terms of bandwidth, delay, dependability, cost) can a particular system offer?
- Do these basic communication parameters allow certain types of location-based applications to be realized at all?

In addition to these architectural considerations, Section 8.7 looks at the location problem from a somewhat different perspective: Determine a "location" in a more general sense based on the available services. But first, the next section gives a brief overview of the basics of wireless communication.

8.2   BASICS OF WIRELESS COMMUNICATION

Wireless communication has two essential problems to solve: (1) how to communicate data between a source and a destination, and (2) how to organize multiple sources that want to send at the same time. This section looks at these two problems in turn.

8.2.1   Wireless Communication Between a Single Sender and Receiver

The basic task of digital wireless communication is to transmit data between a single sender and a single receiver. This communication takes place by the sender generating a sine-shaped electromagnetic wave. The basic property that is exploited is the possibility to detect this wave at a receiver. Moreover, not only the presence of such a radio signal can be detected by the receiver, but it is even possible (with a limited accuracy, as discussed following) to reconstruct the shape of the wave the sender has generated. Hence, by judiciously choosing the shape of such a wave, digital information—zeros and ones—can be transmitted.

Consider a simple example: Sender and receiver agree to use a certain frequency and to represent bit values by the amplitude of the sine-shaped signal: a high amplitude lasting for a certain, fixed amount of time T_0 represents a bit value of "1", a low amplitude represents a bit value of "0". Figure 8.4 exemplifies the transmission of the bit sequence "10010." The amplitude of the signal generated by the sender is shown over time, which is measured in multiples of T_0. The receiver can detect the pattern of large and small amplitudes and can hence reconstruct the transmitted bit sequence. Shaping the form of a sine wave is called *modulation*; this particular example is the so-called Amplitude Shift Keying, as only the amplitude of the sine wave is manipulated to represent information. Other, more powerful modulations exist but are not discussed here.

In reality, the receiver's task is not quite so simple. Some problems common to both wired and wireless communication arise, such as how to decide when a bit actually starts (when to look for high or low signal levels?); these aspects are not considered here. In addition, the receiver faces some problems that are mainly caused by the wireless nature of the communication or are aggravated by it.

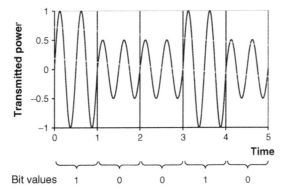

Figure 8.4 Wave generated for the bit sequence 10010 using Amplitude Shift Keying Modulation; time is shown in multiples of bit time T_0, power showing relative to the maximal transmission power.

The first of these problems is that a wireless receiver will not see the identical shape of the signal the sender transmitted. A wireless communication is always exposed to electromagnetic noise (i.e., random oscillations in the receiver circuitry that materialize in small, random deviations of the received signal from the transmitted signal). As a consequence, the decisions whether to decide on a "0" or "1" bit for a particular time period T_0 is no longer certain. Evidently, the degree of uncertainty depends on the relative size of the random oscillations compared to the actually received signal.

Whether a given level of noise is detrimental to a data transmission depends on the strength of the received signal: a more powerful signal can be correctly detected when a weaker one cannot. Formally, this is expressed by the notion of a *signal-to-noise (S/N) ratio*. For a given modulation, the S/N ratio corresponds to the probability with which bits will be incorrectly received—the *bit error rate*.

The strength of the signal arriving at the receiver, in turn, depends on the power that the sender used to transmit the signal, but also on the distance between sender and receiver: Think of the sender as a point-shaped source of electromagnetic radiation. In free space, the power emanated by this source distributes to the surface of a growing sphere as the electromagnetic wave moves away from the sender. Hence, the amount of power that arrives at a surface of constant size (i.e., the receiver's antenna) decreases as this receiving surface is moved away from the sender. More precisely, when the distance is doubled, the arriving power is reduced to one-quarter. This effect of reduced arriving power is called *attenuation*. Putting noise, S/N ratio, and attenuation together, Figure 8.5 shows two examples for small and large amounts of noise where the noise is either small or large compared to the maximal received power.

On one hand, a relationship exists between the S/N ratio and the bit error rate. On the other hand, the received signal depends on the transmitted power and the distance. As the bit error rate basically determines (for a given frequency usage) the amount of data that can be successfully transmitted per unit time—the *throughput*—communication over larger distances requires an increase in transmitted power. Arbitrarily increasing this power is not possible because of both physical and legal limitations. Hence, a direct relationship exists between distance and achievable throughput. A similar relationship exists between speed and throughput: the higher the speed, the lower the achievable throughput

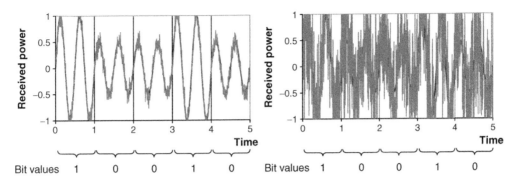

Figure 8.5 Noisy signal seen by the receiver for different signal-to-noise ratios; time is shown in multiples of bit time T_0, power showing relative to the maximal received power.

(this effect is essentially caused by Doppler shifts at the receiver but is beyond the scope of this overview).

But what to do when a higher throughput is desired for a given distance? One possibility is to use modulations that represent more than a single bit in a single period T_0 (e.g., one that distinguishes between four instead of two amplitude levels). The receiver's task to distinguish between these additional possibilities now becomes more difficult, so a better S/N ratio will be necessary to obtain the same bit error rate as before, which in turn requires a larger transmitted power. Another possibility is to use more than a single frequency to transmit information. In principle, a sender can use multiple frequencies to independently transmit information to the receiver in parallel; however, because the frequency range is limited and it is used for many different purposes (e.g., television), frequencies have to be carefully arbitrated among these purposes, especially because not all frequency ranges are equally well suited for all application types.

What makes a frequency range suitable for mobile communication systems are two properties: (1) the amount of data that can be transported with it—it increases with the frequency—and (2) its ability to reach receivers that do not have a straight, *line-of-sight* communication path to their sender: to penetrate walls or to "look around corners." This ability is the result of four essential propagation characteristics of electromagnetic waves: (1) the *shadowing* of waves by obstacles such as a wall or a car, (2) the *reflection* of waves at such objects, (3) *the scattering* of waves at small openings or edges of objects, and (4) the related effect of *diffraction*, which makes wave fronts "bend" at the edge of large objects. All of these effects result in wave propagation paths in addition to the direct line-of-sight

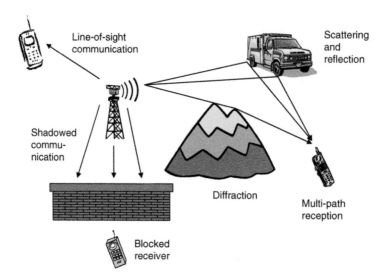

Figure 8.6   Examples of different wave propagation patterns between sender and receiver.

between sender and receiver, the so-called *multipath propagation*. Figure 8.6 shows various examples of these propagation conditions.

These wave-typical propagation effects enable the construction of large-scale communication systems: It is not necessary to place a base station in every little corner or behind every building. Because these effects, on the other hand, are quite different for different frequencies, they limit the range of useful frequencies. Frequencies above about 5 GHz, for example, hardly penetrate walls; even higher frequencies practically behave like light. These frequencies are therefore at best usable for indoor communication systems. Frequencies below about 800 MHz do not provide sufficient bandwidth to communicate with acceptable data rates. Hence, mobile communication systems typically use frequencies between 800 MHz and 5 GHz. Because of legal restrictions and reservations for other applications (e.g., digital radio and television broadcasting), only the frequencies around 900 MHz and 1800 MHz are used for large-scale, outdoor communication systems; the frequencies around 2.4 GHz and 5 GHz are used for medium- and short-range communication systems.[1]

These wave propagation effects are also disadvantageous. In the presence of multipath propagation, it becomes difficult for a receiver to

---

1. The precise numbers vary somewhat among different countries.

correctly decode an incoming transmission as the same signal arrives over different paths of different lengths and, hence, at different times; the signal interferes with itself. For determining locations, this is particularly cumbersome. Whereas in a simple line-of-sight scenario it would be possible to determine the distance from a sender based on the attenuation of the transmitted signal, this is not possible when the signal is reflected and diffracted a couple of times and travels over possibly many different paths. It would perhaps still be possible to determine the length of the signal path, but this has little to do with the geographic distance between sender and transmitter.

Moreover, the simple attenuation model discussed previously (doubling the distance reduces the received power to one-quarter) is also not true in realistic settings: A wave penetrating a wall is much more strongly attenuated than one passing through air; diffraction and scattering also cost power. A simple attenuation model will therefore not result in correct estimations of the distance between sender and receiver. Because of reflection, scattering, and diffraction, the direction from which waves arrive is also at best a misleading indicator of the direction of the sender, unless the line-of-sight communication path dominates.

In summary, wireless, radio-frequency-based communication is a powerful tool to build communication systems; however, many difficulties and pitfalls have to be tackled to enable communication even between a single sender and receiver. The following subsection looks at the problem of how to organize communication between several senders and receivers.

8.2.2 Link Layer for Multiparty Wireless Communication

When multiple senders desire to transmit to their receivers at the same time, a problem familiar from a cocktail party arises: If two senders transmit their signals at the same time to a single receiver, this receiver will see only a very noisy transmission as the two senders interfere with each other's transmissions. No communication will be possible, so at any one time, only a single sender should attempt to communicate with a given receiver.

The same is true for two senders A and B that want to communicate with receivers C and D, respectively (see example scenario in Figure 8.7). Again, A's transmission would add to the noise that receiver D observes

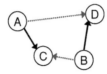

Figure 8.7   Two pairs of nodes attempting to communicate at the same time (black arrows indicate useful transmission, red arrows indicate interference).

and make B's transmission more error-prone.[2] Consequently, the transmissions of multiple senders need to be organized so they do not interfere with each other. This organization is called the *medium access problem*: the wireless medium must only be accessed by a single entity at a time.

Two questions have to be answered: (1) Which entities perform this organization? and (2) What are the possibilities to organize transmissions so that inference is avoided? The first question can be answered with either a centralized scheme—one entity controls several other entities—or a distributed scheme, in which all entities attempt to collaboratively solve the medium access problem. These two options are typically, but not necessarily, reflected by the choice between cellular and ad-hoc-type architectures and are described in these sections, respectively.

Avoiding interference can also be done in essentially two different ways. One option is again analogous to the behavior of polite people at a cocktail party: When one person speaks, nobody else does; the wireless medium is accessed by only a single terminal at a time. Because time for access is divided between multiple users of the medium, this approach is called *time division multiple access* (*TDMA*). Alternately, different senders could use different frequencies for communication as a receiver can "concentrate" on a particular frequency and suppress the interference that is generated by transmissions on other frequencies. This approach is called *frequency division multiple access* (*FDMA*). FDMA can be combined with the fact that radio transmissions are attenuated over distance: Two sender/receiver pairs that are sufficiently far apart can use the same frequency at the same time without interfering with each other. In this sense, a frequency can be reused at different points in space. This

---

2. Strictly speaking, treating noise and interference the same is not entirely correct because their quantitative consequences are somewhat different, but this level of detail suffices for the purposes of this book.

approach is called *space division multiple access* (*SDMA*) and is extensively used in cellular mobile communication systems where neighboring cells use different frequencies for all terminals within the cell, and the same frequency is reused in distant cells according to a fixed pattern.[3]

Once a communication between two entities A and B has been granted according to these multiple access rules, communication can happen only in one direction (*simplex*) or in both directions (*duplex*) between A and B. Similarly to the multiple access system, duplex communication can be organized in time (*time division duplex*, *TDD*)—A and B take turns in sending to each other—or in frequency (*frequency division duplex*, *FDD*)—A and B both send signals the entire time but use different frequencies. Different combinations of multiple access and duplex rules are useful and in use.

Solving the medium access and duplex problem enables the abstraction of a logical link between any two entities. On top of these basic problems, such a link has to be managed, and the transmissions over such a link have to be organized. For example, protocols that proscribe the retransmission of an incorrectly received packet are part of this logical link control layer.

Although these link-layer issues are problems at a rather low abstraction layer, their impact is felt in the design of the entire mobile communication system. In particular, the error-prone nature of a wireless link results in either lost packets or a large variance of the time that is required to transmit a packet over a wireless link if link-layer retransmissions are used. Also, the difficulties in organizing the medium access for a wireless system result in either a flexible system with highly variable medium access times or a strictly organized, hence predictable but inflexible system. Guaranteeing certain levels of quality of service in such systems becomes challenging, and the resulting quality has to be traded off against flexibility and efficiency. The system architectures described in the following sections make different decisions about these tradeoffs.

8.3 CELLULAR-TYPE MOBILE COMMUNICATION SYSTEMS

The original motivation for the design and construction of large-scale mobile communication systems was the support of mobile telephony as

---

3. More complicated approaches, in particular, code division multiple access (CDMA), are beyond the scope of this chapter.

an additional service provided by the traditional telephone network operators. To sell such a service, two conditions were considered important: (1) the mobile communication should provide full coverage (i.e., it should be possible to use a mobile phone anywhere), and (2) the phone calls should have (at least almost) the quality of fixed-network calls, necessitating good quality-of-service support. Moreover, mobile communication should be seamless in the sense that a phone call should not be interrupted by user movement.

A first generation of analog mobile communication systems did not meet all of these requirements. In 1982, development of a second-generation digital communication system was begun, later to be called Global System for Mobile Communication (GSM). GSM is standardized by the European Telecommunication Standards Institute (ETSI), *http://www.etsi.org;* much information about GSM can be found in [GSMA] or [EV99].

These requirements for GSM resulted in the design of a cellular network in which the coverage for mobile user terminals is provided by a sufficient number of base stations (similar to the structure sketched in Figure 8.1). Determining this base station number is a first challenge: Fewer stations result in a cheaper infrastructure but also in larger cells, which can support only a limited number of simultaneous calls, whereas smaller cells are both more expensive and powerful. A heterogeneous cell structure is therefore used: many small cells with many base stations in urban areas with lots of potential customers (typical cell diameters are around a few hundred meters); fewer, larger cells in rural areas (with cell diameters up to 30 kilometers) with a small expected number of simultaneous calls. Because membership of a mobile station within a cell is a rough indicator of location, provided the base stations' positions are known, such a heterogeneous structure results in different resolutions of location information.

With voice as the main application, both the fixed and the wireless part of the GSM network were built to support connections with periodic transmission of small data packets; voice transmissions in fixed networks traditionally consist of 8000 samples per second at 8 bits each, resulting in a total data rate of 64 kbits/second. For the fixed network part, the existing circuit-switched architecture of the fixed telephony network was largely reused. In addition, the GSM network had to ensure that connections were maintained when a mobile user left the coverage area of a single base station by performing a so-called handover of a connection from one base station to another.

In later development, the desire for better support of data communication appeared. Although a circuit-switched architecture can easily provide modemlike data communication, the resulting through-put, costs, and flexibility are not convincing. Therefore, additions to GSM were made to allow simpler and cheaper data communication, in particular, to avoid charging for the connection time but rather to enable a charging mode for the amount of transmitted data to enable an "always on" usage model. These extensions are commonly referred to as 2.5 G systems.

The third generation of mobile communication is targeted to fully integrate voice- and data-type communication as well as to enable greater flexibility in the radio access technology. The Universal Mobile Telecommunication System (UMTS) is currently expected to fulfill this promise.

The following subsections describe these three main generations of mobile communication systems in more detail.

8.3.1 The Second Generation: GSM

GSM organizes the network in several levels of hierarchy to contain complexity. At the bottom are the mobile stations (MS), each of which is in contact with a base transceiver station (BTS). The BTS comprises the actual radio and signal processing equipment but does not contain protocol functions (e.g., for the link layer). These functions are performed for a set of BTSs by a base station controller (BSC). These entities together are responsible for the actual radio functionalities; mobility-specific tasks are provided by the mobile services switching centers (MSCs), where again several BSCs are assigned to an MSC. Some of these MSCs can act as gateway MSCs (GMSC) and provide interconnection with outside networks such as the fixed telephone network. In addition to these active components, a GSM network contains a home location register (HLR) database and, separately for each MSC, a visitor location register (VLR). Figure 8.8 gives an overview of the basic GSM entities. Moreover, a GSM network has several entities used for operations, maintenance, and security, which are not discussed here.

The tasks of these entities are best explained in action. The most relevant events are the setup of a call originating from a mobile station or

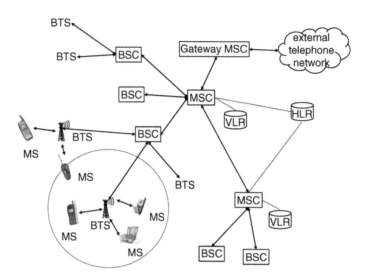

Figure 8.8 GSM network architectural overview (solid lines indicate data flow, dotted lines indicate control flow).

from outside and the handover of an ongoing call when a mobile station moves (the description here is simplified and omits many details; more information can be found, e.g., in [Schi03]).

A mobile-originated call (MOC) to a terminal in the fixed network starts by the MS contacting the MSC via the BTS and BSC, asking for a new connection. The MSC checks the MS's eligibility for such a call by consulting the terminal information in its VLR and checks resource availability within the GSM network. If all checks succeed, the connection into the fixed telephone network is set up.

Setting up a mobile-terminated call (MTC) is more complicated, especially because for an incoming call, the mobile terminal's serving BTS has to first be identified before a connection can be set up. To facilitate this lookup, a moving terminal keeps information about its whereabouts approximately up-to-date in the HLR and VLR databases, even if it is not currently engaged in an ongoing call: An MS X that is turned on registers with the BSC in charge of the BTS with which the MS is in radio contact. The BSC informs its MSC about the fact that X is now in range; the MSC enters this information into its own VLR and updates the HLR (for details see [Schi03]).

Once a gateway MSC receives a connection setup request for MS X, it first contacts the HLR to learn about the MSC where the MS has last been seen. The gateway then contacts this MSC, which then could forward this connection setup to the BSC/BTS where X is currently located. This would require X to always keep its MSC entries up to date, even when just moving to another BTS. To save on signaling costs, X updates its information only infrequently, and as a consequence, the MSC has to *page* X in all of its cells. After X has received such a paging request, it answers the MSC with enough information to allow the connection to be set up.

After a connection has been set up, it has to be maintained even while an MS moves around. Here, the hierarchical structure of the GSM network is helpful. As long as a terminal moves within the coverage area of a single BTS, only actions on a physical/signal-processing level are potentially necessary—a reaction to such a movement is usually not referred to as a handover. If an MS moves to a cell the BTS of which is still controlled by the original BSC, only this BSC is involved in rerouting a connection to the new BTS. Similarly, if an MS moves to a cell that belongs to another BSC but to the same MSC, the rerouting is done in the MSC. In all cases, the rest of the GSM network is unaware of the movement. Only if the MS is switched between cells that belong to different MSCs is more action required. In such a case, the original MSC remains part of the call and only forwards the call to the new MSC; the rationale is to again shield the rest of the network from the effects of mobility and to have the first MSC involved in a call as a stable anchor point for the outside. The original state and the situation after these three types of handovers are shown in Figure 8.9.

The link layer of a GSM network is organized to support this connection-oriented fixed network: For each MS, a connection to the BTS has to be set up, which essentially corresponds to a certain time slot in a TDMA structure.[4] Because supporting the traditional 64 kbits/second data rate over a wireless channel is expensive, lower data rates were used for voice communication, enabled by advanced voice coding techniques. Most GSM networks hence use 13,000 bit/second for a voice call.

For data communication, an even smaller data rate is available: only 9600 bit/second are available using a single connection. Moreover, because of the voice-oriented structure of the link layer (especially the interleaving of channels), high delays are incurred even for small packets.

---

4. In addition, GSM uses frequency hopping for the individual terminals to protect against narrowband interference.

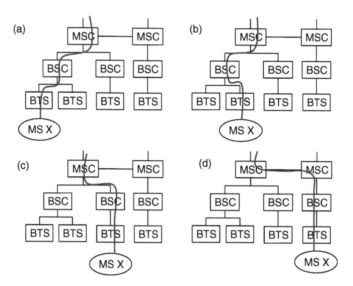

Figure 8.9 Connection after three different handovers in a GSM network: (a) original state, (b) handover between cells of the same BTS, (c) handover between BSCs of the same MSC, handover between cells of different MSCs.

Delays between 60 and 100 milliseconds have to be added to the delay a packet encounters in the fixed network. This would still enable modem-type communication, but this communication model is ill-suited for many data-driven applications: Either a connection has to be open and paid for the entire time, which is expensive, or a connection has to be opened any time data are to be transmitted (e.g., when a user wants to check email), which is time-consuming. Frequently transmitting small amounts of data, which would be useful in particular for LBS, is not well supported or too expensive by the original GSM standard. Therefore, some extensions to GSM have been developed.

8.3.2   Between Generations: GSM Extensions

To better support data communication, GSM has been extended by three main developments (see e.g., [GSMA] for an overview; the standards are available via the ETSI Web site, *http://www.etsi.org*):

◆ *High-speed circuit-switched data (HSCSD).* By using better coding techniques, the data rate of a single connection is increased from 9.6 kbits/second to 14.4 kbits/second. In addition, HSCSD easily enables higher data rates by bundling several modem connections into a single logical connection. HSCSD offers a choice of several possible data rates up to 57.6 kbits/second, but the main disadvantages of GSM—cost and inflexibility—are not solved because HSCSD is still a circuit-switched concept. The advantage is that the necessary changes to an existing GSM infrastructure to introduce HSCSD are small, but new mobile terminal equipment is required.

◆ *Enhanced Data Rates for GSM Evolution (EDGE)*. By further improving channel coding and modulation techniques, the data rates of a single connection can be pushed up to 59.2 kbits/second. These advanced modulation and coding techniques are only possible when the channel between the mobile station and the base station is very good. Consequently, only users close to a base station are likely to benefit from EDGE. By using channel combining such as in HSCSD, theoretical data rates of up to 473.6 kbits/second could be achievable; in practice, data rates of up to 170 kbits/second are expected. EDGE will require extensive changes both to mobile stations and to base stations to be implemented in an existing GSM system.

◆ *General Packet Radio Service (GPRS)*. To overcome the disadvantages of circuit-switched communication and to enable a better integration of mobile communication systems with the Internet, GPRS amends a GSM network with a *packet-switched* network. With packet switching, a mobile station does not have to set up a connection to occasionally send or receive a packet, but can do so whenever data become available. The charging model, correspondingly, can be applied only to the amount of data that is actually transmitted, enabling an always-on usage pattern. GPRS can and typically will be combined with extended data rate via the wireless link, where the allocation of data rates for sending and receiving need not be symmetric—typical values like 53 kbits/second for receiving and 26 kbits/second for sending are expected [Roth02, p. 65].

◆ In addition, GPRS allows specifying different *quality-of-service profiles*, which proscribe service precedence, the user data throughput, a choice between three reliability classes, and several delay classes. The delay classes in particular will have a keenly felt impact on the practical usage because the GPRS standards only put rather weak demands on their implementations that will likely be quite different from the behavior of a fixed Internet. Table 8.1 lists the delay values that the standard proscribes for two different packet sizes. As the table shows, even for low delay classes, there is a considerable chance that the

Table 8.1 Delay classes specified for GPRS (from [Schi03, p. 110]).

Delay class	Packet size 128 byte	Packet size 1024 byte		
	Mean	95% percentile	Mean	95% percentile
1	<0.5 s	<1.5 s	<2 s	<7 s
2	<5 s	<25 s	<15 s	<75 s
3	<50 s	<250 s	<75 s	<375 s
4	Unspecified			

packets will be substantially delayed. This fact renders highly interactive application patterns, which are likely typical for LBS, problematic.

♦ In addition, the variance of the packet delays can be quite high as the differences between the mean and the 95% percentile demanded by the standard is quite high. Large variance in packet delays is a difficult problem for many higher-layer protocols such as TCP to cope with. Actual measurements with the first instances of such GPRS systems corroborate the presence of highly variable delay or roundtrip times.

In summary, GSM extensions will increase the speed of wireless communication, and packet-switched communication is a much more natural fit with the Internet service model. The hope is that GPRS will bring the Internet's success to wide-area mobile telecommunication systems; however, because of the tradeoffs between cost, reliability, throughput, and, most important, delay, a user will still feel quite a difference between mobile and fixed usage. When designing applications such as LBS, these restrictions have to be considered.

8.3.3 The Third Generation: UMTS

In the 1990s, development and standardization of the follow-up mobile communication after GSM was begun. The International Telecommunications Union (ITU), which is responsible for the world-wide standardization of telecommunication, issued a call for proposals for International Mobile Telecommunications 2000 (IMT-2000), which resulted in several proposals, in particular, the European Universal Mobile Telecommunications System (UMTS) proposal prepared by ETSI.

The vision of UMTS is to build a uniform system for mobile multimedia communication, transcending the limited services offered by existing mobile communication systems. UMTS is supposed to integrate various access technologies (e.g., the existing wireless GSM- or WLAN-based technologies) as well as to-be-developed radio access technologies but also wired access systems, and various backbone networks for the interconnection of base stations (e.g., the legacy GSM systems along with TCP/IP-based networks). This integration should adapt to both user needs and technical/financial feasibility in a fine-granular fashion: Urban environments are provided with high data rates for slowly mobile users, and rural highways provide access for quickly moving users at data rates exceeding what would be possible today. This progress is expected to be provided by the UMTS terrestrial radio access (UTRA), which should realize data rates of up to 384 kbits/second at 500 km/h and 2 Mbits/second at pedestrian speeds.

This technical access diversity has its counterpart in a diverse set of services and quality-of-service levels that should be enabled by UMTS. Four main service classes have been identified: (1) *conversational* for applications such as telephony or video conferencing, (2) *streaming* for the jitter-sensitive download of real-time data feeds, (3) *interactive* for low-bandwidth, terminal-type applications, and (4) *background* for noncritical applications such as email download.

These service classes highlight a main trend in the philosophy of UMTS: the tight integration of traditional voice and data applications. Whereas GSM had a purely circuit-switched backbone network, enhanced by an additional packet-switched network via GPRS, the entire fixed network structure of UMTS will be based on Internet protocols (a so-called all IP network), although several quality-of-service problems for such a network have yet to be solved to provide comparable service to a circuit-switched network. The practical consequences for the performance of future UMTS networks for data applications is so far undetermined, but the hope is justified that the unsatisfactory performance of GPRS will be improved upon. At what price, however, is not yet clear.

8.4 WIRELESS LOCAL AREA NETWORKS

The systems discussed so far were designed to support wide-area communication for mobile terminals moving at high speeds and applications with modest data rates, typically telephone calls. The heritage and philosophy of these systems clearly stems from the fixed telephony systems.

Besides telephone systems, data communication via the Internet is the second largest communication system used worldwide. Similar to the telephone companies, the Internet community also went wireless, but with a different emphasis: The original interest was on replacing cabling for end systems (e.g., computers or laptops) in a local area, building wireless local area networks (WLANs) as a counterpart to the well-known wired LANs such as Ethernet. Consequently, the requirements were to support medium to high data rates over short to medium distances— some tens of meters—and a smooth integration into existing data communication systems; mobility support was only a secondary concern. The intended application areas for these systems are the support of data communication in environments such as offices, homes, and factories as well as so-called hot spots such as railway stations, coffee shops, or airports, where many people are likely to demand high data rates but are moving at pedestrian speed at most.

The resulting system concept therefore uses an access point (AP) to connect wireless terminals with a fixed network infrastructure. Similar to the cellular systems discussed previously, such an AP forms a cell for the terminals in its vicinity. From an architectural point of view, such an AP fulfills functions comparable to an Ethernet switch: It offers connectivity to the fixed network and the forwarding of packets to their destination; a terminal is itself responsible for finding an appropriate AP. Within a local network, several APs can be in use (e.g., to cover different floors of an office building). The APs along with other switches and routers act as the infrastructure for such a network. Figure 8.10 illustrates such a structure.

The main conceptual differences between the wide-area cellular networks and the WLAN systems are on one hand a much stronger symmetry within the equipment used in WLAN systems than in wide-area networks: Both terminals and APs typically use identical wireless communication equipment, and it is simply a matter of configuring which entity acts as an AP. On the other hand, the careful planning and organization of GSM-type networks are usually absent in WLAN systems. Whereas in GSM the placement of and resource assignments (e.g., frequencies) to base stations are carefully planned, WLAN APs tend to be installed in a much more random, ad-hoc fashion. Moreover, the radio frequencies that are available for WLANs (in the 2.4- and 5-GHz range) belong to the so-called Industrial, Scientific, and

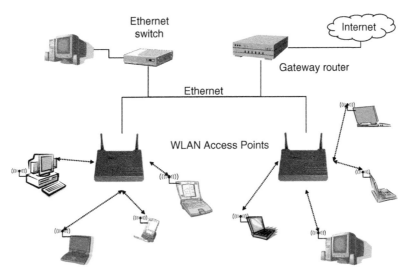

Figure 8.10 Network structure with two access points, connecting several wireless terminals to an Ethernet local area network.

Medical band (ISM) and are open for usage. Hence, when installing a WLAN, one cannot be sure that there will be no interference from other sources.

This uncontrolled environment has consequences for the design of the lower layers of a WLAN system. For example, a tightly scheduled and planned link layer such as in GSM would not be feasible because it has to coexist with other systems using the same radio resources. A WLAN system should also be able—to a large extent—to manage and organize itself (e.g., to select a frequency that is least prone to disturbances from other systems). Today's WLAN systems fulfill many, but not all, of these requirements.

Two main families of WLANs can be distinguished: the ETSI proposal HiperLAN/2 and the IEEE 802.11 family of WLAN standards [IEEE99], [IEEE02]. Whereas the former is often considered to be technically superior and to offer better quality-of-service support, the latter IEEE 802.11 family dominates the market. This system deserves a more detailed description.

8.4.1 IEEE 802.11

The IEEE 802.11 WLAN family, with the two most important members being 802.11b and 802.11a (plain IEEE 802.11 is hardly relevant any longer), is part of the IEEE 802 system concept and hence covers the two lowest layers—physical and link layers—of the ISO/OSI layering structure. The physical layer differs between the various family members (IEEE 802.11b uses direct sequence spread spectrum, IEEE 802.11a orthogonal frequency division multiplexing) and offers different maximum data rates: up to 11 MBits/second for 802.11b and 54 MBits/second for 802.11a; in practice, data rates of no more than 7 to 8 MBits/second and around 35 to 40 MBits/second, respectively, can be expected. Both 802.11 variants contain mechanisms for adapting the data rate to the distance between sender and receiver: 40 MBits/second are only feasible over a few meters, but 1 to 2 MBits/second can be realized over 100 to 200 meters in otherwise good conditions.

The IEEE 802.11 systems offer two different link layers. One of them, the point coordination function (PCF), puts the AP in control over when a given terminal is allowed to access the wireless medium. The goal is to be able to guarantee certain quality-of-service properties by ensuring that each terminal can obtain medium access within a bounded amount of time.

The second link layer, distributed coordination function (DCF), does not use a specific participant as a controller but solves the medium access problem in a distributed fashion: A terminal desiring to send a packet checks whether it can overhear an ongoing transmission. If no transmission is detected for a certain time, the terminal should be allowed to send at once; however, two nearby terminals waiting for an ongoing transmission to end would then be guaranteed to collide. Hence, a terminal has to wait for an additional random time before starting to send. Acknowledgments for a received packet can be sent immediately after a packet to avoid having to compete for medium access again. DCF is enhanced with some other mechanisms to ensure fairness (a backoff timer) or to solve the "hidden terminal" scenario (i.e., two stations can communicate with a third one but not with each other) by employing a simple, temporary channel reservation scheme (the RTS/CTS mechanism).

In most current implementations of IEEE 802.11, the DCF mechanism is used. An important advantage of DCF is its aptitude for ad-hoc deployment, which is discussed in Section 8.6. On the downside, DCF imposes considerable overhead for medium access, which (partly) explains why IEEE 802.11 systems do not nearly realize the physical layer's potential throughput at higher layers. Unlike GSM-type systems, however, IEEE 802.11 systems are naturally packet-switched systems, and as such are a natural fit with Internet applications. Their short range also allows them to easily derive a rough estimate of terminal position from an AP's position.

A major shortcoming of IEEE 802.11 systems is that they lack mobility support. As long as a terminal moves within the coverage area of an AP, the data rate adaptation ensures that the terminal is still connected with the best possible data rate. A terminal moving from one AP to another in the same subnet can still be provided with access under an identical IP address by using ARP/RARP mechanisms, but how to handle long-distance mobility in an IP context deserves a closer look.

8.5   INTERNET-BASED MOBILE COMMUNICATION

In a network based on the Internet protocol suite, a terminal is identified by its IP address. Other entities that want to communicate with a terminal use this address to send a data packet to the terminal. When a terminal moves around, it would be desirable for this address to remain unchanged so that packets sent to the mobile terminal will still arrive correctly. An unchanged IP address would allow terminals communicating with the mobile terminal—so-called corresponding terminals—to be oblivious of the movement.

But the IP address is not only used to identify a terminal; it is also used to route a data packet toward the place in the (fixed) network where the terminal is located. The address encodes network-specific and host-specific information from which intermediate routers can decide where to send a packet. Once a packet has arrived at the last hop, the host-specific part of the address can be used to send the packet to the intended host.

The conflict an IP-based mobility approach has to solve is thus the duality of an IP address: It represents both the identity of a terminal and its location in the network topology. On one hand, the identity should not change to maintain communication with corresponding notes, but on the other hand, the location information must be topologically correct so that packets are not sent to the wrong part of the IP network. Such an approach should, moreover, be transparent for corresponding nodes in that they should not be involved in the management of mobility; it should be scalable and limit the required signaling overhead as well.

One such solution is the Mobile IP approach [Perk96], [Perk02], [JPA02], [IETF02]. It exists in two versions, depending on the version of the underlying IP network (IPv4 or IPv6), which differ in some details but are fundamentally identical; the description here follows Mobile IPv6 (which is still undergoing standardization at the time of this writing). Mobile IP solves the IP's basic dual-address conflict by simply using two different addresses for a mobile terminal. One address is the permanent address—the *home address*—under which the mobile terminal is known to the corresponding terminals and which never changes, no matter where the mobile terminal is located. The second address is a temporary address that is topologically correct and that can be used to route a data packet to the mobile terminal's current location—the *care-of address*. The mapping between these two addresses is done by a proxy for the mobile terminal, the *home agent*, which is located at the topological place of the mobile terminal's home address; typically, the home agent would be integrated into the gateway router for the mobile terminal's home network.

The mobile terminal and the home agent can then together solve the IP mobility problem (compare the overview in Figure 8.11). When the mobile terminal moves to a new AP, it requests a new IP address that is topologically correct for this new AP's network and to which, therefore, IP packets can be sent. The mobile terminal then informs the home agent about its new temporary address. The home agent takes on the role of the

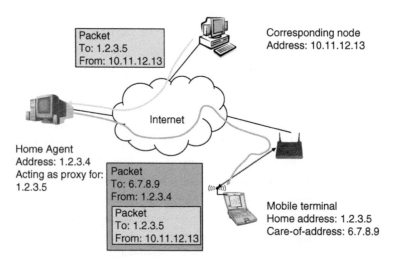

Figure 8.11 Overview of Mobile IPv6.

mobile terminal at its "original" place and intercepts all IP packets that are sent to the mobile terminal's permanent address. The home agent redirects these packets to the mobile terminal's temporary care-of address, where the mobile terminal can receive them. Packets from the mobile terminal to the corresponding node can be sent via the home agent in a similar fashion. Hence, a corresponding node sent the packets to the permanent address, but they arrived successfully at the absent mobile terminal's current location. This solution is transparent both for the corresponding nodes as well as for higher-layer protocols in the mobile terminal (e.g., a transport protocol such as TCP).

Although Mobile IP solves the basic mobility problem, it can be improved upon in different ways. For example, the signaling messages between the mobile terminal and the home agent must potentially travel over large distances in the Internet, incurring high overhead. Similar to GSM, hierarchies for handling local mobility—the most common case—in a local fashion can be constructed by introducing proxies for the home agent within the network [SCEB02]. Also, security and quality-of-service support for Mobile IP–type approaches are still active research areas.

8.6   AD-HOC NETWORKING

Both system concepts discussed so far—the wide-area cellular systems and the wireless LANs—are infrastructure-based. Ad-hoc networks, on the other hand, can solve some communication needs within a group of terminals without recurring to the help of infrastructure. Examples of such ad-hoc networks are disaster relief operations, construction sites, networks between vehicles, or the connection of devices in a personal area network (PAN) into a cellular infrastructure.

Because these ad-hoc networks typically use multihop radio communication—as opposed to the usual single-hop communication between a terminal and a base station/access point—several additional problems have to be solved. Some of these problems have to do with the link layer: It is no longer possible to rely on a central entity to arbitrate the medium access, but rather all entities have to solve it collaboratively. The main problem here is the fact that the sender's observation whether or not the medium is occupied does not necessarily coincide with the medium status at receiver; unlike in a wired network such as Ethernet, the propagation of radio waves is a much more localized phenomenon. As a consequence, issues such as the hidden or exposed terminal problem have to be solved. In practice, link layers such as IEEE 802.11 are capable of solving this problem, but in a dense network with multiple hops, the effective goodput can be severely reduced (e.g., [LDLM01]).

Most of the research in ad-hoc networks, however, has concentrated on solving the routing problem: All terminals together have to ensure that a data packet reaches its destination because all senders and receivers are no longer in mutual radio range of each other. As a result of the specific conditions of an ad-hoc network (mobility of the terminals, terminals failing or being simply turned off) and its environment (changes in the environment impact the neighborhood relationships between terminals), the dynamics of an ad-hoc network are much higher than in fixed networks, and the routing problem is hence much more challenging. Specific routing protocols have been developed that can deal with these idiosyncrasies and achieve reasonable packet delivery rates despite these adverse conditions. A good overview is contained, e.g., in [Toh01].

A specific case of ad-hoc networks are so-called sensor networks [KKP01]: numerous, cheap nodes equipped with simple processing, communication, and sensing capabilities (e.g., temperature) are deployed to form a self-configuring sensor network. Many different application scenarios exist, from environmental control to disaster relief operations and health care. The problems in these sensor networks are somewhat different than in traditional ad-hoc networks in that the required data rates are rather modest (a few kilobits/second), but the scaling requirements are extreme (easily tens of thousands of nodes are projected for typical sensor networks). Because of these large numbers, only the simplest deployment procedures are feasible (e.g., dropping sensors from an airplane over a wildfire), but in typical sensor networks, sensor readings are worthless if the sensor location is not known.

For both ad-hoc and sensor networks, approaches have been developed that can determine the position of nodes in a multihop network even if only a few nodes in the network know their position (e.g., some nodes are equipped with GSM). The idea is to iteratively spread this location information from neighbor to neighbor. Because some nodes will initially have only distance information from a single node with position

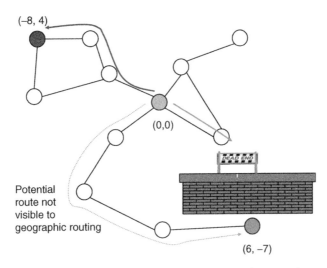

Figure 8.12 Geographic routing example (gray lines indicate nodes in communication range).

information, the challenge lies in building up intermediate information in a fashion that allows reconciling this information when two "waves" of location knowledge meet.

Moreover, in such networks, the location information can actually be used to solve the routing problem. As a typical request could be to communicate with a sensor at (or in the immediate vicinity of) a given position, a simple heuristic is to forward such a request to that node that minimizes the distance to the target. Such geographic routing (e.g., [KV98]) enables powerful routing solutions but has to cope with several potential pitfalls (e.g., obstacles that block the direct way between two nodes and result in a dead end for simple geographic routing protocols). Figure 8.12 shows a simple example: the green node requests information from the blue and red node. While the blue node is easily reachable via simple geographic routing, the red one is blocked, and some mechanism that can find the detour is needed.

In summary, location information in ad-hoc networks is both more difficult to obtain and potentially more useful than in classic mobile communication systems. In addition, making this information available to higher layers is even more challenging because it is not possible to fall back onto databases or other core network entities. Rather, this information has to be maintained and made available in a distributed fashion; it is still an area of much active research.

8.7   LOCATION-BASED SERVICE DISCOVERY

In some situations, a user's location is not so much relevant regarding its absolute position, but rather in the sense that it determines a context from which a user is acting. As a typical example, think of a laptop-equipped user visiting a building where he is allowed to access the network via WLAN. This user might want to print out a document at a close-by printer, but he has no knowledge of how to access such a printer. Manually configuring a printer is cumbersome and error-prone, hence automatic mechanisms are required that enable the laptop to learn which printers are available in such a visited network. Printing a document is but one example of services a network can offer. Other examples include enabling the MP3 player in a PAN to find the earphones; in a sensor network, a mobile user with a PDA should be able to detect which services (temperature or humidity control?) are offered by the sensor network in the first place. Providing information about what services exist and where and how they can be accessed is the task of so-called service location protocols.

In such service location scenarios, the user's location is only implicitly relevant in that it allows determining services that are close-by in a network sense, which does not necessarily coincide with a geographic proximity. For example, the discovered printer might be connected to the same Ethernet network as the AP but placed several floors down, whereas another printer is many network hops away but is located on the same floor. To solve this problem, service location protocols often allow the extension of service location requests by additional attributes such as physical location (e.g., locate a printer, but only one that is located on the second floor).

Service location protocols can be implemented in different ways. Evidently, a global solution is not possible: a database of all the world's printers is undesirable both from a performance standpoint and from a security perspective. Localizing the search for such services is hence required. Such localization fits well with ad-hoc networks and, to a certain degree, with WLAN-based infrastructure networks but is a somewhat more difficult concept in cellular networks; here, the geographic position is often useful information to limit the search for services. In either case, three main approaches can be distinguished:

1. *Request for services are flooded through the entire network.* This is possible and useful if the number of devices is small and the boundary of the network is clearly defined. PANs are an appropriate application domain.

2. *When the network size grows, flooding becomes unattractive.* A possible solution is to introduce a dedicated service directory node that is—by some means—well-known to all other participants. Services can be registered and looked up there. Providing the identity of this node is the challenge here: One option is to leverage configuration protocols (e.g., the Dynamic Host Configuration Protocol (DHCP) [Drom97]) to provide not only an IP address for the mobile node but also the service directory address. An alternative is to search for these nodes by multicast requests to a well-known multicast address (limiting the multicast to an appropriate region is a problem here). A third option is to have the service directory periodically broadcast its identity. Moreover, the service directory can be redundantly implemented to protect against overload and failure. An example of this approach is the IETF-standardized Service Location Protocol (SLP) [GPVD99]. SLP supports registration and lookup of services with multiple service directories; finding the service directories can happen by using multicast in both versions described previously. In addition, SLP supports the concept of scopes, limiting service location requests to given areas of a network.

3. *In some types of networks, having an identifiable service discovery node can be undesirable* (e.g., in sensor networks where nodes often do not have a unique identifier and hence cannot be addressed directly). In such networks, the service discovery has to be distributed. Implementing service discovery on top of sensor-network-specific communication primitives (such as a publish/subscribe infrastructure) is currently an active research area.

No matter how service location protocols are implemented (other examples such as Bluetooth's SDP or Sun's Jini concept [BH00] differ in some details), knowing what services are available in one's vicinity can be an important part of an LBS; however, merging the service information with geographic information is still a question of research and standardization, even though some service location protocols make some first steps in this direction.

8.8 CONCLUSION

This chapter could only give a superficial overview of the basic problems and system designs for mobile communication systems and their consequences for LBS. Some of the physical properties of wireless, radio-based communication (e.g., multipath propagation) pose fundamental problems for determining a terminal's location using the communication system. The fundamental tradeoffs between distance, transmission power/interference, and data rate determine many design decisions for mobile communication systems. On the basis of these tradeoffs, two rather different system families have evolved: (1) the cellular, wide-area systems such as GSM and UMTS, and (2) the short- to mid-range, Internet-based WLAN-type systems. In the future, both a convergence and a continued coexistence of these systems are to be expected.

The complicated task of supporting wireless mobile communication makes both of these families rather complicated. This results in communication services that are still not on par with what is commonly expected from wired communication, and it is not likely that this gap will ever be closed. As a practical consequence, data rates, delay, and cost will limit the frequency with which a mobile terminal can update its location information in core-network-based databases; hence the precision of location information, particularly for quickly moving terminals, will be limited as well. These restrictions of realistic mobile communication systems will have to be considered when designing LBS for mobile communication systems.

References

[BH00]   H. Bader and W. Huber. *Jini TM*. Addison-Wesley, Reading, MA, 2000.

[Drom97]   R. Droms. "Dynamic Host Configuration Protocol." RFC 2131, 1997. *http://www.ietf.org/rfc/rfc2131.txt*

[EV99]   J. Eberspächer and H. J. Vögel. *GSM: Switching, Services and Protocols*. John Wiley & Sons, New York, 1999.

[GPVD99]   E. Guttman, C. Perkins, J. Veizades, and M. Day. "Service Location Protocol, Version 2." RFC 2608, 1999, *http://www.ietf.org/rfc/rfc2608.txt*

[GSMA]   GSM Association, *http://www.gsmworld.com*

[IEEE99]   IEEE. "Standard 802.11: Wireless LAN Medium Access Control (MAC) and Physical Layer (PHY) Specification." 1999. *http://www.ieee.org*

[IEEE02]   IEEE. "IEEE Standards Get IEEE 802." 2002. *http://standards.ieee.org/getieee802/802.11.html*

[IETF02]   IETF, 2002, *http://www.ietf.org/html.charters/mobileip-charter.html*

[JPA02]   D. B. Johnson, C. Perkins, and J. Arkko. "Mobility Support in IPv6." Internet draft, 2002. *http://www.ietf.org/internet-drafts/draft-ietf-mobileip-ipv6-19.txt*

[KKP01]   J. M. Kahn, R. H. Katz, and K. S. J. Pister. "Next Century Challenges: Mobile Networking for Smart Dust." In *Proc. 5th Ann. Intl. Conf. on Mobile Computing and Networking*, pages 271–278, Seattle, WA, August 2001.

[KV98]   Y. B. Ko and N. H. Vaidya. "Location-Aided Routing (LAR) in Mobile Ad Hoc Networks." In *Proc. 2nd Ann. Intl. Conf. on Mobile Computing and Networking*, pages 66–75, Dallas, TX, 1998.

241

[LDLM01]   J. Li, D. S. J. De Couto, H. I. Lee, and R. Morris. "Capacity of Ad Hoc Wireless Networks." In *Proc. 7th Ann. Intl. Conf. on Mobile Computing and Networking*, pages 61–69, Rome, Italy, June 2001.

[Perk96]   C. Perkins, editor. "IP Mobility Support." RFC 2002, 1996. *http://www.ietf.org/ rfc/rfc2002.txt*

[Perk02]   C. Perkins, editor. "IP Mobility Support for IPv4." RFC 3344, 2002. *http:// www.ietf.org/rfc/rfc3344.txt*

[Rapp02]   T. S. Rappaport. *Wireless Communications Principles and Practice.* Prentice Hall, Englewood Cliffs, NJ, 2002.

[Roth02]   J. Roth. *Mobile Computing Grundlagen, Technik, Konzepte.* (In German.) Dpunkt Verlag, 2002.

[SCEB02]   H. Soliman, C. Castelluccia, K. El-Malki, and L. Bellier. "Hierarchical Mobile IPv6 Mobility Management (HMIPv6)." Internet draft, 2002. *http://www. ietf.org/internet-drafts/draft-ietf-mobileip-hmipv6-07.txt*

[Schi03]   J. Schiller. *Mobile Communications.* 2nd edition, Addison-Wesley, London, 2003.

[Stal01]   W. Stallings. *Wireless Communications and Networks.* Prentice Hall, Englewood Cliffs, NJ, 2001.

[Stoj02]   I. Stojmenovic. *Handbook of Wireless Networks and Mobile Computing.* John Wiley & Sons, New York, 2002.

[Toh01]   C. K. Toh. *Ad Hoc Wireless Networks.* Prentice Hall, Englewood Cliffs, NJ, 2001.

ACRONYMS

AP	Access point
BSC	Base station controller
BTS	Base transceiver station
DCF	Distributed coordination function
EDGE	Enhanced Data Rates for GSM Evolution
ETSI	European Telecommunication Standards Institute
FDD	Frequency division duplex
FDMA	Frequency division multiple access
GMSC	Gateway Mobile Services Switching Center
GPRS	General packet radio service
GSM	Global System for Mobile Communication
HLR	Home location register
HSCSD	High-speed circuit-switched data

IMT-2000	International Mobile Telecommunications 2000
MS	Mobile station
MSC	Mobile services switching center
MTC	Mobile terminated call
MT	Mobile terminal
PAN	Personal area network
PCF	Point coordination function
TDD	Time division duplex
TDMA	Time division multiple access
UMTS	Universal Mobile Telecommunications System
UTRA	UMTS terrestrial radio access
VLR	Visitor location register
WLAN	Wireless local area network

Index

Contributor Biographies

Clay Collier is currently the chief executive officer of Iro Systems. Previously, he founded Kivera and served as its CEO. Prior to founding Kivera, Clay Collier developed the first full-featured automotive route guidance system in North America with Zexel and Navigation Technologies. He received his B.A. in physics from the University of California, Berkeley.

H. Arno Jacobsen is a faculty member in the electrical and computer engineering department and in the computer science department at the University of Toronto, where he leads the Middleware Systems Research Group. Dr. Jacobsen received his Ph.D. from Humboldt-Universität zu Berlin in 1999. His research interests include distributed systems and data and information management systems.

Christian S. Jensen, Ph.D., Dr. Techn., is a professor of computer science at Aalborg University, Denmark, and an honorary professor at Cardiff University, UK. He is a member of the Danish Academy of Technical Sciences. Dr. Jensen received the Ib Henriksens Research Award in 2001 for research in temporal data management and the Telenor's Nordic Research Award in 2002 for research in mobile e-services. In addition to his academic activities, he serves on the board of directors and advisors for a number of companies.

Holger Karl obtained an M.S. from University of Karlsruhe in 1996 and a Ph.D. from Humboldt-Universität zu Berlin in 1999, both in computer science. Since 2000, he has been an assistant professor in the Telecommunication Networks Group of the Technische Universität Berlin. His current research interests are mobile and wireless communication, ad hoc networks, and wireless sensor networks.

Xiaobin Ma   is a Ph.D. student in the computer science department at the University of Minnesota. His research interests are database systems, GIS, and data mining, with a focus on spatial databases and spatial data mining. He has been working on several database systems and GIS projects.

Lance McKee   writes on geospatial information technology topics. From 1994 to 2000, he was on the staff of the Open GIS Consortium (OGC). His current interests include technology and policy issues related to spatial data model coordination, spatial data sharing, and the open standards of the Spatial Web.

Jörg Roth   holds an M.S. and Ph.D. in computer science and has worked as a software engineer developing industrial applications. He is currently researching and teaching at the Fernuniversität Hagen, Germany. His research topics include wireless networking, mobile computing, and location-based services with a focus on development frameworks for mobile applications.

Jochen Schiller   is head of the Computer Systems and Telematics Working Group at the Institute of Computer Science, Freie Universität Berlin, Germany, and a consultant to several top 100 companies in the networking and communication business. He studied computer science at the University of Karlsruhe, where he received his Ph.D. in 1996. He is the author of *Mobile Communications*, published by Addison Wesley in 2001 and used as a textbook by more than 200 universities and colleges. His research focus includes wireless, mobile, and embedded devices; communication protocols; operating systems for devices with small footprints; and quality of service aspects in communication systems.

Shashi Shekhar,   a computer science professor at the University of Minnesota, was elected an IEEE fellow for contributions to spatial database storage methods, data mining, and geographic information systems. He has coauthored a popular textbook on spatial databases, serves on the board of directors of the University Consortium on GIS, and is a co-editor-in-chief of the journal *Geoinformatica*.

Sarah Spiekermann   is an assistant professor at the Institute of Information Systems, Humboldt-Universität zu Berlin, Germany, where she teaches IT system design. Dr. Spiekermann received her Ph.D. from Humboldt-Universität zu Berlin in 2002. Before starting her university career, she worked as a consultant with A.T. Kearney for numerous European mobile operators. She has also worked for Openwave Systems, where she was responsible for EMEA marketing intelligence and location-based services.

Mark Strassman is currently the senior director of marketing at Autodesk, where he manages AutoCAD and various AutoCAD-based products. Prior to working at Autodesk, Mark served as vice president of products and services at Kivera, a leading location-based services provider. Mark has also held founding and senior management positions at Tirata, Macromedia, Adobe Systems, and EMU Communications. He graduated magna cum laude from Brown University and holds an M.B.A. from the University of California, Berkeley.

Ranga Raju Vatsavai is currently working as a research fellow at the Remote Sensing and Geospatial Analysis Laboratory at the University of Minnesota. His primary research interests are extending database technology for emerging applications such as spatial, temporal, biological, web services, multimedia, remote sensing, and sensor networks, as well as discovering knowledge from large databases that arise from some of these emerging application domains.

Agnès Voisard is a research scientist at the Fraunhofer Institute for Software and Systems Engineering (ISST) in Berlin and adjunct faculty at the Institute of Computer Science, Freie Universität Berlin. She received her Ph.D. from INRIA, the French National Computer Science Institute. Over the past ten years, her research has focused on spatial databases and interoperability in information systems. She was General Chair of SSD'97 and Program co-chair of ACM GIS 2002. With Philippe Rigaux and Michel Scholl, she coauthored the book *Spatial Databases with Application to GIS*, published by Morgan Kaufmann in 2001.

Jin Soung Yoo is a Ph.D. student in the computer science department at the University of Minnesota at Twin Cities. Her research interests are databases, data mining, and spatial databases.

Printed and bound by CPI Group (UK) Ltd, Croydon, CR0 4YY

03/10/2024

01040339-0019